THE ART OF RUN TRAINING

Lena,

Thank you for the support of
enthusiasm over the years, along
with the reminder that the
Training Notes needed some
editing :)

Mike

THE ART OF RUN TRAINING

Using Sport Psychology & Physiology for Optimal Performance

MIKE HAMBERGER M.A.

ISBN: 1515311546
ISBN 13: 9781515311546

Some praise from runners for Mike Hamberger's

The Art of Run Training:

"...*Mike's first-hand experience as a runner and coach comes through on every page, and I think [people] on the racing circuit as well as weekend runners can benefit from this book.*" –Gary Cohen

"...*[This book] includes all the aspects needed for successful running, including different types of running workouts, cross-training, motivation, and more. It's easy to read and you can refer back to it again and again, always taking away more knowledge and tips as you get deeper into your training.*" –Caryn Ginsberg

"*Mike Hamberger is one of the best running coaches out there so when I saw he wrote a book I immediately picked it up! Having worked with him for a couple of years I was hoping that his personable training style would come through and it did.* –Dr. Ami Lynch

"*As someone who is often caught up in the [data of running, like pace and distance], Mike's approach to sport psychology has been tremendously helpful. I've found more joy in [running], diversifying my workouts while getting faster. Great book!*" –Amanda Nichols

Note: these reviews were posted on the book's original Amazon Kindle page

For the many dedicated, lively, witty, intellectual and inspiring athletes who I've been lucky enough to coach over the years. A large percentage of the material in this book comes from our correspondence, especially the insightful questions that you've all asked. Thank you for your continued support and votes of confidence.

Give a man a fish and you feed him for a day;
teach a man to fish and you feed him for a lifetime.

TABLE OF CONTENTS

AUTHOR'S NOTE

I'VE WRITTEN THIS book in the 1st- and 2nd-peson narrative style in order for it to read more like a conversation with the reader. Having said that, as a university professor and former teacher of grades 5 - 12, I favor the Socratic method of teaching. Therefore, there are many rhetorical questions posed throughout this book, which again, reads better in the 2nd-person. I hope you, the reader, find the alternating of 1st, 2nd, and 3rd-person narratives seamless.

Additionally, rather than overload the book with the inclusive phrase "he or she" or "his or her" when referring to a runner, I have opted to use only one of the gender pronouns in many instances, but with no intended discrimination between the genders.

There are no citations for the empirical studies I reference. I try to make it clear to the reader when I am relying on other sources rather than offering my own views; however, I often take the liberty of assuming certain empirical facts to be common knowledge.

A List of Abbreviations

EM – Extrinsic Motivation

IM – Intrinsic Motivation

HR – Heart Rate

PR – Personal Record

PT – Physical Therapy

RV – Running Volume

ST – Strength Training

XT – Cross-Training

PREFACE

THIS BOOK IS intended as a guide for *anyone* who wants to fully understand the ins-and-outs of running, training, and racing. This book is also a how-to for current and aspiring coaches who want to understand how to apply the principles of sport psychology and physiology (the latter referring specifically to periodization, a systematic training theory) in order to help runners reach new heights. Within the rapidly growing community of runners, relatively few are full-time professional athletes and I tip my hat to those elite runners. However, this book is designed for the *non-professional* runner, anyone who uses running as a means to improve fitness or fuel his/her competitive nature. As a coach since 2006, I continue to work with a clientele who represent a bell-shaped curve of experience—ranging from very fit runners on one end, to couch potatoes on the other, and every demographic in between. The individuals I coach have such goals as qualifying for the Boston Marathon, finishing their first half-marathon, breaking an hour in a 10k, running a 5k under 6- or 7-minute/mile pace, running a mile without stopping, passing military physical fitness tests, and becoming fitter during the off-season as a high school or collegiate athlete.

I've become a chameleon as a result of coaching a diverse group, and it appears that I wear many hats, as each individual athlete requires more attention to specific elements of training in relation to other athletes. The particular element of training that receives more focus will change and evolve for each athlete the longer I coach him/her. For instance, an athlete may reach out to me initially for help in improving her half-marathon time, but the first priority to me (as a coach) might be to improve her running form, accompanied with run-specific strength training. Once the running form is tip-top and a foothold is established with a strength training routine, *then* we can re-introduce a higher volume of run training (frequency x duration). In time, as the athlete learns more about the sport of running and picks up the general training theories from the coach, the main focus can then swing to any psychological skills training that are involved in higher-intensity running and competition.

Regardless of the runner or the goal, and regardless of the color my chameleon self needs to be in a one-on-one conversation, my coaching is always guided by the principles of periodization and sport psychology. In that sense, I am grounded in science by the underlying principles of human physiology and social psychology. Periodization, as a traditional training theory, and applied sport psychology are simply two applications of the decades of research on performance. I try to load an athlete's brain with these general principles over many months of coaching, so that he/ she can eventually be better self-coached. Once the general theories are understood and put into practice more regularly, my role as a coach shifts toward *fine-tuning* the theories in a customized fit for each athlete. The fine-tuning is necessary because each body does not respond the same way to certain types of training, nor does it take much convincing to realize that psychology is a very individualized realm.

Fine-tuning and building a faster machine (athlete) to enhance athletic performance is mostly accomplished through *physical* training (this point should be logical). Applied sport psychology merely oils the parts on this machine. Priority #1 is to take the theories of periodization and specificity of training and build a stronger, leaner and faster athlete. Once that goal is achieved, the next step is to teach the athlete how to let the training speak for itself and to operate on autopilot, without the mind getting in the way. Musicians, public speakers, dancers, and surgeons all follow this same model. It's often said in the run community, "Running is 90% mental." I could not *disagree* more.

A worldwide poll of the general population might show that running would be considered the simplest sport there is in terms of equipment, techniques to learn, and variations (*my* vote would go that direction). So why make running more complicated than it has to be? To those who say, "Running is not easy because it's physically demanding and the pain is self-inflicted," I would agree. However, in terms of actual brainwork and the processing of information, no sport is easier than putting one foot in front of the other. Running allegedly becomes *mental* when we test our boundaries in terms of going farther and/or faster. However, once it's remembered that adhering to the principles of periodization *prevents* a coach (or runner) from prescribing *too much* training, then an athlete is always within their natural element/range and there's not much negative feedback from the body to the mind. Thus, mental processing is reduced.

This relaxed mental state and the elimination of extra processing is desirable in *all* sports; running is no exception. In the instances where there was much mental effort required to finish a workout or race, or hit a certain goal time, then perhaps the athlete was not *physically* prepared, he was under-trained, the goals were too lofty (unrealistic), and/or the coach prescribed the wrong workouts or paces. Proper physical training eliminates extra mental effort. To that end, running should be 10% mental. "Paralysis by analysis" is not desirable in any field of human performance. I am not downplaying the mental aspects of running (or else the word *psychology* would not appear in this book's subtitle), but I offer that it depends on how we define "mental." Applied sport psychology can be defined as the mental management of physical resources. This book will delineate the how-and-why of using the mind to improve performance.

On that note, there are several other aspects of run coaching in which I do not follow suit with what is typically seen in run magazines, online articles, and conversations in running stores. This book is *not* intended to be controversial or experimental; rather, the aim is for it to be educational. Without going into detail (for now), some of those stances addressed in this book include the following:

1) Running should be 10% mental, not 90%.
2) Switching to a new style of run shoe is overrated in terms of changing run mechanics.
3) The instruction to run with "short, quick strides" can do more harm than good.
4) Runners have better form when running fast, not slow.
5) Garmin watches (GPS devices) can hamper running performance.
6) The surging popularity of half-marathons and marathons is causing most injuries.
7) There's a need for a longer, more strenuous off-season dedicated to strength training.
8) A runner should *not* use a race as "a training run."

Another area where I may deviate from the norm a great deal is already evident here in the Preface—I use the term *athlete* as much as I use the term *runner*. Yes, this is a book about running, but there's good reason for my choice in semantics, which I discuss in its own section titled, *"Marathoners"* (quotation marks intended). Briefly stated, one particular off-the-field aspect of running is that not all who attempt this sport feel like "runners." When I address my group as a whole, I am able to be more inclusive of everyone if I use the term *athlete*, which I prefer for another reason anyway. Before I state that other reason, I'll note that it can be easier for one to *feel* more like an athlete instead of a runner, so from a coaching standpoint it's easier for me to initially train folks of all athletic backgrounds, or lack thereof, without self-concept being an issue. But perhaps the more important point here is that the term *athlete* (as part of self-concept) opens the door to more training possibilities. *Runners* are often limited to run-specific training, and while the element of specificity of training is generally positive, it is detrimental if it leaves few or no alternatives. *Runners* want to run as much as possible, which can lead to stagnant training, over-training, negligent training, and/or mental burnout. It is easier for one to embrace off days, recovery weeks, strength training and an off-season phase that has more variety when the mindset is that of an *athlete*, and not a *runner*. So although I use the term *runner* in this book to describe one who is in a race or doing a workout, I typically address the individuals I coach as *athletes*. It's a better practice. In this instance, I am not applying sport psychology to help a runner "push through a mental barrier in a difficult race" (so goes the stereotype of the "psychology of running"); rather, I am using sport (social) psychology to change a runner's self-concept so that *all* aspects of training receive due diligence.

I have included a References page at the end, which includes other educational books, as I don't believe that my own book, or any book for that matter, could offer a *detailed* discussion of *every* topic related to running or performance. Rather than try to reinvent the wheel on some of the solidified topics of running and performance, I created a References page of reliable sources. For example, although I cover some of the elements of physiology in Chapter 2, I don't take the science of muscle contractions too far under the microscope. This choice was my attempt to "keep it simple," while allocating more pages of the book to go into the details of other topics (e.g., running form). Anyone seeking the microscopic details of human physiology would be well served with *Daniels Running Formula* (listed in the References). Additionally, I have not included sections on running while pregnant, anemia, hyponatremia, not to mention a laundry list of other less common situations that runners encounter. Again, rather than attempt to cover the infinite number of aspects of running, the chapters and sections in this book represent the foundational points of coaching, with some of the finer details (e.g., anemia) left up to the individual to pursue elsewhere (not to discount these other topics). Therefore, in covering many viewpoints on training that you won't find in other books, *The Art of Run Training* serves as a complement to whatever else may be on your bookshelf under this general category.

I have opted against putting any sample training programs (for running or strength training) in this book because to do so would contradict a bedrock of my coaching philosophy and coaching services, as I pride myself on crafting *customized* programs for individuals. Furthermore, I make the point very clear in Chapter 5 that a coach should not design a running program until having assessed the individual's running form first. For this reason, many runners who contact me for coaching will inform me that they had previously failed in attempting to follow an online/magazine program, which are cookie cutter programs that can be followed by countless people. Attempting to follow a generic program, while potentially successful for the majority, will be the root cause for others becoming injured due to the inability of the program to account for running form. Running form is the single most important determinant in designing a training program for an athlete, but I have observed that it is otherwise (unfortunately) the last variable to get attention, if at all. This oversight is one reason runners will always keep the physical therapy and chiropractic industries in business. Related to the previous paragraph, this observation is why I dedicated more pages of the book to running form and psychology, rather than too many details on the breakdown of glycogen. I teach proper running form using a more unique language than most other coaches. Every month I am contacted by runners whose form was unable to be corrected by another coach. The devil is in the details, and those details are in the language being used to teach running form.

Each of the athletes I coach receives a copy of this book, which is my attempt to share all the knowledge and education I have on running, training, and racing. I keep no secrets. If I learn something, I share it. *The Art of Run Training* is my brain on paper. This book is largely the culmination of tens of thousands of questions, answers, tips, advice, and feedback shared between my athletes and me throughout my first decade of coaching. I want my athletes to be better self-coached because if they are, then that is a testament to my ability to teach and their ability to learn (a win-win situation). Legendary basketball coach Phil Jackson wasn't teaching Michael Jordan or Kobe Bryant how to shoot a basketball or how to block a shot; rather, he was oiling the links on the machine (a reference used previously). Jordan and Bryant were very well self-coached for most of their careers, like Peyton Manning in football, so Jackson's role changed as his athletes evolved. Similarly, I anticipate my athletes eventually not needing me to micromanage each workout or every aspect of a race, yet I am still coaching them in other ways. Whereas athletes tend to zoom in and focus on the day-to-day fluctuations in their training, coaches tend to zoom out and look for longer-term *trends* over a few weeks or months. Honing in subjectively on the day-to-day aspects of training can cause an undesirable, emotional roller coaster, so my objectivity is another hallmark of my coaching. After reading this book, a self-coached athlete will know how to interpret results/data/workouts with the same objectivity (emotional detachment) as a coach, and then how to make adjustments to the program (if needed).

My athletes receive a group E-Newsletter from me each Sunday to set the tone for the week, which includes thoughts, announcements, musings, brief race highlights, a Tip for the Week, and a Link for the Week. Even though I am coaching a large number of individuals at any given time, I use those E-Newsletters to address everyone as a group, which carries its own tone and purpose, as many of the points I'm communicating for a given week will apply to *everyone*. I address my athletes more individually during my phone calls, emails, small group workouts, and pre-race goals and reminders.

There are some tips given in this book that apply to living in the Mid-Atlantic region, specifically in terms of weather and the seasons. The connection between periodization and the changing seasons is evident for athletes in this region, but the principles can certainly be applied to everyone, as Mother Nature exists everywhere.

Finally, I would not have a full-time coaching career if it weren't for my formal education and the wonderful mentors I had in those areas. I cannot imagine that I'd be able to understand my athletes' questions and to answer them effectively if I didn't have a background in social (sport) psychology. Science-based evidence in areas such as motivation, goal setting, and stress management has given me much peace of mind, credibility, and confidence as a coach. Confidence breeds confidence (from coach to athlete). *The Art of Run Training* is the blending of empirical research with mounds of anecdotal evidence from the field (a.k.a., the race courses and the track) in order to give more confidence to those who want to explore the do-it-yourself route, as well as those who intend to coach runners. In either case, I present some new and different perspectives on the mental approach to training and racing.

Mission Statement

FOUNDED DC Running Coach, LLC in the fall of 2006 as a way to give back to the greater athletic community. I have been fortunate enough to have athletics be an integral part of my life, having *officially* become an athlete at age seven, when I put on my first flag-football uniform. Since that time, I have competed in almost every sport under the sun in some way, shape, or form, with the exceptions of jai alai and team handball. From that first uniform until today, I have been a member of 45 different athletic teams and counting, while competing in multi-sport and running since 2003. Overused clichés about sports being "a metaphor for life" occasionally detracts from the values and lessons learned from training and competition, but nonetheless I *do* owe much of my character to those lessons, as well as to the coaches who instilled those values.

Drawing inspiration from my own coaches and exhilarating sports experiences over the years, I hope to be able to lend a hand in giving you similar experiences when you overcome some challenge to achieve the unattainable. There is something unique about the sport of running as compared to other leisure-time sports. Not only is it a very effective way to lead an active, healthy lifestyle, but it also requires self-discipline and physical toughness, as the adversity is self-inflicted, unlike most other sports.

An alarming 78% of U.S. adults are not physically active, while 66% are overweight, which is largely due to the dropout rate from exercise programs being approximately 50% within the first six months. I am upfront about the notion that I did not start DC Running Coach to help people lose weight or improve how they look. Rather, I feel that taking the approach to train everyone like an athlete is more effective in achieving health and fitness goals, for a multitude of reasons. DC Running Coach caters to an athletic mindset; therefore, everyone should attempt to see him/herself in this light, regardless of his/her experience and background.

Athletics and games are meant to be fun; running should be enjoyable! I believe that running is most enjoyable after having reached some objective, measurable goal. You don't necessarily have to be the fastest runner in the area or the fittest in your age-group, but as long as you are striving to run faster and/or farther, then health and fitness will improve naturally and you will learn more about yourself in the process. Finally, it is not my goal to simply impose my own training routines on others, but to train each individual based on their athletic background and specific goals, all the while using science (and my opinion on occasion) as the guiding light.

I look forward to the challenges and successes that lie ahead for each of you.

Train hard!

Mike Hamberger, M.A., PhD candidate

1

PHILOSOPHY OF A
TRAINING PROGRAM

WHERE TO BEGIN?

EVERY YEAR, MORE than 20,000 people will run in either the Boston, New York, Chicago, or Marine Corps Marathon, and not surprisingly, there are more than 20,000 different training programs in motion on those given days (to use marathons as an example, not the norm). There is no single, best method to train for a marathon (or any race), and although most of the training follows the same general principles, it is healthy, both mentally and physically, to trust and believe in *one* system. This way there is consistency in the progression of the program and/or a coach's feedback. Conversely, as great as endurance sports publications can be, they can also be confusing. Each issue contains new articles written by different authors from different parts of the country with different backgrounds and different philosophies. For example, one edition will contain an article discussing the importance of rest and recovery right alongside an article that preaches the importance of "making this the best month of high-mileage running yet!" After a while, it's enough to make you doubt your own first name.

There have been many great endurance athletes and coaches who've come before me and influenced me, such as Dr. Jack Daniels, Troy Jacobson, and Mark Allen, among others. However, at some point, a coach must develop a consistent approach or system. Coach Bobby Knight, in relation to winning college basketball games (of which he was arguably the best), emphasizes "the belief in a system." There are dozens of offensive strategies in basketball and just as many defensive setups, and to try all of them simultaneously is futile. Just like basketball, it is best to pick one system and believe in it, squeezing everything you can out of it, taking each race and workout as an opportunity to learn/adapt before giving up on it and reaching for new drawing boards.

It's my job as a coach to help guide the training, yet the longer I work with an athlete, the less defined the programs (templates) become, which is usually after a year-and-a-half. How can a coach differ from online programs? Coaching is more than just a program on paper. A coach is a person; I have the ability to get to know the runners' personalities and how their training is going week to week. I am also able to give race goals and reminders, as well as help with race selection, strength training, run form, etc. Chris "Macca" MacCormack is a two-time Hawaii Ironman world champion and he was self-coached, but he consulted with legends like Mark Allen, after which his performances in Hawaii improved. MacCormack's approach to training and racing, *without* all its structure, is very well structured. As you'll read in more detail in the *Running Form* chapter, I believe that running mechanics, specifically, foot strike, should be the first variable considered when contemplating running volume (RV) and intensity, but for the time being let us assume that every runner has flawless running form.

THE TRAINING PROGRAMS & WEEKLY RECAPS

I am a low-tech coach. I don't use computer software or cell phone apps to monitor my athletes' workouts because I don't think it's necessary. I take the "less is more" approach. Although there is certainly a time and place for data, I prefer a large-scale view of a training program, not a small-scale one. I recognize that a goal time is, by definition, rooted in numbers, but I don't want the athletes I coach to get bogged down in numbers week to week and lose sight of the bigger goals on the horizon. The reason I choose to build the programs three months at a time is to allow the athlete to see more of the big picture. Although I do use a week-to-week approach with some athletes, whereas some of them don't actually receive a program at all, I initially lay out a tentative (ideal) 3-month plan to make it easier for both coach and athlete to zoom out and see the progressions from month to month. The longer an athlete and I work together, the less structured the coaching (programs) become. Conversely, I attempt not to *over-coach*, and by this I mean I don't have a fear of not being perceived as useful if I'm not "involved" (or deemed to be highly structured) all of the time.

The key to my own coaching involvement is to receive weekly updates in order to gain a sense of how things are progressing and to know if changes need to be made. Additionally, by routinely answering questions posed in the recaps, I hope to strengthen the belief in the individualized system that was created together. I want runners to look forward to their training, so I encourage them to let me know in their recaps if there are motivational or logistical issues that need to be addressed. As adults, we can successively juggle a schedule, so adjusting certain days here and there is not an issue, but my objective is to ensure that a runner doesn't feel exhausted by the end of the week.

The format of the recaps I ask my runners to send is intentionally designed to be short and sweet. Recaps include the following six elements:

1) Whether all the workouts were completed, or which ones were missed (weekly mileage can be included here).
2) Results/splits from any speed workouts, as well as how it felt subjectively.
3) Results from the longer weekend run, as well how it felt subjectively.

4) Assessment of health and injuries (if anything is noteworthy).
5) Updates to the race and/or travel calendar (if applicable).
6) Questions and comments.

These same elements can also be applied to anyone who is self-coached, as these items will prompt a runner to either take weekly notes or to have an honest conversation with himself about the progress of the training. It's not uncommon for a runner to miss a week or so of training and then not send a recap because "there's nothing to report." On the contrary, knowing which workouts were completed *and* which workouts were missed is of equal importance. To know how many and what types of workouts a runner was *unable* to complete helps me tremendously to keep things in perspective and adjust the program accordingly. It's part of the scientific method: all data is good data. Runners sometimes take a break from sending me recaps and that is certainly permissible and understandable, it's just better that I know that in advance. Otherwise, history shows that when I don't hear from a runner for more than a month, then the training went haywire, a nagging injury popped up, and/or motivation is suffering. I'm not the only motivator in an athlete's life, but I can't help but note this correlation.

A coach and a runner should both be taking notes about the workouts. Some runners keep data records that would make NASA jealous; while on the other hand, others need to recognize that race day cannot—and should not—be the only way to measure success. At the very least, keep score of the speed workouts and long runs, as it allows progress to be monitored over the weeks, months, and years. This will give a definitive answer to the question, "Am I fitter than a year ago?" Data such as this is the main rationale behind seasonal Time Trials and/or repeating a race from the previous year. Similarly, I'll occasionally schedule the same exact workout about 6 - 8 weeks apart. I know the conditions won't always be the same for a duplicate workout, but it's another attempt to get a glimpse of how much a runner has improved (on paper) and/or how much easier the same workout feels the second time around. One could even use average heart rate (HR) and peak HR in this regard.

A program can be altered when things pop up. We'd like to assume this is common sense, but many personalities are tied to structure and rigidness and don't allow for enough freedom in the program. The responsibility rests on my shoulders to communicate this message *before* the training kicks off, but I do like to remind my athletes that nothing is set in stone, nor should it be. Even though the goal is to complete every workout listed for a given week, I don't believe in a strict, rigid schedule. I attempt to target workouts to fall on certain days of the week, and as much as I want the ideal universe to unfold in this regard, an athlete should not bend over backward to maintain strict adherence. It is not always necessary that the workouts be done on certain days or times of day. I always design the programs factoring many variables ahead of time (e.g., races, travel, previously sedentary lifestyle) so that an athlete is not chronically fatigued and so that the schedule is logistically feasible.

We discuss how they can fit workouts into each week, as I am sympathetic toward a busy schedule, but some soul searching is required to determine if one can be active every day. The motto of the clothing and fitness company Lululemon is "Sweat once per day." It's a great motto. A physically active lifestyle is a great value in life because as the saying goes, "There ain't no wealth except your health." I believe in rest days and recovery weeks, and those are mandatory for a program, but generally speaking, being active once per day should be a goal, knowing that the workouts can always vary in terms of duration and intensity. Enjoying an activity for its own sake and making the activities fun (in any way possible) makes it easier to be active each day. Running should be viewed as play, not work. An off-season phase (discussed later) is helpful because one of the goals at that time is to try new activities, classes, and sports.[1] On a personal note, in my long stint as a competitive endurance athlete, I felt out of place on a given day if I missed a workout. It felt odd to not do *something* active on any day. Even if I wasn't jumping for joy to do the workout, I still would have felt off-kilter if I sat around all day (unless it was a scheduled off day or vacation day). Being active (to

---

1. A "phase" is a 3-month program.

feel *alive*) is a wonderful feeling and helps us appreciate the opportunities we have.

SOME INITIAL THOUGHTS ON MOTIVATION

There is a longer section on motivation in the final chapter of this book, but here are some initial thoughts to help frame my coaching philosophy and the training programs. I understand that time and energy can be scarce in some weeks, so adherence to a program should never sabotage one's overall mood. My job description is to be a chameleon and to adapt on the fly, so I need my athletes to not feel abashed about training and life. A coach should aim to be flexible, approachable, and understanding. It's my job to motivate, so I have to find ways to maneuver around obstacles and put the training back on a smooth set of rails as quickly and seamlessly as possible, even if the rails have changed appearance.

When it comes to making time for workouts, a potential motivator (that is often overlooked) is to view a workout as personal time to collect one's thoughts and escape other distractions. This doesn't have to be the primary motivator, but it has its merits. In a technology-laden 21st-century world of constant interpersonal connectedness, embrace some of the workouts as a chance for alone time. As John Blaisman, a famous amateur triathlete, once penned in a poem intended for all of humanity, "Can you be alone with your own thoughts and enjoy the company you keep?" Looking forward to workouts as a way to decompress (versus viewing it as something that *has* to be done) means it's less likely that obstacles will be perceived when trying to make time for one's self. There is certainly room here to insert a plug for not wearing an iPod or Garmin in order to make this personal time more meaningful.

I teach an undergraduate sport psychology course and one of the main objectives is for the students to learn the practical implications of the terms goal setting, confidence, and motivation. Goal setting goes very far to increase motivation, but so does confidence, which is defined as the lack of uncertainty. When we lack uncertainty we are more likely to engage in a given behavior or tackle the task at hand, so of course the simpler the goals, the more confidence we should have (this should sound logical). Subsequently, when we meet our goals, then confidence rises even more, and so does motivation. After even a short timeframe of continued success in this manner (i.e., achieving a series of short-term goals and the subsequent confidence), it's only natural that motivation will increase. Therefore, I try to increase motivation by increasing confidence.

Motivation is enhanced when people perform activities in which there is perceived competence and freedom of choice (autonomy), which are the two hallmarks of intrinsic motivation. No coach can give motivation on a plate (I wish it was that simple), so a coach must ask, "How can I make the athletes feel more competent and give them a sense of autonomy?" Although coaches play a large role in motivating athletes, the motivation ultimately has to come from within, and now you know *how* I help runners increase their own motivation.

SCHEDULING & PRIORITIZING SPEED WORKOUTS

Any program will have one to two key workouts per week (e.g., a speed workout and/or long run) and these are the workouts that get priority even when scheduling gets tight. In one sense, scheduling *is* prioritization. If there is value placed on race performances and/or improving fitness, then priority must be given to certain workouts. Typically, this priority goes to high-intensity workouts (a.k.a., speed- or track workouts), with or without a race on the calendar. If you want to race fast, you have to *train* fast! In other words, if you want to be *more* fit, then you must do workouts that challenge your *current* fitness. This doesn't mean every run should be at a blistering pace; rather, it means that a runner should be dedicated enough to his hobby that he prioritizes the more important workouts. At a minimum, the HR needs to be *significantly* elevated once per week.

The *quality* of speed workouts is also important. Therefore, generally speaking, if a track workout is going to follow another type of workout on the same day, then I suggest keeping the first workout relatively light so that there are fewer variables to consider when the track workout begins. Being relatively fresh for the track workouts means that proper pacing, or intensity, will be learned more easily.

STRUCTURE & ACCOUNTABILITY

Runners and athletes invest in DC Running Coach (DCRC) for many reasons, including structure and accountability. Runners are more apt to hit the workouts and stay dedicated to training (and live an active, healthy lifestyle) if they have someone to guide them and hold them accountable. To that end, the training programs are designed with the general assumption that the athlete will hit *every* workout on the program, knowing that rest days (written in this book as OFF to avoid confusing an "off day" as a bad day) and recovery weeks will be built into the program. Rest days and recovery weeks are part of the mantra, "train smarter, not harder." OFF days are designed with the assumption that they're needed at specific points during training.

A scheduled OFF day is different than missing a workout. Missing a string of workouts will most likely alter the program. Depending on which workouts are missed and how that coincides with the race calendar and vacations/travel, there may be a major overhaul to the program. This is a primary difference between following an online program vs. having a personal coach who can adjust the program on the fly and account for reality. No program should ever be set in stone, so we have to account for missed workouts.

On the other hand, I also assume an athlete I coach won't *overdo* the training. Generally, I assume that a runner won't add any extra running into the program that wasn't already scheduled. This is my reminder to runners not to go above and beyond the call of duty. The practical implication is to avoid doing too much, too soon. However, what counts as "too much" is not the same for every runner. In other words, an hour run doesn't affect each runner the same way. I tend not to be an overly conservative coach, but I lean toward the conservative side based on the fact we are not professional athletes and we have a higher number of (specific) limitations than our immortal counterparts. This is the bottom line: A runner should not try to compete against the training program by doing more than what is designed. Weekly recaps are how to have this conversation and they provide the coach with a constant pulse on the training; therein is the accountability being sought.

Are athletes allowed to improvise or be spontaneous? Absolutely! Freedom of choice and flexibility are the most powerful tools in a training program. Embrace the freedom that can exist within a program. I frequently schedule "open" days and almost always give a range of minutes or reps for workouts. This is because we have subtle changes in our schedules each week, not to mention changes in how we're feeling on a given day. An open day on the schedule, whether weekly or monthly means do anything—swimming, tennis, taking the dog for a walk, watching TV, using it as a make-up day for a missed workout, or for taking a rest day if needed. No worries. I'm here to guide the training, which, to me, means keeping a healthy balance between freedom in the training and keeping the training from flying off the rails. With that said, my definition of "significant deviations" from the program is usually what would cause an athlete to "draw outside the lines" and risk a nagging injury.

Finally, a coach differs from a cookie-cutter training program by having the ability to answer questions. I am not the only expert out there and am certainly not *the* guru, but I vow to be consistent in my feedback. I help to make sense of the seemingly endless array of articles found in magazines and the Internet, so in that sense, it's my job to keep it simple and practical. The two best things a runner can do to maximize his/her training with DCRC is to send me weekly recaps and do the speed workouts. I am candid in saying that the athletes who have the most success with me are the ones who prioritize the speed work and the ones who check in frequently to let me know how the training is progressing. In turn, they get feedback from me more frequently, which helps develop a solid mental approach to training and racing—the main service of DCRC. So there is the looser definition of the word *accountability* that I prefer.

VACATIONS & CREATIVITY

Americans have a bad reputation for not taking enough vacation days in comparison to the other industrialized (1st-world nations), and also for what we do on vacation (work), or what we don't do *enough* of on vacation (unwind). How much actual vacation time do you give yourself each quarter, or even during your vacation itself, even if it's a "stay-cation"? In other words, how much downtime do you give yourself each day, week, and month? Are you a guilty vacationer, not allowing yourself to enjoy your time away from work? Keeping busy is good, but many Americans claim to be too busy for endeavors not related to work or family (I'm aware of the role that parenting plays in the amount of free time someone has). Perhaps that's why I view my own coaching goals as important. Can I convince my athletes that they have plenty of time outside of their work hours to accomplish their athletic goals? Or, have I adjusted their goals accordingly to match the amount of training time they *do* have?

Just as some people feel guilty during their time away from work (as evidenced by the percentages of people who take their work on vacation with them), an often-overlooked aspect of the "psychology of running" is that runners can experience guilt from taking time off from training, or missing a workout, like a long run (the "magic bean" of running, right?). My rationale for not scheduling any group track workouts the last eight weeks of the year and the reason I promote an off-season to everyone is not only to prevent overtraining and injuries, but also to help prevent mental burnout and to allow the brain to mellow out from data, numbers, and pacing for a while. For instance, this is why I'm not concerned about wintertime racing. As a coach who envisions longer-term goals when it comes to racing, I'd want the individuals I coach to embrace *planned* time away from both work and training.

I typically schedule athletes' recovery weeks around their vacations and travel. The method behind my madness (rationale) is fairly obvious: When they're on vacation I want them to *enjoy* vacation. If we need to take recovery weeks anyway, why not take them while we're supposed to be decompressing on vacation? This does not imply that traveling and training are in conflict with one another, nor does this mean that one has to turn into a couch potato while on vacation or traveling for work. But for the most part I am scheduling downtime (away from running) during vacations so that they can explore, do other activities, and perhaps enjoy some boredom and let their minds wander, which can be healthy, both physically and mentally. There is interesting research on how boredom enhances cognitive ability via creative juices that are released during boredom. To this end, even though running isn't boring, the fact that it (ideally) requires very little mental capacity allows runners to use it as a chance to brainstorm and gather thoughts.

I'm aware that some athletes need to capitalize on the increased free time away from work. These runners might actually train more during vacations, but this appears to be the exception and not the rule, to which the following phrases apply: "a time and place for everything," "to each their own," "everything in moderation," and "keeping the balance." Each phrase applies, and whichever one you subscribe to, hopefully you don't lose sight of the major point. Allow for unstructured time away from work—time to be bored and to therefore brainstorm, which is where we tend to engage in synthetic learning (tying concepts together), a great skill set for an employee at any job (agreed?). If running is when the mind is most free to wander, then so be it, but don't be averse to time away from training either.

When it comes to taking a break from work on a smaller timescale (on a day-to-day basis), consider how often you give your brain a rest while "on the clock." Brains need breaks. If a student told me she studied an ungodly amount of consecutive hours for an exam, then I'd question the *quality* of that study session. First, I know that the brain typically doesn't operate at peak capacity for periods longer than 1 - 4 hours at a time (cramming isn't a very effective way to study). Second, taking a break will allow the mind to play around with the learning material. Think about how this might apply to your own professional career. Do you allow yourself a lunch break? How many consecutive hours do you work without any downtime to collect your thoughts on the project or task? Are you working long hours or have work piling up *because* you're not taking occasional breaks to reset your brain? In other words, does your work quality decrease as you increase the number of consecutive hours worked? Would your productivity (efficiency) and energy levels change if you changed your work pattern? What are your options? I'm not privy to all the ins-and-outs of your professional duties, but consider what you can do to unwind while at work, like napping.

Naps are routinely shown to have a plethora of health benefits, including cognitive functioning. Approximately 20 minutes continues to be the unofficial rule of thumb for the optimum nap duration because it will typically avoid a REM cycle, which is what causes the grogginess upon waking. For those working at an office, consider this: I have a friend who works in the IT field and a few times per week she'll stick a post-it on her computer that reads: "Taking a power nap, be back in 20", as she puts her head down at her desk. The first time the CEO saw her sleeping at her desk with the post-it note above her head, he commended her for it.

TOTAL WORKOUT VOLUME

Your doctor and I both want your HR to get up around 70% of maximum (or higher) for at least 30 minutes, three times per week. That's basically three jogs per week. For beginners, I refer to this short-term goal of running three days per week for 30 minutes as the "doctor's orders program." The runners I coach ask me on occasion if yard work or mowing the lawn counts as cross-training (XT), or if hiking counts as strength training (ST). My answer is that it depends on whether or not the HR increases. Meaning, it depends on who is asking and the nature of the hike or yard work. For some folks, a hike is a blistering workout (no pun intended), so if the hike drives up the HR then of course it's XT. However, if the hike was equivalent to "a walk through the woods," then no, in a technical sense, it wasn't a workout. If hiking is going to count as ST, then the individual most likely needs to take "the path less traveled" so that the leg muscles are working to overcome rocks and/or steep hills. This ensures that elements of the hike are equivalent to elements of ST. This same rationale applies to yard work. Someone's HR while in a kneeling position is probably no different than when washing dishes (hardly XT). However, depending on other elements of the yard work, it may be a good hamstring workout, especially if bending and lifting movements are done with flawless form, as in not overusing the back muscles. So in this instance, yes, yard work may be ST, the same way shoveling snow may count as ST.

As it relates to total work, yes, I want my runners to be as active as possible without the risk of overuse injuries. ST and XT have a very low likelihood for causing any injury, so when I talk about increasing the total volume (work) in a program, it is these two elements that can get more attention off the bat. The off-season is typically where total training volume (all elements of training combined) is, or should be, at its highest in order to change body composition and prepare the body for the increased RV that lies ahead. At any local gym, the body builders (whether professional or just a pseudo body builder) do longer workouts than everyone else. Their ST sessions may be 60 - 90 minutes from start to finish. That's a great deal of total work. I'll ignore the dietary and psychological aspects of their approach for now (it's not important to the main point), but their bodies show the results of their high-volume training. Similarly, elite Ironman triathletes do lots of workouts during the week, are active all day, every day, and they're as fit as fit can be.

Recalling the expression "Sweat once per day," I allow runners to choose any activities that make them sweat—it could be hiking, yard work, or a Zumba class. Open days are the days for my athletes to explore this option. The total time spent moving around each day is what is meant by *total work*. It doesn't have to be run-specific all the time. Make time each day to be energetic. A body in motion will stay in motion. The more someone trains, workouts, or exercises, then the more he/she will want to do so in the future. Fitness is invigorating and it perpetuates itself, and there is much scientific evidence to support this claim. A workout does not have to cause one to be tired for the rest of the day (long runs might be the exception). On the contrary, training typically increases energy levels for the rest of the day and the next day. Walk around at the office, take the stairs, bike commute, try a group exercise class—the list is endless. Fluffy words like "dedication" and "motivation" can be measured by the ability to make the time for physical activity, even with a busy work schedule.

INJURIES

Most running injuries are overuse injuries and are usually due to improper foot strike and/or doing too much, too soon. In addition, cutting body weight down to a healthy weight also goes a long way in injury prevention because of less stress on the body with each foot strike. As they relate to injury prevention, these three major topics (i.e., foot strike, training programs, and body weight) will be discussed later in their own chapters and sections; therefore, this section will discuss the *mental approach* to understanding and coping with injuries.

Muscle inhibition is a weak signal from the brain to the muscle and usually occurs at the fullest range of motion of the muscle, which causes instability at the joint. When the body senses instability, other muscles tighten up as a form of protection, and this protection is beneficial to some degree. However, this chronic tightening is ultimately what causes the reduced capacity for these same muscles to contract fully/optimally. The end result is either an inability for the muscles to properly stabilize a joint and/or increased muscular tightness. When high RV is added to this equation, it's easy to see where the problems can escalate.

The symptom (a tight muscle or the area experiencing pain) is usually *not* the origin of the problem. The underlying root cause(s) of the injury must be discovered. In other words, the real culprit of an injury is likely to be a weak neuromuscular signal stemming elsewhere in the body. When attempting to heal the body or make strength gains, address the areas that are connected to painful area. Any form of massages helps alleviate the extra tightness in the muscles that are overcompensating (being over-stressed); however, the best preventive medicine and cure for this problem is strong off-season dedicated to correcting problem areas through specific ST exercises for the particular movement or muscle. This is the value in having knowledgeable physical therapists (PTs), chiropractors, and trainers (2nd opinions are fabulous). Knowledge is the foundation of attitudes. The more we know, the more our attitudes change for the better, which can mean staying positive through an injury.

In determining whether or not to shut down run training at the first sign of pain/discomfort, a coach or PT should be looking for trends, not a single, isolated event. In other words, there is no need to shut down running the first time a minor pain presents itself. How do you know if you can run through the pain? On a 1 - 10 pain scale, it's okay to run if the pain is 0 - 3. Obviously, pain scales differ among individuals, but everyone knows what a 0 and a 10 feel like as two anchoring points. Using a traffic light analogy, pain that decreases with activity indicates a *green light* (keep running). Pain that increases with activity is a *red light*. A pain that neither increases nor decreases with pain is a *yellow light* (proceed with caution and be prepared to stop if needed). Having to alter walking gait and/or running form is a clear signal for a red light.

If an injury occurs, my goal is to take a conservative approach so that it doesn't linger. I don't always believe in "training tough." Training through joint pain is not a sign of mental toughness. It's better to train smarter, not harder. Taking a few weeks off from running is sometimes what is needed. It's a short-term loss for a long-term gain. In the grand scheme of things, that short time frame away from running is insignificant compared to what's accomplished once back to running consistently at 100%. Besides, for a non-professional runner, a layoff from running for a few weeks does not warrant the mentality of "losing fitness." Olympians might lose fitness in such a short time frame because they are the pinnacles of human fitness. The *ceiling effect* offers the teaching point here. We are not Olympians, so we can abandon the "losing fitness" mentality; otherwise it will only harm the psyche.

A hidden benefit from an injury is that it sometimes acts as a rest period that otherwise might not have been taken. Call it a blessing in disguise. If an athlete is injured then perhaps there wasn't a long enough recovery phase following an intense long-distance race. If the injury occurs late in the race season and one is still able to run, albeit a change in the program, then the situation is better than might be expected. Meaning, if a solid base was built during the majority of the year, then missing some workouts for about two weeks (while obviously not ideal) will not *significantly* alter performance. When resuming running after an injury, run and walk as naturally as possible, as if the injury is not there, or else there is a risk for some other nagging injury due to an altered gait caused by over-compensation.

In my coaching experience, 25% of athletes' injuries are new injuries stemming from some underlying problem, 25% are recurring injuries, 25% of are non-running related (e.g., bike accidents, softball games), and 25% are the result of going above and beyond the call of duty (*significant* deviations from the training plan). This breakdown strengthens the case for ST, PT, and embracing breaks in training, no matter how long the breaks have to be. Cutting a run from 60 minutes to 20 minutes isn't necessarily "resting the injury." Consider a complete hiatus and getting an official diagnosis/treatment on the underlying source of the pain, as opposed to constantly coping with the symptoms. The problem area "feeling better" is different than it actually being 100%. Similarly, there is a fundamental difference between muscles soreness and joint pain. Be sure to respect the difference. My athletes know their bodies better than I do, but I offer more emotional detachment from the training than they do, so a consistent dialogue is key in keeping the balance between what the athletes knows about themselves and what I know about them. I *am* empathetic (not just sympathetic) to anyone who has to miss enjoyable run workouts, but we need to listen to our bodies by taking pain and injuries seriously.

Muscle soreness from running and/or ST is an inevitable experience, but the body adapts to stress. Eventually, the body doesn't become as sore even following a strenuous workout; it's a wonderful physiological adaptation. Avoid the mentality, "If I'm not sore, then I'm not working hard." This has steered many runners down the path of overtraining. To quote Dr. Jack Daniels, "The champion runners aren't always the fastest runners; rather, they're the ones who trained properly over many years and were able to avoid injuries as major setbacks."

The programs I create are *not* designed to be strict and rigid. I love freedom of choice; however, that assumes a runner is staying between the lines (within the constraints) of the program. I'm not here to control anyone's life or tell them what they can't do, but if they invested in me to help them reach their goals, then I owe it to them to offer my objectiveness when I design the programs. That means keeping the long runs, workout paces, and total mileage within reason. For instance, I'll sometimes get a recap that includes something like this, "I had off work on Friday so I decided to add a 90-minute run to my week and then did my 2-hour run the next day. Now my knee hurts." Another example of this is "cramming" when training, as in missing 3 - 4 days in a row and then trying to make up all the distance/miles in a much shorter timeframe. You can see where a scientific mind would point to the new variables in these equations.

Adding an extra run or some extra miles here and there isn't terrible and I would hate to curb anyone's enthusiasm, but just consider how much out of the ordinary the new variable/workout might be. Many times this happens when trying a new group exercise class where the instructor doesn't consider individuality of training and it's entirely too much that day for someone, or when someone tries a new ST class *after* a long run (when the muscles are already fatigued). Don't be afraid to speak your mind to a group exercise instructor about your limits. Group instructors are there to push people beyond their limits so that they get a great workout and challenge themselves, but there is such a concept as "too much." Everything in moderation is fine, but in these instances, it only takes that one time to overdo it. Runners don't need a coach's permission like a parent, but drop the coach a line before you bite off more than you can chew.

I often hear runners say with a wry smile, "Yeah, I get injured all the time, but don't we all? After all, we're runners." What a tragic acceptance.

I don't agree with this philosophy that injuries are inevitable in running. Running would certainly be easier on the body if it were merely restricted to the "doctor's orders program" mentioned previously. While some people take this approach, others have greater goals in mind and a willingness to test their competitive drive, so therein lies the *potential* for a nagging injury. However, I do not think it's an inevitable reality that can't be avoided. Again, preventive medicine is the best medicine. In that case, be sure to budget for this active, healthy lifestyle. Massage, PT, a gym membership, ST sessions, a new bed for a healthy back, and new shoes are all part of prioritizing this leisure activity that has many long-term physiological and psychological benefits. If someone is in this sport for the long haul, then it's easier to embrace this holistic approach to training.

When assessing your overall fitness and run goals, ask yourself how long you've been running pain-free and training consistently, and what steps you took to arrive at the point of pain-free running. Occasionally remind yourself of those steps. If you're just getting back into running due to a previous injury or otherwise, use the scientific method and control variables. Be careful about increasing both speed and distance at the same time.

Finally, as it relates to sleep, I've attended clinics on injuries and heard one PT, whose opinion I respect, say that sleep should be a perquisite to training, whereas if a runner didn't get adequate sleep the night before, then they shouldn't train that day. Perhaps a strongly worded message, but he was trying to make a point. Tissue inflammation (injury/overuse) and its repair are related to sleep, as sleep is when the body is restored. Sleep quality and quantity are correlated with a faster healing time (generally speaking). Good sleep can also make the body more resilient to pain, as the nerve endings become more "sensitive" with a lack of sleep. Earlier in this chapter I gave an anecdote about a friend who routinely takes 20-minute naps at her desk in order to boost her efficiency the rest of the day.[2]

---

2. As far as exercising when feeling under the weather, the unscientific rule of thumb is that if the symptoms are "above the neck" a person can still try to exercise, but at a low intensity, while "below the neck" symptoms mean rest. In any case, when attempting to get back into exercise after illness, keep it short and easy for a few days.

2

PERIODIZATION

A YEAR-ROUND TRAINING PROGRAM, regardless of the sport, will follow the principles of *periodization*, meaning the volume, intensity, and specificity of the training are varied throughout the year in order to reach a peak level of fitness at one or two particular points in the year. It is generally accepted that the body can maintain a peak level of fitness for about three weeks, which is logical, given the definition of the word *peak*. Here is an overview of how the year could be divided into different phases (periods) of training:

1. Recovery phase (active rest) ~ 1 - 2 months
2. Off-season phase ~ 2 - 4 months
3. Preparation and Base phase (pre-season) ~2 - 4 months
4. Speed, Power and Maintenance phase (in-season) ~ 2 - 3 months

(After the in-season phase, the cycle would repeat again with another recovery phase.)

RECOVERY PHASE

Assuming a competitive season has just ended, the first phase is a planned recovery period, which some coaches refer to as "active rest" (light running, flexibility training, walking the dog, hanging out in the pool, shooting baskets, etc.). The goals of the recovery phase are to rest the muscles and joints that have been trained hardest during the competitive season and to give the body a general break in order to prevent overtraining (overuse injuries) and/or mental burnout. Even with occasional recovery *weeks* built into a program for different reasons, it's also healthy to take one or two recovery *phases* in the year, as in a 1 - 2 month period of intentionally low-volume training, or at least low-volume *running*. For about a month or so following the end of a season, an athlete would be doing right by engaging in *unstructured* physical activity (i.e., doing what you like, when you feel like it) and enjoying life away from training and competition. For this reason, it's common to see NFL and NBA players enjoying a short golf season immediately after their competitive season ends.

In the Mid-Atlantic region, the late fall or early winter is the best time for this recovery phase. It's an intentional time to mentally reboot and physically recharge. A recovery week is a microcosm of this approach. There's a time and a place for everything, so recovery phases are actionable plans in following the mantras, "Train smarter, not harder" and "Train hard, rest hard."

OFF-SEASON PHASE

Picking up where the recovery phase ended, the months of December and January typically begin the off-season for most endurance athletes in the Mid-Atlantic region. As a coach, I make it *mandatory* that athletes find something to do in the off-season so that running does not become a stand-alone activity. In the off-season I prefer to emphasize strength training (ST) and cross-training (XT). A benefit of ST and XT that is often overlooked is improved athleticism via increased muscular strength. Similarly, I want an athlete's hand-eye coordination to be tip-top. Sports and activities that force one to be aware of where the body and limbs are in space (kinesthetic sense) naturally improve athleticism. This approach doesn't mean shutting down running altogether (I would not recommend that), but everyone can benefit from more athleticism. Athleticism, in turn, improves technique for ST and also improves coordination, like bike handling skills and swim technique, which allows for improved XT. Above all else, athleticism will improve the ability to do dynamic warm-up drills correctly prior to a speed workout. If there is value placed on running performance then improving athleticism should be a goal.

The reduced running volume (RV) early in the off-season does not mean one will "lose fitness"; rather, it's simply a different mental approach to running. Fitness can actually improve in the off-season if the total workout volume increases, which is the goal. At some point, "Sweat once per day" becomes "Sweat twice per day." Logistics and a personal schedule always set the parameters, but where there's a will there's a way. Here is a quote related to the off-season that I picked up from a physical therapist, "Most people run to get fit, whereas most of those people should be getting fit in order to run."

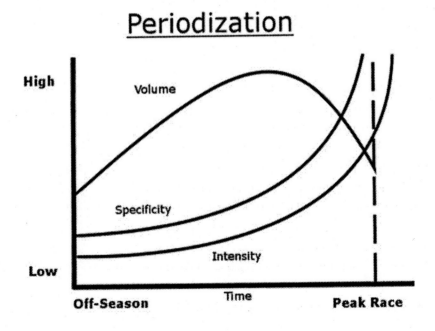

Periodization

High

Volume

Specificity

Intensity

Low

Off-Season

Time

Peak Race

PREPARATION & BASE PHASE

The preparation phase is the longest and potentially the most important phase. Its two main objectives are to build a sufficient aerobic base via high-volume training and to increase muscle mass, or lean tissue (to a degree), while reducing body fat. The increase in training volume at this time certainly includes ST. In short, the goal is to reshape the body in order to be able to handle the months of training that lie ahead. During the preparation phase, the volume of training is high, while intensity is relatively low and/or not as frequent. In the popular literature, this is commonly referred to as the base-building phase. As an athlete nears peak race season, the emphasis will be reversed, so that the training volume is significantly reduced and the intensity of the workouts increases and/or becomes more frequent.

The main physiological adaptations that will take place during this phase are an increase in the density of the capillaries per muscle fiber and an increase in the size/number of mitochondria, the cellular structures that store energy for the muscles. The significance of these adaptations is that (eventually) the muscles can work harder and more efficiently for longer durations (the best of both worlds). A higher capillary density in the muscles means that more blood (carrying oxygen and nutrients) can be delivered to the working muscles. Simultaneously, waste products are removed from the muscles more efficiently. If an athlete were to start high-intensity running workouts without first having a solid aerobic base (or at least a modest base), then the waste products that cause muscular fatigue would *not* be thoroughly flushed from the muscles after the first set/interval and the adverse physiological effects of each successive set/interval would accumulate to the point where the workout would suffer in quality. The result of this non-ideal, hurried approach to training is that the body has been trained to move *inefficiently*, and the workout does not yield the intended results. The reason some people are able to run fast at the end of a long race (or game), seemingly running on fresh legs, is because they *are* running on fresh legs (relatively speaking). Most likely, they have put in high-volume training, so that when there normally would be signs of fatigue during the competition, their legs have been continuously removing the waste products from the muscles, as if the muscles were never stressed in the first place. Also, as mentioned previously, an increase in the size of mitochondria allows more energy to be stored for the latter stages of the event, so endurance improves for this reason too.

SPEED, POWER & MAINTENANCE PHASE

The last phase of a traditional periodization cycle is the in-season phase, where the goals are to maximize speed and power (more so for the power sports/athletes), and to simply *maintain* the strength that was built from the high-volume ST that was done in the off-season and preparation phases. Typically, the in-season phase of training is geared specifically toward the main event for which one is training ("specificity of training"), so it's also commonly called the "peak phase." Here, the training volume is *relatively* low, while the intensity of the workouts is at its highest in order to train the body to be in its fittest form (peak conditioning). Because specificity of training is at its highest in this phase, ST and XT become secondary priorities (a.k.a., maintenance work). However, depending on the nature of the sport, the ST exercises may also attempt to cause similar stress levels for muscles specifically used in competition.

As stated in discussing the preparation phase, a more efficient cardiovascular system means increases in both capillary and mitochondrial densities, along with more efficient removal of waste from muscle fibers. These adaptations are largely dependent on the aerobic system (e.g., longer distance running and tempo workouts). When it comes time for speed workouts, the *quality* of the reps will determine the boost to running economy (efficiency), but the reps will *not* be high quality if the aerobic system is dragging, hence the benefit of an approach using the general principles of periodization, which means having a solid base phase prior to a speed phase.

The terms *speed* and *speed training* are always relative to the individual. The most common way runners improve their speed is through a combination of aerobic conditioning and anaerobic conditioning. Most workouts that a runner will do will fall into the aerobic category, and that goes for most track workouts. The duration, intensity, and rest intervals of the speed workouts in this phase are often dependent on the specific distance of the peak event. For instance, the workouts can be expected to be more intense than usual, but the rest periods within the workout may therefore be intentionally longer, so that the body has enough time to recover in order to do each repetition/set at the required intensity. In order to achieve a desired running pace at the peak race, it's imperative to train at that pace (or faster) for select workouts. Hence, there is a necessity to ensure proper recovery within the workout itself and then between workouts. There are still long runs during this final phase of the training year, but the *total* mileage may be lower compared to other parts of the year. "Train hard, rest hard." This tactic of embracing more rest is often a new piece of the puzzle that's introduced to runners.

PEAK TRAINING

Many athletes invest in me to help them raise their game to the next level. In the grand view, this mostly involves a change to running form, structured speed work, run-specific ST, embracing recovery periods, and help with selecting a race calendar. On the smaller scale (the peak phase in particular) it involves the little tricks of the trade, which are discussed in all of the following chapters of this book. Some of those tricks are directed toward reaching a peak level of fitness.

Because of its favorable weather (cool temperatures and low humidity), the fall is typically referred to as "running season" and therefore labeled as "race season." Upon entering the fall race season, runners should obviously begin to shift their focus more to their peak races and those related goals. This focus applies to both physical training and mental training. About two to three months prior to the peak race, there is likely an increase in the number of key (high-intensity) workouts on the schedule while the run mileage begins to peak. Additionally, intensity and specificity of training will both begin to climb at this point for most runners. If a runner is following the general principles of periodization, then this escalation needs to be embraced, so as a coach I'm more stringent on getting rid of the excuse making during peak season. There needs to be a sharper mentality during peak season to match the sharpness of the training.

Any imagery/visualization sessions (if they're being done) should now be more specific to the peak event.[3] For instance, instead of imagining in general terms that "I'm going to feel good and run well," hone it down to "I'm going to feel _____ on that hill at mile _____" (the first blank is typically a unique/specific word for the individual, called a *cue word*, and the second blank is usually the toughest part of the course). Through individualized pre-race e-mails, I give my athletes specific race strategies to help them tackle whichever race they're doing. Additionally, I offer insight into proper imagery, which is related to using perceived exertion during races versus being governed strictly by the time on the watch. This mental strategy is also very much rooted in what are called *process goals* (more on that later).

During the peak phase, closer attention can be paid to diet (used as a noun, not a verb). If there are more rest days scheduled during peak season in order to recover from key workouts and/or rest for the next day's key workout, and if the RV is gradually reduced from peak mileage to maintenance mileage, then diet should account for these changes; control the caloric intake on rest days. Moreover, the pre-race and in-race fueling strategies should be solidified. These relevant questions should be answered several weeks in advance, as race day is not the time for questions or experimentation.

Whenever the summer Olympics are in full swing, I challenged my athletes to see how long they can train like an Olympian and take care of all the "off-the-field" elements of their training, such as diet, hydration,

---

3. There is an *Imagery* section in Chapter 6.

massage, and sleep. If someone is taking running seriously enough to where there is value placed on performance, then more thought can be given to how one's diet can boost performance, such as adjusting diet for the days with shorter runs or no running at all. To feel like an Olympian, carry a winning mentality through the entirety of race season and take your diet to a healthier place. Train hard when it's time to train; rest hard when it's time to rest. You're not an Olympian, but you can treat yourself like one when peaking.

TAPERING

In anticipation of the week of the peak race, the few remaining weeks beforehand will have more rest days with perhaps shorter, higher-intensity workouts. This process is generally known as tapering. However, when talking with other runners during race season and/or reading magazines and online articles, make sure to take the term *tapering* with a grain of salt. It's an often misused and overused term. For many reasons, not all the athletes I coach "taper." Instead, I prefer the term *recovery*. Professional athletes taper for three to five weeks because they often have been working more than 40 weeks toward one race and they train much harder than we do, which is logical if it's their full-time job. Make sure not to mislabel a restful week before the race with the term tapering. I say this only to save confusion when considering what another source is stating about tapering. The term tapering doesn't always apply to non-professional runners. Non-professional runners often need every week of training they can muster in order to achieve their race goals. The exact duration of a taper, or pre-race recovery period, is dependent on the length of the race, the athlete, the type of training that has been done and how many consecutive months he/she has been training.

Even with the distinction in nomenclature about tapering, restful weeks are still a necessity before peak races. It is important to have OFF days to simply let the body recover and adapt—nothing more. As a coach,

I want my athletes to trust that they have done all the training (done it the right way) and to avoid thinking "I am losing fitness" when training volume reduces. During the recovery period, some people may feel a reduction in energy levels for the first few days, but keep in mind that there are many subsequent days to adapt to this feeling, along with other workouts that will keep the energy levels up. The goal is to feel rested and revived for race day. The physiological adaptations that result from the preparation/base phase last a long time as long as one remains physically active. For instance, there is not much a runner can do the week before a marathon to make him/herself much faster. The work has already been done at that point. Running fairly consistently on a year-round basis (including speed work) requires giving the body ample time to absorb the training, as there is a time lag between the stimulus and the adaptation. Doing a combination of high volume and high intensity training is expected, but it's best not to tease this line for too long.

Finally, during the final lead-up to a peak race, run-specific ST can still be done one to two times per week, which is part of the *maintenance* approach. Continue to do regular lower body ST until about three weeks prior to the peak event, assuming this ST does not conflict with other races. Upper body ST during this time should be short and sweet, if done at all. At the risk of sounding repetitive, these alterations are aligned with the principles of specificity of training.

PATIENCE & PEAKING MENTALLY

Assuming runners are aiming for a peak race that's in the fall season, I don't encourage them to focus on this race during the other seasons. I know the training will get more intense as the big event draws near, so I don't want athletes consumed all year long by a single event. Otherwise, mental burnout may be around the corner. Instead, during other portions of the year a runner would focus on the journey (the training) and not the destination (peak event), which means it's beneficial to back off in terms of how much mental energy is put into these races. This is how to avoid mental burnout—let the mental engagement *build* throughout the year, rather than having it to be omnipresent from the onset. As the peak/fall race season approaches (e.g., less than 2 months away), *then* a runner can change gears and begin to focus on the peak race for most workouts.

The spring season is often the time for other peak races. During the winter off-season phase, a runner can make subtle shifts month-to-month in terms of prioritizing certain types of workouts and how much emotional energy is given to spring racing. However, a primary reason I encourage athletes to delay this mental shift toward "race mode" is due to the weather and the principle of specificity of training. The winter off-season is the phase of training farthest away from the peak race, so a runner doesn't need to be thinking too much about spring or fall races when winter weather is in full effect and there is still snow on the ground. When it's January, keep the focus on ST. Carry this gym-rat approach through the end of February with the goal of transforming the body as much as possible via ST, XT, and PT. Moreover, if the specificity of training is still relatively low in January, then mentally I doubt that runners are *feeling* their spring races during their winter workouts so they should stop trying. There's no reason to put dents in confidence; put that mental energy back into ST, XT, and PT. Rather than dabble in a grey area of "mental training" (or lack thereof), I encourage runners to wait until late February or March 1st to get fired up for spring racing (assuming they have a peak spring race on the books).

Knowing that all the off-the-field aspects of training were solidified in the winter will lend itself to enhanced confidence at the start line of spring races. But without legitimate dedication to these aspects of the off-season, the changes won't happen. It takes many, many run workouts to build a solid fitness base, and the same truth applies to ST, XT, and PT. No physical therapist or chiropractor has ever said, "Just do those exercises here and there once or twice per week and you'll be fine." That would be rubbish. You can't fake fitness and you can't fake functional corrections in the body. It either is, or it isn't. Injuries are not mysterious; no person is "unlucky" in that regard (unless perhaps it's a matter of rolling an ankle in an unseen pothole, for example). Stronger, leaner, more resilient athletes become stronger, leaner, and more resilient with less chance of injury because they beat the hell out of their bodies (in a good way, without *over*doing it) for a long, dedicated off-season. This is evident when reading/ listening to post-race championship interviews. Therein lies lots of motivation to prioritize ST in the off-season.

When peak season rolls around and the training priorities have shifted, confidence will increase for a few reasons. First, the legs will feel fresher due to less intense and less frequent lower-body ST. Second, the key run workouts (i.e., track work and select long runs) will begin to resemble races (specificity of training). And third, it can't be ignored that the winter and summer weather significantly impact training (for most states in the U.S.). To reiterate from points made previously, in one of my weekly E-Newsletters each summer I encourage everyone who is registered for a peak fall event *not* to be in race mode yet. Why? It's because a two-hour run in 90-degree weather with 80% humidity offers zero resemblance of the *feel* of a marathon that is run on a crisp autumn morning. For a runner to think otherwise may be causing unnecessary dissatisfaction with the summer workouts. Again, there's no reason to dabble in a grey area of mental training that will detract from confidence. Regardless of how well someone trains in the winter, the winter is not the spring (for most parts of the U.S.), so don't compare apples to oranges. Don't compare summer slugfests to perfect fall weather. Don't compare how your body feels in 35-degree weather on slightly fatigued legs to perfect spring weather on fresh legs.

Patience is a virtue, but in this respect, the real virtue is in understanding the body-mind connection because specificity of training applies to the mental training too; it has to build toward a peak, just like the physical training. The physical and mental aspects of training go hand in hand, and there will be more connections between mind and body when the specificity of training is peaking and the weather is consistently favorable. You'll later read my thoughts on Garmin watches and attempting precise pacing during the winter/summer and how both of those topics relate to this section. A final strategy for avoiding mental burnout and putting too much mental energy into racing is to not let other runners pull you into too many conversations about big races that are not on the immediate horizon. Tune out and be patient.

YOU HAVE THE RIGHT TO REMAIN SELFISH

There is a time and a place to be selfish. I'm aware that the term *selfish* has a negative connotation. Research shows that as long as there isn't any *guilt* attached to a seemingly selfish behavior, then we are happier as a result of that behavior, and as long as our selfish behavior doesn't detract from anyone else's happiness. What does this mean for running? If you believe in reaching a peak level of fitness at some point in the year, then you have to act like it—by being selfish. This implies that at a certain point in the year, namely, peak season, a runner may have to put him/herself first when it comes to altering the weekly schedule and prioritizing aspects of his/her life, especially in terms of key workouts and meal selection. During other times of the year, when key races are far away on the calendar, there is much more room for leniency with workouts and meals. Because of the ceiling effect, it becomes harder for experienced runners to hit a PR, so these runners need to be firing on all cylinders in order to peak. All aspects of the training must be in tip-top shape. If we accept that advanced/experienced athletes can only be in *peak* condition for about three weeks, then that's a relatively small window. Therefore, athletes should take steps to ensure that the build-up to the A-race, or peak race, is not sabotaged. True beginners need not pay as close attention to this premise.

In practical terms, being selfish might mean deviating from the usual workout done with a training group, such as a runner skipping a group long run if she is instead scheduled for a shorter, faster run. Or a runner may need to do a scheduled run when he would otherwise choose a social activity detrimental to training that day. Learning how to say "no" becomes a skill, like saying "no" to some activities if/when they conflict with morning workout plans, or saying "yes" to social activities if a recovery day was needed anyway. When people talk about "keeping the balance" among running, work, and leisure, I can't help but remark that following a periodized training program *naturally* builds this balance into the equation. Of course, this all assumes a runner is following a training program to begin with, no matter how structured or unstructured it may be. If there's no general plan being followed, then this section probably won't resonate.

During the tapering period, a runner should be less concerned with what everyone else is doing and be more concerned with how he is feeling day-to-day. It's okay to skip a group workout if it conflicts with a personal schedule or energy levels. If a runner has sacrificed much of his time, energy, and money in the past year in hopes of achieving some meaningful running goal, then he shouldn't let it be sabotaged in the final lead-up to the race. Be confident in telling training partners that you need a day of rest, or that you want to run on your own in order to hit the target pace for a workout. We claim that exercise and health are strongly correlated with positive self-esteem, so let's put that self-esteem into action! Have enough self-esteem that your friends and family will still be there for you as you engage if some "selfish acts" in the few weeks before an A-race. Make some "me time" for yourself. As much as running does add a social element into many people's lives, running is very much an individual endeavor. During peak season, stick to *your* workouts on *your* specified days of the week and eat *your* chosen foods/drinks at *your* chosen time of day, especially in choosing the specific meal the night before the main event. Your body will thank you for it on race day, and you'll be able to thank yourself. Selectively during the year, treat yourself like an athlete.

Those are some of the practical tips as it relates to "taking running seriously." Many runners go overboard with this mentality and it becomes socially maladaptive, but all I'm encouraging runners to do is to put their race goals in the proper context. If someone isn't training like an athlete and/or doesn't have a peak-race slated, then there's no need to develop this approach. Otherwise, a runner should take a month out of the year to do it all his/her own way. After the peak race, there is usually a recovery period where the opposite approach takes places and there's much more time for to catch up on aspects of one's personal and professional life.

As peak season nears, ask yourself what kind of social support you have (or could create) to help you reach your goals. I certainly enjoy being a part of a runner's support crew, but consider how friends, co-workers, and family can pitch-in. Are they aware of your goals? Do they need to be? Support goes a long way with goal setting. There may come a time during race season when you need to be a bit selfish. Don't wait until the week of a big event to consider how your routine may significantly affect family and friends, or vice versa. Talk to your support crew early; give them an advanced heads-up on your plans (if needed). This does not mean you'll ignore your loved ones and neglect your pets that week; rather, it's just the subtleties that need consideration. These steps are part of what it means to be good to ourselves, which we, as humans, need to do.

More Thoughts on the Off-season

On the heels of sections devoted to understanding peak training, let's keep the chronology flowing and revisit the components and rationale for the off-season phase, which, along with the recovery phase, follows the peak phase. Elite endurance athletes consistently credit their successes at peak races to smart training or proper recovery, which typically entails a month of two of planned recovery. Once it's time to jump back into training, then that signals the beginning of the off-season.

The off-season is about experimentation. Experimentation in this sense can (at the least) mean new challenges for the body. A logical first place to turn is ST because it corrects muscular imbalances and helps bio-mechanics, endurance, and athleticism. However, there are other modes of physical activity that enhance athleticism other than ST. Therefore, in keeping with the model of periodization, and to reiterate from above, it is mandatory for athletes to add one of the following to their routine in the months of November through February: yoga, Pilates, Zumba, boxing, racquetball, step aerobics, circuit training classes (e.g., boot camp), swimming, kick boxing, rock climbing, ultimate Frisbee, spin classes, and the list goes on. Additionally, plyometric routines ("plyos") are a great way to increase strength, power, coordination, and athleticism.[4] This approach is also a method to keep the fitness lifestyle fun. Nobody should be a one-trick pony.

Many runners' ST and XT options are limited in the winter due to a lack of coordination. Scroll through the Group-X classes at your gym and sign-up for ones that will challenge balance and coordination, but always remember that strength helps balance (strong muscles allow for greater bodily control). In turn, balance helps coordination, which in turn improves athleticism. An off-season routine *must* include activities besides running and generic ST, or else one becomes stuck as an "exerciser" or "runner," and less like an "athlete." The latter term has many implications for long-term health and fitness, as well as improved run performance.

Peter Reid, a 3-time Hawaii Ironman winner, said, "The Ironman World Championship is raced in October, but it's *won* in the spring." He did serious amounts of ST and XT in his winter off-seasons so he was prepared for serious training and racing each spring. Reid also won Hawaii one year despite a nasty virus the month prior, and now you know *how* he was able to accomplish that feat. Make the effort to put more time/energy into ST in the off-season and the benefits will be apparent the entire year. This is also the time of year to focus on changing body composition. This has nothing to do with vanity; rather, having a leaner build will benefit running mechanics and endurance.[5] Yes, running can develop a leaner build more effectively than ST, but there are additional benefits we get from ST. These benefits include strength, power, endurance, balance, coordination, lean muscle, and variety in a routine.

---

4. I offer my athletes a designed plyos routine. There is a *Plyometrics* section in Chapter 3.

5. I recognize there is a limit to how lean an individual can become. There is a section titled *Body Types* in Chapter 4.

The off-season is the time to find "the missing links" in one's training or body and to fortify these weaknesses. What are the missing links, or where is the weak link in *your* chain? What element of training are you lacking that would take your game to the next level? Specifically, is it finally embracing run-specific ST or speed workouts? Is it scheduling more sessions with a physical therapist, personal trainer, nutritionist or masseuse? Do you need to purchase a foam roller, The Stick or a gym membership? All of these components would boost performance. The obvious considerations are time and money. Save money on the junk apparel/gear that's not needed and spend it on something more functional and performance-related.

Experimentation also means it's time to try new meals for breakfast (or pre-workout), new run sneakers (if that was an option), or anything else that would be new or different. I recommend that most, if not all, runs during Nov - Dec be done without a watch (that's only an 8-week period). If the run is less than an hour, do you really need to time the run, especially if it's a route you know like the back of your hand? Because the run doesn't need to be timed, and because pace should neither discourage nor limit a runner, this is a good time of year to run based on perceived exertion without numbers being a distraction. This would be a tremendous mental skill to take into spring racing (*lots* more on this skill in Chapters 6 and 7).

In order for an off-season to be effective and to accomplish its goals, we need it to be relatively long. Eight weeks would be the absolute *minimum*, but as non-professional athletes, we tend to need much more time for catching up in terms of general strength, specific strength, flexibility, coordination, balance, and athleticism. These attributes are all related to the ability to make the ST sessions dynamic and functional, which in turn improves running performance. Therefore, the off-season should be ~16 weeks in order to better prepare the body for the harder training during the remainder of the year.

Finally, recall the expression: "Most people run to get fit, whereas most of those people should be getting fit in order to run." Another helpful quote to keep in mind during the winter and off-season is as follows: "The biggest mistake that people make in the off-season is feeling like they are going to get a head start on the next year by training a lot. Part of getting a head start is to put energy back into your body, which means you stop taxing it." –Mark Allen. If Allen won the Ironman World Championship six times, then I think we can heed his advice.

MASSAGE

Massage can be discussed within this greater context of recovery and making corrections to the body. During a massage, the soft (connective) tissue "knots" are broken apart and blood flow increases to the massaged area to pull away waste products. In this sense, getting a massage means a *professional* massage, versus a mere shoulder rub after a long day at the office. Getting a relaxing shoulder rub is one thing, but a professional massage is a better way to reshape the connective tissue. It doesn't necessarily have to be a "sports massage" either. I frequently receive massages from people who aren't even aware that people ran as a sport, but they knew where the problem areas were without any conversation. As mentioned in the *Injuries* section last chapter, the area of the body that hurts usually isn't the underlying problem; rather, that's just where the symptoms are showing up. Massage, Active Release Technique (ART), Muscle Activation Technique, and ST are all designed to correct muscle imbalances or misalignments. I am yet to meet an athlete who did not feel like a new person after a legitimate sports massage or ART session.

"How often should I get a massage?" I suggest that an athlete *treat* him/herself to a massage every six to nine weeks, which happens to be the same timeline that recovery weeks should be taken. Self-massage is certainly a great tool, but treat yourself to the "real deal" during your recovery weeks. Don't hesitate to try a new masseuse each time or to try a new massage therapy practice. A different massage therapist is like getting a 2nd opinion on how your body is aligned.

Self-massage (self-myofascial release) is what most people refer to as foam rolling. Foam rollers and The Stick (a different product with a similar aim) can be used before and/or after any workout to stimulate blood flow and break up tight muscles and tissues. Foam rollers come in different densities; I recommend the denser ones. There are online videos for learning how to use the roller on almost every area of the body, or a trainer at the gym can cover a great deal in a five-minute review session.

Massage, or self-massage, is also a great way to increase flexibility. Massage, as a form of muscle manipulation, is typically superior to static stretching in terms of correcting the body. Stated alternatively, in terms of increasing flexibility of a joint, if given the choice between static stretching and self-massage, I would encourage the latter. Both can be beneficial, but self-massage or any form of muscle manipulation (e.g., Graston technique) is more beneficial because it addresses the root of the problem. Because the connective tissue encasing each muscle (the fascia) is strong and requires constant stress to change its shape, only direct pressure can change the shape of the fascia. Static stretching does not provide this type of pressure. As our muscles become tight by sitting frequently and/ or months or years of being sedentary, the muscles conform to these positions. If muscles are going to move into new ranges of motion and we intend to lessen the tightness that the muscles have developed, then direct manipulation of the muscles is needed. Again, this is accomplished through some form of massage, not static stretching, though the latter has its merits.[6]

Massages can also be used as a lesson in *how* to relax. Get in tune with HR and breathing, and learn what it takes to achieve a state of relaxation in a very quick timeframe. Use massage sessions to practice positive self-talk to relax the body. The masseuse is just there to assist that practice, like a shaman of sorts. There is a strong connection between mind and body, and any lessons learned in this regard while lying on the massage table can be applied to race day. Additionally, also pay attention to any differences in tension/tenderness between each side of the body. Yes, it's nice to space out during a good massage, but stay aware.

---

6. There are more details to this paradigm shift covered by other sources. Static stretching is discussed again in Chapter 5.

CLOSING THOUGHTS ON PERIODIZATION

A training program in December should look much different than it did in September. Similarly, March training should look different than December training, and so on. The different training phases are never set in stone, and there is certainly room for displacement of these phases, as well as crossing over of the phases. This is essentially due to the fact that speed work needs to be done year-round to avoid *completely* losing the speed that was developed ("use it or lose it"). However, an element of "de-training" is typical for most endurance athletes, even the world champions. The goal is to end the race season on a high note, at peak fitness. Following the last race of the season, take the next few weeks off from structured workouts and allow for more rest than usual. Now we've come full circle with understanding the flow of a yearly training cycle. Think about new activities to try (or get reacquainted with) during the winter/ off-season.

In addition to a recovery phase following the peak fall race, a similar recovery phase can be planned at some point in the late spring or early summer, which is natural if a runner just finished a solid bout of winter training and spring racing, especially at the full- or half-marathon distance. For instance, a runner training all winter for the Boston Marathon could back off the training for a few weeks to let the brain reset (avoiding mental burnout going into the fall) and to recharge the body (avoiding overtraining and injury). Again, this assumes that several months of consistent training took place beginning back in November/December. Yes, we take scheduled OFF days here and there, and also have the occasional recovery week, but similar to the short break taken after the peak fall races, I suggest a short break after the spring race season. This brief layoff does not mean that training shuts down altogether; it just means that one can mentally back off for a few weeks. This brief phase is when to catch up on work, sleep, social life, family life, or to take a weekend getaway. Take a short break from track workouts, recording data, and sending recaps, and keep the racing to a minimum. Preventive medicine is the best medicine. Ask any runner who has been successful year after year and they will surely credit this planned approach to their success and their injury-free, happy running.

There is no "get rich quick" scheme in running, and there are no miracles on race day. Once the majority of the learning and growing pains are under an athlete's belt, performance can improve exponentially. Patience is a virtue. Furthermore, there is no need to think (in an absolute sense) that we slow down with age; it's all relative. It's not uncommon for me to coach runners over age 40 who beat PRs set a decade (or more!) earlier. Experience, wisdom, and maturity help a great deal, meaning we learn as we go and our bodies adapt over a lifetime.

3

Strength Training &
Cross-Training

General Thoughts on Strength Training

When I first began coaching amateur runners in 2006, I would frequently hear statements from them suggesting that professional runners don't do strength training (ST) or that the pros don't need to do ST. The Internet has made it increasingly easier to tap into the training regiments of professional athletes, so we now know that those previous statements were a myth. Back in 2010, when I had a chance to have a brief chat with Ryan Hall, a top U.S. marathoner, I asked about his ST routine. In short, he replied, "We're in there five times per week, year-round mostly." He mentioned his focus is on run-specific muscles and exercises, including plyometrics (plyos), or as he phrased it, "short bursts of fast-twitch muscle work." These words from one of the world's fastest marathoners should fuel your motivation to do ST (I hear similar answers each time I talk to one of the elite runners I meet). Also consider *why* they are elite runners. They likely have been running most of their lives, but they also maintain a lifestyle that doesn't include sitting for most of the day. Therefore, they haven't developed bad posture or tight hips and hamstrings, which are some of the obstacles to be overcome by mortal runners. The elite runners have also been naturally strengthening the run-specific muscles over a lifetime, at least more so than us. Because we typically need to correct muscular weaknesses and imbalances, we have to play catch-up via ST.

Increases in strength and muscle (lean tissue) are commonly cited reasons for ST. ST for muscle growth (hypertrophy) does *not* mean you will look like a body builder, unless you specifically train (and eat) that way. ST for muscle growth can mean a simultaneous gain in lean tissue and reduction in body fat, thereby increasing body metabolism, causing the body to burn more calories at rest (see next paragraph). However, people typically do not achieve these *significant* changes in body composition until at least six weeks after starting a ST program (genetics pending). The first changes that take place are neuromuscular. After the initial neuromuscular changes, the body adapts by increasing the size of muscle fibers. The actual increase in the size of the muscle fibers depends on the specificity of training. If you want to look like a body builder, then you have to train like one. I never have met nor will ever meet a runner whose ST program resembled anything like that of a body builder. To be candid, I find that females are more likely than males to shy away from using appropriate loads (heavier loads) for ST, and it's often rooted in the misinterpretation of how the body responds to ST (they fear they will become "bulky"). Most of the female personal trainers I've met, many of who are great runners, agree with this observation.

Body metabolism is directly related to the amount of muscle tissue (the more muscle, the faster the metabolism). A body with an increase in lean tissue will begin to burn more calories at rest. This is an obvious benefit of ST. It is common knowledge that running generally burns more calories than most other activities. Therefore, running combined with ST creates a simple formula of moving toward a more slender build. To take this surface level muscle physiology a step further, endurance athletes tend to release more cortisol (a hormone) into the body, which breaks down muscle (to a modest degree), so the muscles may thin for that reason too. Additionally, the slender build associated with avid endurance athletes is also theorized to be a result of the muscles thinning to make the capillaries more efficient in circulating blood and oxygen, which is to say that the blood would have less distance to travel within the muscles.

PROGRAM DESIGN

A ST routine depends on a number of variables. The number of days per week of ST, the duration of each set, the number of sets per exercise, the number of exercises per muscle group, the rest period between sets, and the order of exercises are all equally important and determine how the body will respond. It should be noted that there is an upper limit for how many sets should be done in one workout. The mantra that "more is better" is only true to a certain degree. If it is assumed that each set is performed to failure (as in generally the goal), then there may be a point of diminished return if the total sets for a specific muscle is higher than 15, or higher than 30 total for all muscle groups in one workout. Body builders often tease these lines as they experiment in training.

The ST program I create is structured for an ideal universe, in which a runner is able to do four days (or more) of ST for the first six to twelve weeks, and then gradually reduce the frequency. If ST is only being done once or twice (for whatever reason), then it's best to salvage the lower body and core workouts. In that case, the upper body workouts can be mixed in if possible, with the variety for those guided by selecting different upper body muscle groups each week. A ST template should leave much room for individual progressions and improvisations as needed (e.g., technique or equipment).

ST should be done twice per week as a minimum. Once per week just isn't enough to elicit significant changes in body composition and strength for amateur athletes. During some weeks, ST might only be scheduled once or not at all. Those are called recovery weeks and are part of the bigger picture. Otherwise, I will only reduce an athlete's ST frequency to once per week during peak season(s), the length of which varies from person to person. This rationale explains when ST takes on its *maintenance* phase. However, a true maintenance phase only exists if there was a true *base* phase (high volume) in the first place.

There is a real difference between ST once per week vs. twice vs. three times and so on. I encourage all runners to make that transition to ST four to five times per week so they can feel how much fitter, leaner, and stronger they can become. Obviously, logistics are the main factor in that transition, and I pride myself on creating programs that are challenging, *yet* feasible. How can you make more time for ST? Do you even want to? The answer to the latter predicts the answer to the former, as people typically make time for the activities they *want* to do. Remember that a legitimate ST workout can be done in as few as 20 minutes as long as you are fatiguing the muscles.

In terms of fatiguing the muscles, the appropriate load or difficulty setting to use for a given exercise is that which is *moderately difficult*, which implies there is a challenge imposed to the muscles, yet the set can still be successfully completed with proper form. Each set having an appropriate level of difficulty is how lean body mass and strength are attained. If the end of your set is not difficult, then you are stronger than you think. The body must be stressed in order to adapt (insert the "no pain, no gain" cliché here). If it is the first time performing a particular exercise, then a person may have to start with trial and error, but certainly erring on the conservative side for safety. The same difficulty setting can be used for each set or the load can be gradually increased each set. Keep in mind that many exercises don't require the use of weights or machines, so the difficulty setting in those instances would rely on the duration of the set and/or technical progressions to make the exercise more advanced. As mentioned before, there is a generalization that females tend to choose settings that are not challenging enough, whereas males gravitate toward the opposite side of that spectrum, often sacrificing proper technique while using difficulty settings that are too high. Fatigue *and* technique are paramount, so hopefully both genders can benefit from this chapter.

Assuming a runner is prepping for a peak race in the fall, September is typically the final month of intense ST. In other words, one to four weeks prior to a peak race is too little time to *begin* correcting muscle imbalances; the real hard work needs to be completed by that point. Sure, ST can be done on a year-round basis, but as specificity of training dictates, late September through early November ("race season") is all about running, with ST and XT mostly set aside in favor of high-intensity run workouts and more rest. During other seasons, when ST and XT get priority, a runner might accept short-term losses in run training for long-term gains in overall strength and athleticism. Therefore, some run workouts (especially in the off-season) will be done while feeling sore from ST and that is acceptable. However, during peak season a runner should not want any extra soreness from ST/XT because the goal during this time is to feel like a million bucks for every run, at least in a relative sense (i.e., like a thousand bucks). In sum, you're allowed to be sore during run workouts, you're allowed to forget about exact pacing, but once the final lead-up to the peak event begins, you have to welcome the added rest days and embrace the fact you're letting the body recover to absorb the past few months of training. That is a crucial coaching point.

There is a potential drawback to doing too much of any type of XT during the week, yoga and Pilates included. Not to contradict earlier points about increasing total training volume and doing more ST to gain further adaptations, but the point is that there may come a time when doing too much ST or isometric contractions will conflict with run training due to the extra fatigue. The athlete or coach has to be objective in deciding how important those run workouts are in relation to the bigger picture. This is related to why XT eventually doesn't make it through the funnel we call tapering. Meaning, if the mileage is cut down in order to recover before a peak race, piling on extra XT will have defeated the purpose of the taper.

Whether or not ST and running are on the same day depends on one's weekly routine. If these workouts happen to be done on the same day and there is a choice as to which one to do first, then I would recommend doing ST first. One reason for this rationale is that load bearing exercises typically require more skill and concentration than running, so it's better to do ST exercises while you're mentally and physically fresh. Additionally, based on both empirical and anecdotal evidence, the run workout will produce greater muscular fatigue and have a greater adverse effect on the ST workout if done back-to-back, whereas ST workouts don't typically adversely affect a subsequent non-key run workout. In other words, you can still have a high quality run session following ST, but are less likely to have high-quality ST after a run. Speed workouts would be an exception to this rule, in that one should avoid ST right before a speed workout. I generally want my athletes to treat speed workouts like gold.

RUN-SPECIFIC STRENGTH TRAINING

It's important to remember that because running is essentially a series of single-leg squats or single-leg stances, the ST should reflect this specific demand. ST exercises performed one leg at a time, such as single-leg squats or walking lunges, is the essence of a run-specific ST program. Because we don't run with both feet on the ground at the same time, our ST needs to include isolated, controlled, and single-leg stances and motions.

When performing ST exercises with a self-selected additional load, like free weights or weight-stack machines, performing 6 - 15 reps is a general rule of thumb for gains in strength and lean tissue. However, varying the number of reps within that range from week to week causes new adaptations. With that in mind, the number of reps (or duration of the set) is not listed in the ST template I create. This is partly because freedom of choice can be built in here, but it's mainly because when it comes to the core exercises that use only the athlete's body weight as resistance I have no way of knowing how long an individual can perform a set, nor do I want to impose a number of reps. These core exercises (akin to Pilates movements) are relatively difficult, so the number of reps that can be done with *perfect form* (key phrase) will vary from person to person.

Form needs to be near flawless for it to be effective, so an athlete can simply guide him/herself by performing as many reps as possible while maintaining flawless form. For instance, when I coach an athlete through a ST session, I'll point out all the little details of the mechanics that need to be corrected. I am notoriously a stickler for ST technique and pride myself on being absolutely militant in this area. There is an exponential difference between ST done with good form and ST done with *perfect* form. Tiny adjustments here and there (often a matter of an inch or two) make all the difference in the world. Even the speed of the movement is something to consider. The way I quiz my runners on whether or not their form is flawless is by asking if they are competent enough to teach a 45-minute run-specific ST class for ten runners and be able to correct the technique of everyone in the class and make the key points about each exercise.

Here are two final coaching points regarding proper form. First, before you think you are strong, ask yourself if there a reason the set/exercise felt so easy. Was your technique incorrect, to the extent you were unknowingly cheating and therefore you were able to do many reps of an exercise that is traditionally difficult? If it feels like too many reps or the duration of the set feels too long, then there should always be a way to make the exercise more challenging, dynamic, and progressive. Second, before you think you are weak or uncoordinated, ask yourself if there a specific reason the set/exercise was unnecessarily hard? Was your form so poor that it made it impossible to do a given exercise for even a few reps or a few seconds?

CIRCUIT TRAINING & CROSSFIT

Circuit training, as in hitting many or all muscle groups in one workout with little or no rest between sets, is a great option if you are pressed for time.

Otherwise, resting an extra 10 - 30 seconds (or longer) between sets can increase the quality of the sets and allow you to occasionally work on your *maximum* strength. Maximum strength is increased when using heavier loads and higher difficulty settings, which is sometimes compromised during circuit training because of the lack of full recovery. However, any mode of ST can be effective for decreasing fatty tissue while increasing muscular tone, strength, and endurance. Another option when time is scarce is to target two muscle groups in a given workout (instead of all muscle groups), as in performing 2 - 3 sets per exercise and 3 - 4 exercises per muscle group.

Regarding CrossFit training, which is typically high-intensity circuit training combined with some explosive, dynamic movements (e.g., Olympic lifts), I generally agree with many of its principles and think it has many benefits for certain populations. However, with individuals that are relatively new to ST, I'd rather they build a more solid base of coordination and strength before moving into CrossFit. In addition, the world of CrossFit can be very competitive. Workouts are often based on how quickly they are completed and/or pushing for extra reps at the sacrifice of proper form, especially at the amateur level. That said, be careful when doing CrossFit and always keep technique the priority. Although it places an emphasis on core/functional movements, much of the CrossFit training is not specific to running in terms of lower body exercises. It can help running performance, but wouldn't be as optimal as true run-specific ST, like Pilates.

CORE TRAINING, PILATES & YOGA

As a coach and personal trainer, I am asked too often about "how to get a ripped 6-pack." I'm more inclined to help an athlete achieve a stronger core than get "ripped abs." Having a strong core has nothing to do the appearance of your mid-section. Your core refers to the your abdominals, back, glutes, hips, and every muscle surrounding your thigh. These are the muscles that help control posture and stride length. Posture and stride length are strongly associated with running performance among sprinters and distance runners alike, but a strong core is also important for power athletes, as a body in poor alignment would not generate as much force for a given movement. Many of the world class athletes in track and field's throwing events could be considered overweight, but their core strength and power are ten-fold compared to athletes in other sports. Therefore, in order to generate higher forces, the biomechanics of the movement must be ideal. Biomechanics is aided by proper body positioning via a stronger mid-section. If a ST routine is kept dynamic and functional, then virtually every exercise performed could be considered core training, namely for the same reason that running is a great core workout. When performed with proper form, both dynamic ST and running generate high forces, which leads to a great core workout.

Pilates and yoga are both great for core strength and posture. They both emphasize body awareness as it relates to the principles of proper running posture and rhythmic breathing. Another benefit of these two modes of training is that they teach one *how* to focus on pain and discomfort, which is vital in learning positive self-talk, a skill I discuss in other chapters of this book. I am a strong proponent of Pilates and yoga, but if push came to shove in terms of building strength, then I would choose Pilates over yoga. Both are challenging, both require coordination, but Pilates is more specific to running, as it incorporates more true strength work for the leg muscles, even though this exists to a degree in yoga. Furthermore, doing more yoga "to gain flexibility" isn't necessary unless a physical therapist or trainer has diagnosed you with a range of motion limitation. If a person is already flexible enough to establish proper running mechanics, then improving flexibility does not further enhance run performance. To reiterate, I prefer Pilates because there's more emphasis on strength work rather than on isometric contractions and range of motion.

POSTURE

I discuss posture in more detail in the *Running Form* chapter, but here are some initial rhetorical questions. Do you sit up tall at your desk, or do you slouch? Do you lean your head forward toward the computer screen? Is your screen significantly below eye level, or can you move it up closer to eye level? How often do you take breaks at your desk to stand and stretch, including neck rolls, ankle rolls, wrist rolls, and "heart openers" (from yoga)? Do you find that your shoulders are constantly shrugged upward (too much stress in your life)? Do you stand with one shoulder lower than the other? When you stand, is there more body weight on one foot? Do you think about these points while running or doing ST? Pay attention for a week and see what you discover.

A strong core will improve your posture tremendously, but as with any correction to form, being aware of the body is the first step ("detection then correction"). Develop a cue word or phrase to be able to correct your posture more immediately, as in classical conditioning. I coach a several runners who have pinned a reminder post-it reminder to the wall at their desk that reads, "Posture!" However, if you want better back posture, "thinking about it" will only take you so far. One has to strengthen the neck and upper back muscles to allow the muscles to maintain proper alignment over a period of time.[7] Popular media wants us to have great front side to the body—abs, quads, biceps, chest, and front shoulder muscles. However, the muscles on the back side of the body are vital for running form, with the hamstrings and glutes being the important running muscles.

BALANCE BOARD TRAINING

A balance board (or wobble board) is definitely run-specific ST. Extra equipment isn't necessary for balance training, as a flat surface with the shoes off will suffice. A session of balance training will strengthen the feet, ankles, calves, abs, adductors, and glutes. A good place to start is with

---

7. I recommend the book *8 Steps to a Pain-Free Back* (listed in the References). Although it virtually never mentions running, the practical connections are there. It also addresses why adults in the U.S. and other industrialized countries report back problems compared to non-industrialized cultures.

30-second sets, alternating legs. There should be a slight bend in the leg, mimicking the amount of bend in the leg when the foot hits the ground when running, but sets can be done with a straightened leg. If using a circular, wooden board then some sets can be accomplished by "surfing" with both feet on the outer portion of the board (with a slight bend in both knees). Otherwise, using a BOSU ball or the flat, rubber discs are just as beneficial.

The goal in balancing is to keep the "free foot" off the ground the entire set. Use the leg that is on the ground/apparatus to regain balance. Meaning, it is okay to not be perfectly balanced as long as the free foot stays off the ground. Because it is very difficult to maintain a perfectly balanced state (in the truest sense of the word) during these sets, the strength benefits are gained by the act of regaining balance with the muscles in the feet, calves, glutes, and abs. The goal is to steadily increase the time that the free foot can be kept off the ground. Some circular wobble boards have three difficulty settings and I suggest using the lowest/easiest setting and keeping it at that setting until you can keep the edges off the ground for at least 20 seconds.

PLYOMETRICS

Plyometrics ("plyos") are typically a series of jumping and bounding movements of which the aim is to increase the strength of the joints, tendons, and ligaments in the legs, as well as to increase muscular *power*, as differentiated from strength. The difference between strength and power is the speed of the movement, with powerful movements being performed more quickly. A plyometric exercise is a quick, powerful movement using the spring-like action of the tendons (jumping rope and sprinting can be considered plyometric exercises).[8] Power has been associated with im-

---

8. Jumping rope is a good warm-up for ST, as well as a good way to strengthen the lower leg muscles and tendons that used when running with a midfoot strike (discussed in Chapter 5).

provements in running economy (RE).[9] Studies have appeared in the scientific literature demonstrating that eliminating portions of endurance training in favor of explosive activities or adding plyos to an existing running program for six to nine weeks can improve RE and performances in short-distance racing without needing to see an accompanying change in VO_2max. These benefits are evident regardless of ability, gender or age.

These results are best understood in that any time a muscle group becomes stronger and more powerful, fewer muscle fibers are recruited to perform the given task, thus allowing the muscle group to have more fibers in reserve for continued work. Basically, this means that less energy is used to cover the same distance. Since the discovery of this concept, it has been shown that power training, not just ST, will lead to enhancements in running economy. Of course there is no substitute for running if one wants to run faster and farther; however, during peak racing season, as the RV gradually decreases, plyos are another option for maintaining high-intensity workouts (in addition to speed workouts).

A plyos program is typically done one or two times a week and is based on the total number of foot contacts, or "touches." For beginners, the recommended range is between 60 - 100 touches for a few weeks, before progressing toward 100 touches for a few more weeks and then beyond (capping the total touches at 140).[10] Reps can be performed as double-leg exercises (both feet jump, or contact the ground, at the same time) or as single-leg exercises, although single-leg plyos should be reserved for experienced athletes. Sometimes additional equipment can be used to add variety and difficulty into these workouts, like small hurdles and boxes.

---

9. Running economy, as defined by Dr. Jack Daniels, involves the amount of oxygen being consumed relative to the runner's body weight and the speed he/she is running. Simply stated, an athlete who requires less oxygen to maintain a given speed/pace is operating at a lower heart rate.

10. Jumping rope, if performed as a warm-up for a plyos workout, does not have to be counted when considering the total foot contacts.

Plyos are a great compliment to ST but don't underestimate how strenuous these exercises can be. For many of the exercises, it's not necessarily the muscles that are the target for strengthening; rather, it's the joints, tendons, and ligaments. With that said, these aren't always muscle-burning exercises or workouts, so don't mistakenly take that mentality into a plyos workout. Additionally, before starting plyos training, I recommend completing at least six weeks of general ST in order to strengthen the body parts that incur more stress when performing various jumping and hopping exercises. I recommend plyos as long as an athlete is familiar/comfortable with jumping exercises in general. Do not do plyos unless there is 100% certainly on the landing mechanics for each exercise. Similar to how I frame a discussion on proper ST technique, if you couldn't teach jumping and landing mechanics to a small group, then your plyos form probably isn't ideal.

MOTIVATION FOR STRENGTH TRAINING

If there is a value on running goals, then a value should be placed on run-specific ST. If there is no longer any motivation to do ST, then perhaps it needs to be more challenging. If so, how can it be made more challenging? If the spirit of human nature is to embrace and accept new challenges, then making ST more dynamic, progressive, varied, and (fun)ctional should cure any apathy. Activities are boring when they're too easy. This notion is confirmed by decades of social psychology research. Yes, we also lose motivation when activities are too challenging, but in terms of ST, I'm willing to bet that anyone who is struggling to find the motivation isn't working hard enough. That's not reverse psychology at work; that's my expert eye at work.

I designed my athletes' ST template to flow in a certain order, but runners can stand the template on its head if they wanted. Just ensure each set is performed to fatigue and that technique is graded strictly, as if a trainer were hawking over you. The possibilities of adding variety to ST are endless. The prospect of endless possibilities lends way to yet another plug to increase athleticism and coordination in the off-season. Variety, fun, challenge, getting faster, getting leaner, getting stronger, losing weight, dedication, sweating once per day...be mindful of your reason for ST, not your excuse for skipping it!

For those training for a marathon, ST may determine race-day performance more than actual run mileage. Non-professional runners miss goal times and bonk in marathons for many different reasons. However, it's rarely because they ran out of breath or did too few miles. At the marathon distance, subpar performances are often because the joints/muscles became painful and the runner had to slow down or walk (sound familiar to anyone?). Increased RV certainly helps, but only to a degree. Running doesn't strengthen every aspect of the body. Running 26 miles is hard work and the body needs ST to prepare. As the goals become more ambitious, running form and strong joints/muscles become more important in handling a more intense workload.

4

NUTRITION & FUELING

AFTER HEARING ENOUGH presentations on this topic, I am convinced that diet is the most individualized sport there is. The more I read, the more it seems that one person's pleasure is another person's poison and vice versa. Our bodies are very unique and I think nutritionists are great diet coaches. The notes below on nutrition are general (e.g., refueling, eating breakfast, hydration), as I am not a licensed dietician. What to eat pre-race or mid-marathon is something to be answered on an evolving basis. This chapter merely offers general reminders for healthy eating habits and fueling practices.

WATER & HYDRATION

The most important nutrient for athletes is water. The main effect of dehydration is an increase in body temperature, which places additional stress on the cardiovascular system. When blood flow throughout the body is reduced due to dehydration, muscles don't receive the fuel and oxygen they need. Therefore, dehydration ultimately causes pre-mature muscle fatigue. Here is a crude outline depicting how dehydration operates, using "»" symbols to show causal relationships:

Less water in the body » decreased blood volume » decreased blood return to the heart » decreased stroke volume (amount of blood per beat) » decreased O_2 to working muscles (because O_2 is carried in blood) & reduced blood flow to the skin » increased body temperature » increased HR to attempt to pump more blood to skin for sweating/cooling » decreased aerobic metabolism (muscles in need of O_2-carrying blood must now compete with the skin to receive blood) » body overheats and muscles fatigue.

As outlined above, when exercising in a dehydrated state, blood flow to the skin is reduced, which is problematic because blood flow to the skin is what enables sweating, in turn cooling the body through evaporation. When dehydrated, blood flow to the rest of the body (not just the skin) is reduced, which certainly has an effect on working muscles and HR. Dehydration is not simply whether or not there is cottonmouth, although that is a sign. Feeling thirsty is an indicator of a state of 1 - 2% dehydration, which means the muscles are already in a less-optimum state (no need to call the emergency room though; 5% dehydration is where trouble begins).

Regarding how much water one should consume over the course of a day, there is no precise answer. During exercise, the rule of thumb is to consume approximately 24oz of water per hour. However, other variables increase that number, such as duration and intensity of exercise, level of fitness, body weight, weather conditions, and sweat patterns. With this in mind, I prefer the simple mantra, "Drink *before* you are thirsty." This tip is practical because the body will not absorb as much water if it is consumed in larger quantities at one time (we can *absorb* ~8 - 10oz every 10 - 15 minutes). For instance, the goal on race day is to sip fluids the hour leading up to the race and during the race (the water cups at aid stations are typically 3 - 6oz).[11]

The concentration of a sport drink, including the amount of powder added to homemade concoctions, is dependent on the intensity of the

---

11. I encourage any distance runner to purchase a FuelBelt or similar hydration belt, which also comes with a small pouch to hold the fuel, keys, etc. sparing unnecessary muscular tension by having to use the hands.

workout or race. This tip definitely applies to triathletes and ultra-marathoners, who are typically equipped with their own bottles of sport drink during the race. The body prefers a weaker concentration (less scoops of the powder) for high intensity races because it's harder for the body to process higher concentrations of fuel during high intensity efforts. An athlete can get away with a higher concentration sport drink when going slower/longer. As always, these questions should be answered during training.

ALCOHOL AND CAFFEINE

Regarding other fluids, alcohol and caffeine are obviously not the ideal choices for athletes but to delve into those details is beyond the scope of this book. However, I will mention that alcohol limits the absorption of some vitamins and minerals, like calcium, iron, and zinc, and also contributes to the loss of these vitamins and minerals through urinary excretion. Therefore, excessive alcohol intake is a double-whammy. Caffeine and cocoa have a similar effect on mineral loss, as the tannins they contain bind to certain minerals, like calcium and iron. Despite the popular belief, caffeine is not conclusively linked with dehydration or significant increases in urinary frequency; however, it is still not a healthy choice for a beverage. As with some soda brands, coffee can be marketed as zero-calorie and zero-fat, but on the other hand, what nutritious value do soda and coffee offer? What do they contain that is considered healthy? Additionally, how does your caffeine intake affect your sleeping patterns? If this point is well taken, then all the more sense to stick with water and nutrient-enriched drinks.

For athletes seeking the extra boost from caffeine, it is important to understand that the benefits of added alertness and endurance are only realized for those individuals who are *not* regular coffee drinkers, and even then not everyone receives these benefits. This should be logical, as there is a desensitization effect with coffee (similar to any drug) in that the more it's used, the less it stimulates the brain. Eventually, more coffee is needed to get the same stimulus, an underlying cause for habit-forming behavior. Many gel flavors contain a serving or two of caffeine, and some long-distance athletes drink flat soda at the midpoint of a race. These two strategies are worth considering—to have some caffeine (in a tolerable form) on occasion during a longer event.

FUELING STRATEGIES FOR ENDURANCE ATHLETES

To perform well in a long-distance event, high-quality training sessions at the longer distances are required; therefore, proper fueling becomes vital. I understand that the term *long-distance* can be relative, so I'll define it as longer than 90 minutes. Avid endurance athletes can usually get through a workout of 90 minutes or less without needing to fuel. However, beyond that, a general rule of thumb is to fuel with carbs (e.g., a gel pack) every 45 minutes. In practical terms, studies show that it is vital to fuel *before* the presence of fatigue because of the principle of "too little, too late." This means fueling before it's actually needed, similar to hydration strategies. It's best to fuel at the exact same time during each long workout, and it's better to fuel based on minutes, not miles (e.g., running six miles on a flat course might be 48 minutes, on a hilly course on a hot day, it might be 54 minutes). Due to the ease of digestion, the body prefers liquids and gels (versus solids).

Experienced runners can do the occasional long run of two hours or more without any fuel (other than water). This is a good strategy in training the body to burn more fats throughout the event, sparing the much-needed storage of carbs as much as possible for as long as possible. This strategy can leave many runners borderline on bonking, so I don't recommend it every week, but it's a good way for a runner to test the limits for how long and intensely a run can be done without fuel, an *indirect* measure of improved fitness.

The quality of longer workouts is determined not only by proper fueling, but also by how well a runner recovers from weekly training in general. The latter (recovery) is largely determined by daily diet. Having healthy eating habits is more realistic if one thinks of him/herself as an *athlete* because it fosters a mentality that gives practical reasoning for a healthy diet. For example, if diet has benefits and consequences on a daily basis, then it's more likely to be monitored. This becomes a better strategy than simply stating, "I want to eat right," which is a psychologically useless goal.

You may come across the phrase *periodization for nutrition*, which states that a diet should be structured throughout the year to parallel the energy demands resulting from periodized training (discussed in Chapter 2). I tend to agree with this system. Basically, during the preparation and base-building months, an athlete can consume more calories to support the extra calories burned. One could also stand to eat more meats and protein in these months to help rebuild the muscles, as muscle breakdown can be greatest in the high-volume ST months. When the training becomes low-volume and the caloric intake is therefore reduced, a healthy reduction in body weight (be it great or small) can occur. Fat intake should be significantly reduced as training volume is reduced, especially since carbs become the primary fuel for workouts later in the year. Periodized nutrition helps runners reach a healthy race weight during the peak season.

FUELING FOR A MARATHON

During an endurance event, stored muscle glycogen (carbs *stored* in the muscles) is the preferred source of energy compared to blood glucose (carbs gained via fueling *during* the event). The former is more efficient in terms of carbs entering the blood stream and muscles, and it yields more calories. This is the main rationale for carb-loading the days before an event lasting three or more hours. Fats take too long to be broken down and transported to be considered an efficient energy source, so it is not a preferred source of fuel. Plus, to use fat as a fuel implies that the intensity must be low. Fats can't be metabolized anaerobically (e.g., the last 10k of a marathon) mainly due to the decreased blood flow to adipose (fat) tissue. At that point, blood flow has already been dramatically increased to the working muscles and to the skin for sweating.

Smaller continual feedings during a marathon are preferred because, unlike *larger* feedings, blood and water don't need to be excessively pulled into the intestines to aid in digestion and absorption. This is also another rationale for trying to fuel with liquids and/or gels compared to solids, as solids require more blood and water to digest.

Studies have shown that in the later stages of a marathon, blood glucose may make a larger contribution to race performance than hydration. Tentatively, this can be interpreted to mean that carbs may be more important than water in the final 10k of a marathon. It would be wise for a runner to assess his/her individual needs in those moments because too much or not enough sodium (contained in sport drinks, where a runner may be getting her carbs) can be dangerous, as in hypernatremia and hyponatremia, respectively.[12]

There is no need to fuel within the first 30 minutes of a long-distance race because energy stores aren't compromised at that point, and the extra calories won't significantly improve performance. This explains the general set of instructions on fueling products to begin fueling around the 45-minute mark. However, a runner can certainly *hydrate* before that time. A runner can get calories/carbs from the sports drink available at the course's aid stations, but as far as gels are concerned, he/she should stick to the regular timing used in training, which might roughly be the 45-minute mark, 1:30, 2:00, and 2:30 (for a sub 3:15 marathoner). Again, the doses should *not* be large, so for example, one gel or a half-pack of Sports Beans might do. This means hitting the start line fully "carb-loaded," knowing energy will naturally be running low the last 10k regardless. Experimentation in training should guide fueling plans for the race, so some weekend long

---

12. Anyone attempting to run a marathon should research these terms.

runs need to be done at predicted race pace, whereas some runners do *all* of their weekend long runs at a pace much slower than they hope to do on race day.

CARBOHYDRATES & PRE-RACE MEALS

As athletes, we can generally agree that we need to consume our carbohydrates to some degree. Carbohydrates are the primary fuel for *all* types of exercise, regardless of duration or intensity. For exercise lasting less than 45 minutes, there is no significant difference in performance *during* exercise based on a pre-workout meal, and that's regardless of the nature of the workout (e.g., endurance, strength, power), assuming one has not overeaten. For these shorter workouts, the timing of the pre-workout meal and the type of fuel is more important in benefiting the body *afterward*. In other words, the ingestion of nutrients and energy (carbs) within two hours *before* exercise spares the glycogen already in the muscles, which can then be used to minimize post-workout breakdown of protein. Therefore, in these instances, any meal will suffice, granted it's approximately two hours prior to the workout, contains carbohydrates and is easily digestible.

Regarding carb-loading for events three hours or longer, the research does not promote a *significantly* larger meal (~800 or more calories than usual) the night before the event, given that studies have not conclusively shown a significant improvement in performance for a carb-load group compared to those who ate a regular-portioned meal. Also, consider that it is probably not best to experiment with a significantly larger meal the night before a big race because the digestive system might not be able to tolerate the meal. More calories can be consumed at each meal during the two to three days before a long-distance race, but regular-sized meals should be eaten the day before, with perhaps a *slightly* bigger dinner (~400 - 500 calories extra) and an *extra* 150 - 200 calories than normal at breakfast on race morning. Also consider that if an athlete is tapering before a long distance event, then the body is naturally storing more carbs in that preceding week(s) due to the reduced training volume.

I suggest experimenting with the pre-workout diet far in advance of peak race season, so it can be utilized later for competitions; therefore, there is a consistent approach throughout the year. Record the timing of pre-race meals, as well as what was consumed on race day, and note how the body reacted. The questions, "What should I have for breakfast before the race?" and "How should I fuel during the race?" should be answered prior to the race based on personal notes following key workouts and races.

REFUELING

Refueling immediately after a workout is pivotal in maintaining energy stores and reducing the degree of muscles soreness. Research has shown that in order to optimize nutritional intake, a meal high in carbohydrates *and* protein should be consumed within 15 - 20 minutes after the workout (the "metabolic window"). As soon as exercise stops, the muscles are breaking down, which usually causes muscle soreness a few days later (the term is *DOMS* and stands for Delayed Onset Muscle Soreness). Getting carbohydrates and protein into the bloodstream will reduce these effects by helping the muscles repair and grow. A short explanation posits that there is a post-workout release of insulin into the bloodstream, which aids in the absorption of carbs and protein into the muscle cells. This insulin release peaks within 20 minutes post-workout, and this is when the muscles are primed for absorbing carbs and protein, like a sponge. Insulin also increases blood flow to the muscles, which removes the substrates of muscle fatigue. Every 20 minutes, after the first 20 minutes following the workout, becomes more and more critical in minimizing muscle breakdown and maintaining lean tissue; after two hours the muscles are insulin *resistant*. The combination of protein and carbs is greater for stimulating insulin secretion versus the independent effects of these two fuel sources.

Not to be contradictory, but research shows that refueling within 20 minutes is less critical if the next workout is more than 24 hours later and if an adequate amount of carbs will be consumed during that period. In that case, glycogen levels (carbs) will return to normal by the next day. So if an athlete is resting the day after a workout and trying to watch his/her caloric intake, then it is logical to cut down significantly on the post-workout calories, especially if the workout was relatively short (less than 90 min).

Because it is natural to have a suppressed appetite following a high-intensity workout, it is easier to ingest the carbs and protein in liquid form (e.g., recovery drinks). Supplemental recovery drinks, which typically have many servings of protein, are increasing in popularity. Consuming more protein above the recommended dietary allowance does *not* lead to enhanced muscle mass, nor have creatine products been able to consistently show improvements in muscle mass or performance across populations. Because of this finding and coupled with the fact that the long-term studies on creatine are still in the works, I am *not* a proponent of creatine products.

THE PALEO DIET

The Paleolithic (Paleo) diet is also called the hunter-gatherer diet. The original Paleo diet eaten tens of thousands of years ago has a different definition than what we can readily duplicate today, so that is one reason to take it with a grain of salt. There is yet to be unequivocal evidence that paleo strategies enhance athletic performance, but if it works for you, then go for it! Carbs are needed for athletic performance, especially the longer and more intense the workout becomes. This is due to muscles relying on glycogen stores already within the muscles, which led to the original theory of carb-loading. When glycogen stores drop and additional carbs haven't been consumed, this can cause the "bonking" sensation. Exercising in a carb-depleted state can also lead to greater increases in circulating stress hormones (i.e., cortisol), impairing the immune system. Athletes who over-train while using a low-carb diet are at a higher risk for getting sick due to the release of cortisol into the body during strenuous activity. Consider a modified paleo diet that doesn't restrict carb intake as much. The amount of carbs needed comes down to the type of running being done. Put simply, the faster the pace and the longer the distance, the more carbs that are needed.

Any diet can be healthy if everything is kept in moderation (a familiar catch phrase). I think the Paleo diet, similar to a multiple-day juice cleanse, can be a good reset button or wake-up call to begin a healthier diet. It's a good place to start in that sense and it can have positive, indirect effects on running performance for that reason. I don't think it has to be a way of life, but such diets have their merits, especially as a kick in the butt (if needed) for one to love his/her body more.

BODY WEIGHT & BODY FAT

Exercise should be a regular part of everyone's routine because of its importance for a healthy heart and regulation of body metabolism. The Basal Metabolic Rate (BMR) is the minimum amount of calories burned each day through the simple, daily activities (excluding exercise). Most Americans eat more calories than is required by the BMR. Weight management boils down to the balance between caloric intake and calories burned, with routine exercise helping to maintain this caloric balance. Reducing caloric intake is often the first step to losing weight and it's a logical first step. However, if caloric intake is restricted too much (i.e., 600 - 800 or fewer calories per day), not only will the body not get sufficient nutrients, but also the body will respond negatively in many ways. To name a few examples, there would be decreases in white blood cell count, bone density, vitamins, proteins, with impairments of the digestive system, immune system, brain functioning, and a likelihood for increased cholesterol.

Therefore, anyone attempting to lose weight by "not eating" is obviously at risk for other health defects. Moreover, what is often overlooked is the fact that "not eating" can lead to a slower BMR in order to conserve fats, which is an evolutionary survival mechanism based on the vital roles that fats serve within the body. The initial weight loss experienced by someone virtually starving him/herself is certainly due to fewer calories, but once metabolism slows and body fat percentage increases, these individuals are actually *un*healthier at a lesser weight. Ultimately, the increase in body fat percentage is the result of not eating enough calories. During this time the body will get its energy from proteins, which means muscle is broken down to supply energy, further enhancing the unhealthy body composition. These negative effects begin to initiate after only a few days of too few calories.

When someone first begins an exercise program, there may be a nominal increase in body weight due to an increase in lean tissue (muscle tissue is denser than fatty tissue), so it would be a healthy weight gain. Then, in turn, body weight typically reduces due to the increased rate of fat burning, which is a result of the increased amount of lean tissue on the body. For this reason, measurements of body weight and body fat (or waistline measurements) should be done together so that the results are kept in perspective. The healthy body fat ranges for young adult males and females is 15 - 20% and 17 - 27%, respectively (the healthy ranges increase slightly with age). Anything lower than these values is indicative of an experienced athlete or a lifelong exerciser. As an aside, females *may* run into other health problems if this value is below 10%, while males may have health problems dropping below 5%. The hand-held devices and bathroom scales using electrical impedance as the means to measure body fat tend to read a bit high and are only moderately reliable. The most accurate way to measure body fat percentage is with a "bod pod" ("dunk tank"), which is essentially an underwater body weight assessment.

Runners will typically get faster and be less prone to injuries when they shed some pounds and have less weight to carry around. This advantage is obvious, but sweat patterns also improve, meaning a person won't sweat quite as much, which allows more blood for the working muscles (improved performance). Due to the *ceiling effect*, someone who is already at a healthy body weight would see fewer gains in performance as a result of weight loss.

In terms of achieving a healthy body weight by maximizing calories burned, consider the phrase, "Becoming fit is hard; staying fit is easy." This argument is made because once a substantial level of fitness is achieved (measured by resting HR, VO$_2$max, body fat percentage, race performances) the body is more likely to use fats as a fuel throughout the day. This preference for fats as a fuel is realized because for activities done at less than 60 - 70% of maximum HR (low-intensity activities), the body will use a higher *proportion* of fats as the fuel (carbs will still be utilized, but not as much as during high-intensity workouts). Because most (daily) activities will become less stressful and therefore low-intensity for the fitter folks, it's easier for them to burn a higher proportion of fats during the day.

Do not misinterpret that last paragraph and think that low-intensity activities are better for improving fitness. This is not true. Higher-intensity activities burn more total calories than low-intensity activities and therefore use more *total* fat as fuel. Again, regardless of intensity, carbs will comprise close to 75% or more of the energy expenditure, even though there is a higher *proportion* of fat burned during low-intensity activity. Therefore, anyone attempting to reduce body weight and body fat should choose activities that burn more *total* fat and more total calories, which means higher-intensity activities (i.e., greater than 70% of maximum HR).

We should all be aware that being healthy goes beyond a body weight measure. When I talk about health or fitness, I'm talking about HR. If the HR never goes above 60 - 70% of max, then the heart (a muscle) is being under-trained. We want a strong, healthy heart with a low resting HR, which means a high stroke volume (amount of blood pumped per beat). Having a stress-free life, flexible joints, a healthy diet, and proper hydration are wonderful, but those are not the markers of fitness. Running usually takes the HR over 60 - 70% of its maximum and can therefore be viewed as a way to be good to the body. Even while they're traveling, I strive to help my runners maintain at least a modest run routine, as I know many of them look forward to running in new locations with new scenery.

BODY TYPE

Midway through one particular hill workout I was coaching, we arrived back at the bottom of the hill and were greeted by a woman walking her superbly fit looking dog, who had a ton of energy. I greeted the owner (and the dog), who said, "Oh, I bet he could keep up with you going up that hill." My initial thought was, "I bet you dollars to gel packs that this dog would not only keep up, but this dog would smoke us up that hill and never be seen again." I had that thought because I noticed this dog looked like a running machine: the legs, the muscles, and even its "eye of the tiger" look! Body type has an effect on ability and performance. In the breeding of animals, we do breed some types of dogs and horses to be faster and stronger. We have the capacity to be very direct and selective with animals, yet not so much with humans. So what control *do* we have in morphing our body type?

As you read in Chapter 2, a goal of the winter off-season should be dedication to reshaping the body, which includes not just its strength, but also its composition. This doesn't imply vanity. Although I recognize that "looking good" is motivating for some people, the research shows this is one of the least successful motivators for sticking with a fitness routine. There is certainly no harm to self-esteem when someone is happy with how he/she looks, but the better motivators lie in the realm of tangible performance measures. Confidence in one's abilities is a better motivator than one's perceived physical appearance. That's a fact.

Sports Illustrated continues to print its popular "Body Types" issue each year, where athletes representing the full spectrum of different sports are posing in their skimmies. You get to see what the body types look like across various sports (I'm not sure about the amount of photo-shopping involved; it's rampant in the modeling world). Some body types are more advantageous for basketball, some are better for discus throwing, and others are better suited to sprint up a hill like a wild dog. My observation about that same dog came on the heels of finishing a well written book,

The Sports Gene, by David Epstein, who was a pretty good collegiate runner himself.

Epstein's book highlights how our very long genetic evolution has made certain populations of humans (based on ethnicity and/or region) primed for certain athletic pursuits. Nature vs. Nurture? It's always both, but this book delves more in detail about the who, what, when, where, why, and how of elite performance from the point of view of genetics, height, muscle fiber types, leg length, ankle circumference, and you name it. Epstein is an outstanding writer. He presents clarity in his points and is very clever and witty, and he's on-point with a scientific mind that helps dispel many myths we once held about elite performance. He even covers the game of chess in the opening chapter when he explains the vision/eyesight of elite athletes and why/how it's different than the general population. For those who have no interest in reading about "sports," you will find this book only uses sports as a backdrop. If you're like me and you become excited reading about evolutionary biology, evolutionary psychology, anthropology, and history, then add it to your list.

To come back to the main point, without becoming obsessed with your body, continue to brainstorm and be brutally honest with yourself about how you can change your body, or if you even want to or need to. Consider how it can help you reach your goals. Are your nagging injuries due to weak muscles, not enough muscles/strength, and/or extra weight you're carrying around? Explore options such as hiring a personal trainer, trying a juice cleanse, and cutting out caffeine. The previously mentioned *Sports Illustrated* issue reminds us that mom and dad gave us our body types, which we can only change by so much (or so little). However, even though your upper and lower limits are set, that middle portion in between is large! Maximize it! "Most people start running in order to get fit, whereas more people should first be getting fit in order to run." This quote is a reminder to take ST and XT to heart if ambitious running goals exist. You don't have to look like "a runner" to perform your best, but you should revisit your checklist of what it is that you can do to love yourself (your body...that thing that hosts your consciousness, the essence of who you are).

5

RUNNING FORM

RUNNING SURFACES

Proper running form is more important than running surfaces in determining the likelihood for injuries, but the location of runs shouldn't be completely overlooked. Low-volume runners don't have to be as concerned with where they run because their likelihood for injuries is less, but in any case, gravel and dirt paths are best in terms of lessening the impact on a runner's body. Even though the concrete sidewalks aren't the best option, "everything in moderation" is an acceptable rule of thumb that applies here. For the city runners, as long as safety isn't an issue, the asphalt road is a better option than the concrete and brick sidewalks.

To keep the terminology consistent, true *trail running*, as its own sport within running, is more than just a jog on a path that cuts through a local park. Trail running is more like cross-country (XC) style running, going over logs and rocks, through creeks, off beaten paths, etc., and therefore usually requires a specialty shoe for various reasons. So trail running is different than "running on trails," the latter of which is more common amongst runners. It sounds like a small difference in semantics, but it may save confusion in conversation.

If a trail's beaten path is only the width of a shoe (or even a few inches wider), then be careful not to run on that particular portion for too long.

This would be related to one aspect of non-ideal running form where each foot lands on an imaginary centerline. Running in this manner is what I call "monorail running." We don't want both feet to hit the centerline, yet these very narrow (often man-made) trails can force us to do so (at least in our minds we feel forced to do so). This monorail style of running can potentially lead to ITB problems and/or a nagging pain in the hip/glutes if done long enough on one run (30 minutes or more) and/or on a frequent basis (two to three times weekly). The feet should land on a "thin railroad," which implies two tracks, not one. In other words, if running down a painted line on a road, then the inside portion of both shoes should contact the outside portion of the line. I doubt these very narrow beaten paths are frequently encountered, but they're worth mentioning.

SHOES

Most running injuries are accounted for by non-ideal running form and/or muscular weaknesses and imbalances (more on that later); however, some injuries are the result of shoes either in poor condition or not being fitted properly. Traditionally, run shoes are good for about 300 - 400 miles, which usually equates to about 3 - 4 months. A runner with a proper foot strike and a healthy (or low) body weight can get up to 700 - 800 miles (or more) in a pair of shoes without injuries entering the picture, as I've seen in many runners I've coached. Once a runner finds a pair of shoes he likes, he should buy more than one pair at a time to last him through the year so they can be switched/rotated at any time. Shop for shoes at a store that allows them to be test-run (ideally outside) before being purchased. When scouting for a new type of shoe, the best time of year to do this is in the winter off-season because the run volume is relatively low. Introducing a new style of run shoe when the RV is high is not ideal because there would then be two new significant variables in the equation at the same time (high mileage and shoes).

The book *Tread Lightly* offers a history of not only running shoes, but also of shoes in general. Modern shoe design, with relatively narrow toe boxes and elevated heels, is the cause of many problems arising in the feet and spine. Females have certainly heard this spiel more than males. I suppose there is a time and a place for all footwear, but the less the feet are jammed into wedge-shaped boxes, the better. I admire females who pack sneakers as a preventive medicine for their work commutes.

Danny Abshire, founder of the Newton shoe company and author of the book *Natural Running*, says that running barefoot, or running with minimalist shoes, allows the feet to feel the ground in a more direct way, which helps the body balance more naturally. In other words, the feet are most sensitive at the midfoot, so when the midfoot hits first, it sends a stronger, more direct signal to the brain. In turn, the brain communicates immediately with the rest of the body as to how to balance or compensate (if needed). The argument against traditional shoes is that the extra cushioning that is sworn to protect us actually inhibits this foot-brain communication. Although Abshire puts emphasis on foot shape and function, he is not a strong proponent of barefoot running, although doing barefoot activities has its merits (a separate section on barefoot running is next).

Another adverse effect of the thicker, traditional running shoes is that the extra cushioning material allows the foot slightly more movement upon impact, which does not occur when running barefoot or minimalist. The extra movement, or sliding, causes a runner to be less in tune with the ground, thereby causing *extra* compensations (e.g., extra rotational forces in the knees) that can lead to injury. Feet that are weak or predisposed to leaving a runner "unbalanced," like low- or high arches, and/or bones in the feet that are too short/long, create additional compensating factors, or forces, upon foot strike.

Traditional run shoes will continue to be made and will never go off the shelves because not everyone can run in lighter-weight shoes, and even fewer people can run barefoot. Empirical studies do not show that the style of run shoe can predict faster runners and slower runners, so the individual comfort/match of the shoe must be considered. Additionally, studies attempting to demonstrate individual performance gains while running barefoot or in minimalist shoes are still inconclusive. This is an important data point and is part of an overall mental approach to training, in that we should *not* try to mimic what the pros do or what somebody faster than us does. Just because "so and so" runs in a type of shoe and is really fast, it doesn't mean that changing shoes will improve performance.

Regarding *motion control shoes,* understand that ankle pronation is natural and is not a culprit in and of itself. The book *Tread Lightly* is critical of motion control shoes and also of running shoe stores in general, and the authors Larson and Katovsky present good reason for it. I won't say that the staff at a running store isn't helpful, but a good running store will not push products that aren't suited to the runner. Unless you have flat feet and/or orthotics have not proven beneficial, I recommend neutral shoes instead of motion control shoes. The neutral shoes can perhaps be viewed as a transitional phase into something more minimalist, if that's the ultimate route.

Running barefoot or in minimalist run shoes (e.g., Vibram Five Fingers and Newtons) are theorized to help prevent injuries by changing a runner's foot strike, but this change is *not* guaranteed and warrants special consideration. A minimalist shoe, or running barefoot, is not for everyone, especially if one tends to be a heel striker because there is less protection for the heel. Most runners will continue to heel strike in these shoes unless coached properly on mechanics. Shoes, in and of themselves, don't change foot strike. A 2014 class action settlement against Vibram only strengthens these points. It appears a runner has to already have proper running form (a midfoot landing) in order to wear these shoes, a catch-22. In that case, the prerequisites for wearing minimalist shoes are good strength in the core, hamstrings, and glutes, along with hip and ankle flexibility. Otherwise, without those functional attributes, it's tougher to land midfoot. Unfortunately, it's passed off too often as common knowledge that wearing minimalist shoes will change mechanics by transitioning a runner into a midfoot landing, which would allow for a softer landing, less shock to the joints, and increased cadence. It's a good theory; however, it's not a guarantee that the change will take place. My personal coaching experience in having seen hundreds of runners show me their running form in minimalist shoes before we start working together indicates that the desired change to a midfoot strike *rarely* takes place until their mechanics are address more in-depth.

Minimalist shoes are not a cure-all, "one size fits all" solution. I do not think everyone should run in minimalist shoes, and I agree with the authors of *Tread Lightly* in that "if it ain't broke, don't fix it." I also agree with these authors in that if you have a *history* of injuries then you probably want to make a change to your form and/or the shoes. This is something I discuss with new runners I coach. I prefer to change the form first, then the shoes, in order to control variables. I abide by this format under the premise that the shoes do not necessarily have a cause-effect on run form (foot strike). That last point of mine is perhaps where the *Tread Lightly* authors and I would have a friendly debate, but I make a living *teaching* people how to run. The authors do ascertain that the shoes may not change foot strike, but it's not a strong case when they present it. I present this case more persuasively, or at least that is my intent.

When transitioning to lighter shoes with less material, make it a gradual process in terms of how much running is done in the new shoes. It's not necessary to "break the shoes in," like many adults were told as kids, but what needs breaking-in is how the body adapts to the shoes. Achilles injuries can increase during this transition phase because the Achilles now has to take on a more active role in absorbing elastic energy from the new, midfoot landing. So if the change to a midfoot strike does occur, then there is certainly an adaptation period needed for the muscles and tendons. Similarly, going from traditional run shoes to minimalist is a big enough jump for some, while going barefoot is a *huge* jump that can be counterproductive.

Ethiopia's Abebe Bikila made barefoot running world-famous by mistake. Days before the 1960 Olympic marathon in Rome, where he won gold, he was supposed to pick up run shoes at a nearby location, but they had run out of his size. Rather than run uncomfortably in a half-size too small, he decided to run barefoot, which he had some experience doing while growing up in Ethiopia. He won the *subsequent* marathon while wearing shoes again and he never went back to barefoot.

Regarding racing shoes, or *flats* (different than minimalist run shoes), they are noticeably lighter because there is less material. This significantly reduced weight is what allows the legs to turn over faster; however, the same reason they improve performance can also lead to injury—the fact they have very little material/support. Running too much in these lightweight shoes can develop overuse injuries, especially if the lower leg and feet aren't strong enough to withstand an increased RV. They should really only be used for racing short distances, especially if one's landing mechanics do not promote the use of flats.

Minimalist run shoes look more attractive to purchase because the professional runners are so fast. It's not the shoes that make the pros fast; rather, it's the fact they are very talented athletes. For example, did Bikila win Olympic gold *because* he ran barefoot? No. He was so darn fit he might have won that race in boots. Therefore, when you see ads with pro athletes in digitally cropped images telling you how much their run shoes contributed to their successes, don't forget how freakishly fast they are in the first place. I'm not downplaying the good work of Danny Abshire and his Newton company, nor orthopedists and orthotics for what they've done for athletes, I'm merely reminding everyone to always have a healthy dose of skepticism when it comes to advertising. Dr. Jack Daniels coached many hall of fame runners, but out of the more than 200 pages in his book *Daniels Running Formula*, there are only a few paragraphs dedicated to running shoes and all he mentions is that you should occasionally do workouts in your race shoes. With this in mind, we can tentatively reason that shoes are not the secret ingredient for championship success.

In sum, running in lighter shoes helps to mimic barefoot running, which theoretically promotes a softer impact and higher cadences, in turn reducing injury. However, the shoes do not automatically teach one how to run properly. There is another skill set involved to do that. If a proper foot strike *is* developed while running in minimalist shoes, then there must be time allowed for those relevant muscles to also adapt (i.e., a transition phase). So when is the ideal time for this transition phase, to try a totally new style of shoe? To repeat from earlier in this section, the answer is in the off-season because of the cardinal rule of all sports that states not to try anything new on race/game day, or once the mid-season training is under-way with relatively high mileage. Make major changes when specificity of training is at its *lowest* point, the off-season, which typically brings about a planned reduction in mileage. A beginner or a low-volume runner can probably make the switch at any time and be unaffected. Following a consistent mental approach (a system) and having an understanding of training *phases* will always help one understand when and how to make such changes.[13]

BAREFOOT RUNNING

To follow-up on points made in the previous section, running barefoot isn't something that needs to be avoided; rather, it's simply overrated. There is a difference between running barefoot and running in minimalist sneakers, for which I would argue much more support for the latter (if I had to choose). There isn't anything that can be accomplished barefoot that can't be accomplished in sneakers, other than perhaps getting some nice puncture wounds from debris on the ground. Granted, a runner can do some laps or striders on the grass infield at a local track; however, I don't think any coach would promote those instances as legitimate stand-alone run training (it's simply not enough volume, agreed?). So while I do think there can be a time and a place for barefoot running (hey, I grew up as a kid with a big backyard), I also think it does more harm than good, given the type of training an adult runner would try to implement with today's city streets and layout of state roads. I find that Abshire communicated similar points in his book *Natural Running*. He acknowledges the proprioceptive benefits of barefoot running, but also acknowledges it's not very practical in the environment of today's cities.

As a dual-role coach for running and ST, I promote the proprioceptive benefits that come with ditching the shoes during ST, but I will assert that moving into barefoot running is not worth the grief that would be experienced from a resultant injury. Despite that last point, injury from taking a wrong step is not the more important argument against barefoot running. For instance, there is some research to suggest that running barefoot

---

13. When it comes to buying socks, make sure they are *not* the low-cut ankle socks that barely cover the anklebones. If the socks are too low, then there is a risk for blisters on the back of the heel/Achilles.

imposes more stress on the lower leg than running in shoes. One of the studies done by Dr. Daniel Lieberman (Harvard University) showed that barefoot running did not change foot strike in all runners (not surprising to me), and led to increased impact forces when continuing to heel strike (as one might expect). In short, "it's not about the shoes."

ORTHOTICS

Orthotics and heel cups can be helpful in alleviating some aches and pains associated with running, especially runners who have low- or high arches, yet orthotics can also be viewed as a crutch, a detriment to improving foot strength. This is why many physical therapists (PTs) don't promote their use. They would rather see a focus on improving foot strength and foot strike. Improved foot strength can cure many foot, ankle, knee, and hip injuries, which is why many runners are given a prescription of working on foot strength following PT sessions. Everyone's goal in the off-season, when RV is theoretically at its lowest, should be PT appointments and correcting technical issues. Run-specific ST helps make this transition easy, as does a reduction in training volume. As stated above, minimalist shoes can do more harm than good if the feet aren't strong enough to wear them. The book *Natural Running* has taught me much about the importance of orthotics made correctly. I can see the rationale on both sides of the orthotics debate, but, either way, foot strength should be a priority.

PHYSICAL THERAPY LINKED TO RUN FORM

PTs are not miracle workers. They cannot fix a runner if the runner doesn't back off the training to some degree. You have to help them help you. For instance, I once chatted with a former elite runner who thought proper shoes were the answer to all of his injuries and that PTs are "a hoax" and he went on and on about his three decades worth of PT treatments that never worked. After he finished his thoughts, I had one simple question for him, "Did you ever stop training while you were receiving treatment?" His answer, "No." C'est la vie.

As a coach, I consider a PT appointment to be *mandatory* in the off-season (2nd and 3rd opinions are fabulous) and if/when the PT makes specific recommendations, don't be surprised if he/she also encourages a reduction in RV. The rationale is simple: How can a muscle (or neuromuscular pattern) be re-trained if it's constantly under too much stress? Even a 10-mile training week can be considered too much running if each mile (each step) is impeding the healing process.

PT isn't restricted to curing injuries; it's also about preventive measures and making gains in endurance and speed. I find that few people view ST and PT as a way to get faster, whereas most people still have the old mentality, "Oh, those are things I do when I'm *injured*." Change your mental approach to ST, PT, and the off-season in order to make significant progress. Even for an athlete who is 100% pain-free and on top of his/her game, it's beneficial to get some baseline testing done (for future frame of reference), or to find out where weaknesses are so that performance improves even further!

Changing run form is a holistic approach that requires total body strength, run-specific strength, correct technical instruction at the right times, and a smart approach to building volume. A physical therapist, run coach, personal trainer, nutritionist, and massage therapist all become equally important in this regard.

FOOT STRIKE

Most runners who come to me for coaching are landing on their heels, but this doesn't mean I'm only working with a unique subset of the running population (heel strikers), as there are many more categories to which these runners belong. Therefore, the runners who come to me for help with either running form or training programs are *representative of the whole* (of non-professional runners), and to that end, the overwhelming majority of runners are heel strikers. Foot strike is the popular topic in the running world these days, and the correction I make is for runners to land *midfoot*, rather than "forefoot" (more on that in a moment). Landing midfoot means landing with a "flat foot" and that is a good teaching point to keep in mind. When landing midfoot, the heel will either contact the ground simultaneously with the rest of the foot or make contact a fraction of a second *after* the midfoot hits the ground; thus, the spring-like action of the Achilles tendon that is mentioned often.

(Landing midfoot)

Before continuing, I'll point out that I don't think everyone should change to a midfoot strike and I partially addressed my rationale in the *Shoes* section above. If a runner has been injury free while maintaining relatively high mileage in his/her current foot strike and shoes, and if the legs still hit the ground with a slight bend in the knee, then I don't think foot strike changes *need* to be made. Many heel strikers are passing all of us at local races and running injury-free. However, if a runner complains about run-specific injuries even when the mileage is low, then I think running form is a major variable to change. Because most runners experience overuse injuries, and because I consider improper foot strike the enabler of overuse injuries, I will discuss foot strike in various sections of this chapter.[14]

(Landing on the heels)

---

14. After averaging the results of various sources, approximately two-thirds of runners experience an injury of some sort each year.

Heel striking can be caused by many factors, some mechanical and some psychological (the phrases/terminology the runner repeats in his head cause him to move his legs a certain way). First, to examine one of the mechanical causes, heel striking is often related to a runner's posture being *too* tall. Running with *too* tall of a posture is an issue only because it resembles our posture when walking, and walking is heel striking (and always will be). *Running* with this same tall posture, or even leaning back a tad, lends itself to heel striking. Coaching runners not to be straight-up-and-down while running is a basis of the Chi Running method, which I echo in some ways. When runners are told to "run taller," it's usually because they initially have poor posture in the sense that their backs are rounded and their shoulders slouched, similar to how they probably sit at their desks all day.[15] Running tall is a good initial focal point for most folks with a desk job and/or bad general posture, but from there the goal is to develop a *slight* forward lean, which is natural as long as we're not running *too* slowly (more on this in the *Posture, Pelvic Tilt & Leaning* section).

To follow up on that last point, a main contributor of heel striking, which goes hand-in-hand with running too tall, is running *too* slowly. Most of us desire to run farther, so it's logical that proper pacing is needed to eventually extend the distance of each run, as we all remember the moral of *The Tortoise and The Hare*. However, there is such a thing as running *too* slowly. It is the reason most beginning runners or those training for a marathon land on their heels. Because the pace is so slow, it resembles walking, which, by design, only lends itself to heel striking. This doesn't mean the runner now has to become overly competitive or obsess over the pacing of every run. It just means that it's impossible to run with a (natural) total body lean when jogging too slowly, for which I tag a pace slower than 10-minute miles as the unofficial tipping point for when the form breaks down in this way. Slow and steady may get someone across the line, but the body may be worse

---

15. A weak upper body can cause a rounded back.

off if it was *too* slow, due to the cause-effect relationship of heel striking and injuries.

If we imagine that each runner has five gears like a car, I'll encourage most of my beginning or unfit runners to stay out of 1st gear (their "slow jog") at the beginning of their new training program because it may be too slow, to a detriment.[16] Second gear is a "fast jog" and that's where I guide my many of my beginning runners (whose previous form resembled a fast walk) until the midfoot strike is automatic.[17] The runners I coach who have a good midfoot strike get my blessing to run in 1st gear because they'll keep that form no matter the pace and are therefore less likely to develop nagging injuries.

Heel strikers are more likely to transition to a midfoot landing as they run faster (not slower) because, although it may sound counterintuitive, runners usually have better mechanics at faster paces. I see it all the time in my Running 101 sessions (one-on-one running form sessions) or anytime I see kids running. Once kids are past the wobbly infant stage of running, and before they get into a significant growth spurt, they have perfect run mechanics. Barring the two subgroups just mentioned, you'll see great form in kids anytime they're running around playing tag or any ball-sport that requires sprinting. When kids are asked to do a "distance run" (which for many of them might just be a single lap on a track) then that's when you'll see more of them develop some improper mechanics, especially as they get tired and the pace slows significantly. When I work with runners for the first time and get them "running like kids again," they notice how natural it feels to run faster than they're accustomed.

Runners should go shorter and faster in their first year of running. They'll be thankful later. This approach to using a slightly faster pace during endurance runs also means that some runners have to temporarily accept being out of breath more quickly than they're accustomed

---

16. Most endurance runners don't dabble in 5th gear (true sprinting) in training.
17. Third gear can loosely be associated with tempo pace, a term with which most experienced runners are familiar.

and/or cutting down the duration of the long runs. Patience is a virtue. Many runners struggle to cope with the idea of not doing a weekend long run, which is related to another problem—signing up for marathons (or even half marathons) too soon.

The increasing popularity of marathons and half-marathons contributes to heel striking. People who normally wouldn't run these long distances are now training to do so. Generally, more running is a healthy idea; however, when we're unable to run with good form for the required distances, we'll naturally figure out a way to keep going, which for most runners means jogging slower and slower. If we jog *too* slowly to help our endurance then we may end up doing more harm than good because, as stated previously, running *too* slowly breaks down running mechanics into a heel strike. This is the irony of it all. When many runners write to me for help with their form, they include the phrase, "My form breaks down when I get tired." Hopefully it's now apparent *how/why* the form breaks down—pace. If I sound like a broken record in this section, then amen (anything worth knowing is worth repeating).

I don't use the term *forefoot* because it encourages the runner to run on the balls of the feet or the toes. Because of the increased demand on the calves, Achilles, and ankles, the average person running on the balls of the feet, or the toes, is just as undesirable as heel striking. Additionally, the pace for a forefoot striker is often slower than it could be, and this is related to lower leg strength. In other words, because the runner senses (even subconsciously) that his/her feet and legs are not strong enough to support his/her body weight when landing solely on the forefoot during faster speeds, the easy correction to make is to simply slow down. With the foot traveling less distance into the ground at slower speeds, it's easier to maintain a forefoot landing, and that is why I almost always see forefoot runners running a 9-minute mile pace or slower, no matter the actual fitness of the individual. On the contrary, a distance runner who *can* handle appropriate pacing on his/her forefoot is most likely at a healthy body weight (or lightweight) with lots of lower leg and foot strength. I'll admit that the distinction between forefoot and midfoot is sometimes splitting hairs, to the point we could move a large percentage of forefoot runners into the midfoot category, but the differences are significant enough to warrant careful attention. Even though I teach proper leg mechanics for jogging by first teaching good sprint mechanics, the *sport* of sprinting, or a sprinter, is a whole separate beast; therefore, sprinting (as its own sport in a way) on the forefoot is an exception to the rule, not the norm.

In fact, when we hear about sprinters running on their toes, we must remember that true sprinters, trained in college or the higher ranks, run with different mechanics when they land forefoot compared to the average non-elites runner attempting to sprint. In short, sprinters can also get away with a forefoot landing because they are only running 100 - 400 meters with that style (maybe 800m), an important difference compared to endurance running. When runners overcompensate for their heel strike and run on their toes or the balls of the feet they will often develop injuries in the foot and ankle because their feet and/or lower leg are not strong enough to support that type of foot strike. This problem is made worse by being overweight or attempting speed work.

There is more stability in the entire leg when landing midfoot, as compared to landing on the heels or toes. Most people know this intuitively and it's the reason why squats are done with the entire foot contacting the ground, without having to think about it. Stable contact with the ground can save many overuse injuries. *Unstable* contact, seen in most heel strikers and some forefoot runners, places additional rotational forces on the knee, along with braking forces on the ankles, calves, shins, quads, and lower back. That's wasted energy, and in order to overcome this we must become "efficient at moving inefficiently," as Abshire phrases it.

(Landing on the forefoot)

An often cited 2007 biomechanics study looking at elite Japanese runners mid-race showed that midfoot and forefoot strikers were landing with their feet under their hips (or center of mass), while the heel strikers were mostly landing with the foot in front of the hips, causing a braking action (whether slight or severe). This braking action and the strain absorbed by the leg can be responsible for injuries as the body adjusts to absorb the extra impact; it's also a proposed cause of tight calves and shin splints, which are often synonymous. I'll make a quick point here that the foot does not have to land *directly* under the hips, even when running with a good midfoot strike. Therefore, "landing with the foot under the hips" is not a focal point I encourage. Running with a midfoot strike and a decent pace (faster than a 10:00-minute mile) typically produces a slight total body lean, a "natural lean." In this case, the foot lands under the slightly protruding *chest*, not the hips, which also implies the foot *is* landing under the center of mass—the chest. In essence, the foot landing *slightly* in front of the hips is not problematic when running with a midfoot strike and total body lean; a subtle yet key distinction to be made when answering questions about *where* the foot should land. The other important consideration here is whether the leg lands with a slight bend in the knee (typical of a midfoot strike) versus a leg that is straight upon impact, which is typically of most (but not all) heel strikers. Landing with a straightened leg is one of the primary causes for running injuries and a good reason to switch to a midfoot landing.

A benefit of a midfoot landing that is often overlooked is that it allows a runner to use a simple heel-flick to start the next stride. Think about how much energy that saves the muscles in the back of the leg when those muscles don't have to *propel* a runner forward, as in walking and heel striking.[18] Rather than relying on an actual push-off using the calves and hamstrings, which becomes tiresome in heel strikers, a midfoot runner can think about flicking the heels up, similar to the butt kick warm-up drill. When it's time for the foot to come back down, let gravity help the feet fall into the ground—this should help with a gentler landing. A gentler landing is desirable, as it reduces the impact with the ground, but I rarely encourage a runner to "run more quietly". The reason for refraining from this phrase is that I typically see runners who were instructed to run more quietly do nothing more than simply slow down, yet they maintain their heel strike. Slowing down and running more quietly are two different actions. Many runners will sense a "softer landing" only because they've slowed down a great deal, again, without actually correcting their foot strike.

PRANCING AND JABBING

The final points I usually make during individual Running 101 sessions is that there are two ways for runners to be fooled into thinking they're

---

18. Calf tightness in heel strikers is common for this reason.

running with a midfoot strike, yet actually still landing on the forefoot. One way is by *prancing* while running; the other is by *jabbing* the feet into the ground. Knowing what it means to prance or jab will enable a runner to self-coach his/her new form. In describing prancing, I relate it to running too slowly, not in the sense that it's causing a heel strike (as outlined previously), but by the fact the runner is running too high up on the balls of the feet. In order to run on the balls of the feet, a runner must slow down. Otherwise, as mentioned above, a runner's lower leg strength and/ or body weight will contribute to injuries. Our brains are usually smart enough to figure this out ahead of time, so when one part of the brain wants to land on the forefoot (as in prancing), the other part of the brain says, "Fine, but the only way we're going to accomplish that is if we run very slowly." This rationale would explain many of the super-fit looking runners prancing around at 10:00/mile pace (or slower) while wearing Vibrams, Newtons, and other minimalist shoes. Prancing can also cause the foot to land too far in front of the center of mass. So even though a runner may sense a "soft landing" in this way, he/she may also be unaware that the foot is overextending.

The term prancing conveys the image of someone running gingerly down the street. As you can now probably visualize, the instruction "run more quietly," which I do *not* use, is a common cause of prancing. We can also "run more quietly" by slowing down, but then again slowing down doesn't solve any of the problems of improper mechanics. Prancing usually causes a runner to point their feet down toward the ground immediately before impact (plantar flexion), usually an attempt to land on the forefoot. Instead, runners should be running with the ankles dorsiflexed, which helps the foot to land flat. Another subtle change that goes undetected while prancing is that the runners will fan/spread their toes in their shoes, which overly engages the calves. You can try this now as you read this sentence: Simply lift a foot off the ground and spread your toes and notice how much your calf flexes. The real culprit for tight calves in this case is the plantar flexion (the prancing) because in order to run at faster paces while landing on the forefoot, a runner usually has to engage the muscles in the feet and calves more. The toes should be mostly relaxed when running, which means the calves relax too.

When it comes to jabbing, this is when a runner *aims* the foot into the ground to ensure a forefoot landing. Here, like prancing, the runner may actually believe he is landing midfoot. This jabbing motion is the runner's way to *guarantee* that he lands midfoot, much like a baseball pitcher *aiming* the ball and changing his arm mechanics to do so instead of *throwing* it with more of a natural form. When runners jab, there is usually an accompanied sliding forward of the feet in the shoe and/or the legs will not have as much bend in the knee upon the recovery phase of the stride (leg action after toe-off), so it will resemble a stiff-legged motion.[19] I remind runners at the conclusion of run sessions with me that one way they can ensure that the new midfoot strike "sticks" is for them to periodically ask themselves if they are prancing or jabbing while running. If they are, then there's still a forefoot strike instead of a midfoot strike.

On a related note, if a runner is unable to accelerate and run faster upon command, then that's another way to tell that he/she is most likely still prancing or jabbing onto the forefoot instead of landing midfoot. When the brain senses less stability, as in landing forefoot, the brain won't want to put the additional stress/load on the legs that comes with an increased pace. Increasing the stride length when running faster means the foot will have more distance to travel into the ground, which means more force. Therefore, most forefoot runners will not increase their pace beyond 2nd gear because their brain is subconsciously protecting them (the brain knows there would be too much instability upon landing forefoot at faster paces). The result is that the runner's 3rd, 4th and 5th gears (when told to "go faster") are not significantly faster than 2nd gear. This is one method I use to test whether the runner is still too high up on the balls of the feet (in case the point of impact can't be detected with the naked eye). Moreover, there is much more stability landing midfoot (using squatting

---

19. The recovery phase of the stride refers to the action of the leg from when the foot leaves the ground to when it is pulled upward behind the body. A recovery phase as it relates to periodization (Chapter 2) is obviously a different concept.

as a quick example once again), which means the brain has more trust in running faster and I usually see a change in speed in these instances.

STRIDE LENGTH & STRIDE RATE

Stride length is very much related to foot strike because when the foot comes *relatively* high off the ground (increased stride length) it then has a better chance to fall into the ground with a midfoot landing. Stride length refers to the action of the leg *behind* the body, not the action in front of the body (a.k.a., the recovery phase of the stride). Longer strides lead to faster paces via an increase in the distance covered between foot strikes, such that the recovery phase of the leg goes through a greater range of motion. In short, the faster the pace, the greater the range of motion of the leg (picture Carl Lewis or Usain Bolt). Once the foot leaves the ground, the thigh extends backward via hip flexibility and glute strength. Next, the hamstring pulls the lower leg upward before the entire leg is swung forward.[20] The hamstring is used again to decelerate the thigh, from which the foot drops back into the ground—the foot should not continue to reach forward as in heel striking. These mechanics are practiced with the Paws drill (described later). The distance that the leg (thigh) can extend backward is related to hip flexibility, glute strength, and spinal flexibility (though I won't discuss the latter as much). How quickly the leg can be pulled forward and dropped under the center of mass is primarily related to hamstring strength. This is why the hamstring is considered "the running muscle" and why ST for the hamstrings is important for effective speed work.

The fastest sprinters are usually the ones whose legs have the fastest recovery phase while maintaining a maximum stride length. In other words, stride rate does not have to be sacrificed as we increase our stride length. In fact, it's taught in high school science class that (all else being equal) shorter levers move faster than longer levers (I'll make this same point later when discussing proper arm swing). As the stride length is increased, the foot is

---

20. This is referred to as the *swing phase* of the stride.

pulled/tucked higher underneath the body as it is swung forward. In effect, this creates a shorter lever (leg) and allows the cadence to remain high.

Even though individuals have their own unique gaits, the first major change in mechanics that is true of *all* runners once fatigue sets in is a shortened stride. This is true regardless of age or ability. This doesn't mean a runner needs a long stride; it just means that the stride should not become *too* short (shuffling would obviously be the extreme case). Distance runners, in order to be most efficient, should be running with *relatively* short, quick steps. Ideally, a runner should be taking close to 84 - 90 steps per minute with each leg (also called cadence or RPMs). Similar to cycling, think "easy gear, high cadence." However, when we want to changes speeds, either faster or slower, it's done via stride length, not stride rate (true sprinting would be an exception to the rule, as we all note our own increase in cadence in our finishing kick or during 5th gear sprint workouts). Stride rate will remain unchanged from 5k through marathon, regardless of pace. This is good news for the brain, knowing that there aren't *significantly* different cadences for different paces. Rather, a natural lengthening or shortening of the stride is used to go faster or slower, respectively.

Higher cadence may be correlated with a shorter stride and less injuries, but correlations are not cause and effect. I agree with the authors of *Tread Lightly* that 90 RPMs is *not* a magic number. That number partly comes from methodological biases when studying cadence using *elite* runners. If a runner has proper foot strike and a cadence of 84 RPMs, then I don't force the issue to get to 90. "If it ain't broke, don't fix it." As it relates to a midfoot strike, having a faster cadence (a.k.a., higher turnover) is *not* the answer. This point is contrary to what's written most often in articles about running form. Go down to the National Mall in DC and sit on a park bench and watch hundreds of runners in bright, neon-colored minimalist shoes running with a cadence at 90 RPMs (or higher!) and observe how most of them are still landing on their heels or prancing. Increasing cadence without knowing what to do with the feet doesn't correct foot strike problems. In fact, it is this very mentality of "fast cadence, fast cadence…" that can lead to a heel strike. Why? The answer is because in order to move the legs faster and faster, the feet must remain relatively low to the ground, and although this is generally a good practice, it leads to a heel strike when there isn't the proper cue for *how* to land midfoot.

In attempting to move the feet into a very high cadence (90+ RPMs), many runners end up moving the lower half of their leg like a pendulum, which implies that the foot only swings back and forth, with the lower leg merely hinging at the knee. Without any real lift into a proper recovery phase of the stride, this "pendulum swing" is often the main cause of a heel strike. Additionally, without any backward thigh extension at the hip, the glutes are left out of the equation, which isn't desirable considering that the glutes are the biggest, strongest muscles in the body. This latter observation also applies each time a runner goes to a PT or chiropractor and hears the expression, "You don't engage your glutes enough when you run." For anyone who has heard this before, you now know what it means—your stride is *too* short. Again, to imagine the correct style, picture Carl Lewis or Usain Bolt sprinting in the 100m dash. If those 100m sprinters gradually slowed down to a jog, then their form would resemble that of Ryan Hall, a top U.S. marathoner.

With the exception of true sprinters, the only difference in mechanics when running in 5th gear versus 1st gear would be the actual *range* of motion of the leg during its recovery phase, and similarly, of course, the range of motion of the arm swing (see *Arm Swing* section below). Many runners don't realize this and they instead draw a drastic distinction between how they should look while running at different speeds. Keep the general mechanics the same all the time. Posture, cadence, and foot strike remain pretty much constant at all speeds/distances.

Finally, as it relates to stride length, a potential culprit for preventing someone from achieving an optimal stride length is *sitting*. Sitting at work for many consecutive hours spells bad news for running form. Prolonged sitting leads to tightness in the hips and hamstrings, which makes it harder for the thigh to extend leg backward when running. This means the glutes can't fire, which means the biggest, strongest muscles aren't being engaged. This limitation can produce an over-reliance on smaller, weaker muscles, which lends itself to an overuse injury, regardless of actual mileage.

PAWS DRILL

The Paws drill is done to help learn a midfoot strike and proper sprint mechanics. It gets its name due to the "pawing" action of the foot, but it can also be named its homophone counterpart as the Pause drill. All that is needed is a wall, fence or tree to aid in standing on one leg at a time.

Begin by facing a wall with one foot on the ground ~12 inches from the wall, with the other leg in front of you at a near-90-degree angle (this is the start and finish position for each rep, but when running naturally your knee will never come as high as it does during this drill). Drop the foot straight down in slow motion so that the foot hovers in midfoot striking position, but do not scrape the foot on the ground (keep the foot an inch off the ground). Next, to enter the recovery phase of the stride and to mimic what happens after toe-off, extend the leg (thigh) backward in slow motion as far as it can go while keeping the leg straight or slightly bent and without moving the upper body (this will also test hip flexibility and glute strength). Next, bend the leg to pull the foot upward and then forward under the butt and back into the starting position. The foot should be kept high ("tucked") under the body during the swing phase.

Do 5 - 10 reps in slow motion to learn the mechanics. At the end of each rep, freeze once again in the "pause" position. Then do 5 - 10 reps at normal speeds so that it feels smooth and fluid. You'll feel the hamstring working when you do it in slow motion, so this can also be viewed as a hamstring warm-up even when you have good run mechanics. You are now learning how to sprint, which is easily translated into proper jogging form.

When extending the leg backward during the Paws drill, the goal is maximum hip flexibility and glute engagement, which are largely responsible for stride length. Again, stride length is what goes on behind the body, not in front of the body. Therefore, increasing hip flexibility is often a goal for improved running form (foot strike) and achieving faster speeds. A series of 7 pictures is given below to demonstrate the drill:

(PAWS drill)

Remember that this is simply a drill to train the foot how to fall downward into the ground in a midfoot fashion. If you were to do this drill facing a wall, you should *not* kick the wall in front of you. Otherwise, that would resemble the mechanics that the lower leg undergoes during heel striking (or walking) and would defeat the purpose of the drill. This drill is not the magic bean to cure a heel strike, but it does help. To visualize the effect of this drill while actually running, imagine there is a glass window a few inches in front of your entire body as you run. You should be dropping your foot down to the ground sooner (rather than later) under your center of mass so that you don't kick the imaginary glass window directly in front of your body.

POSTURE, PELVIC TILT & LEANING

In addition to a shortened stride, the second major change that occurs in all runners when they become fatigued (regardless of ability) is that they get "top heavy." This means they start to *bend* forward at the waist (bending is the key word), running with an *anterior pelvic tilt* (hips angled down toward the ground). This bend, which is different than a *lean*, is both the cause and the effect of being fatigued. In other words, bending forward doesn't allow the core muscles to fire optimally, so the core muscles either fatigue more easily or aren't engaged at all. When runners fatigue and start to bend over, this incorrect posture can also be observed in that their butts stick out behind them.

For practice, here is a quick way to see what is meant by the phrase *anterior pelvic tilt*. Walk over to a mirror, stand sideways, roll your shirt up above your waistline and check the angle of your pant line at the waist. Is it angling downward in front of you? If so, this means you need to correct your posture in general to get rid of that pelvic tilt (assuming your pant line is being worn level to begin with) because in this case your pelvic bones are not level (as they should be) to stabilize the hips. Sitting long hours at a desk usually exacerbates this problem. Another way to think about anterior pelvic tilt is that if the pelvic girdle was a bucket of water, then it should be positioned so that the water does not spill forward. If there is an anterior pelvic tilt, the correction is to "crunch" the belly button up toward the chin, similar to how one keeps good form during elbow planks.

In addition to downward-angled hips, lateral (side-to-side) hip movement upon foot strike is also problematic. Taken together, when the pelvic tilt is downward, then lateral hip movement becomes exaggerated. This exaggeration of lateral hip movement while running is due to the lack of pelvic stability caused by the anterior pelvic tilt (read that again). When the RV is high enough, this combination can cause lower back problems, from which other problems could arise due to subsequent overcompensations.

Looking at the two pictures below, there is a noticeable anterior pelvic tilt in the first picture, as the hips (waistline) are angled downward (the horizontal bar in the background offers a good frame of reference). In the second picture, the waistline is level with the ground, or horizontal bar, and is the desired hip posture.

You can experience the relationship of these different hip movements by doing a simple test. Stand up and stick your butt out a few inches so that you allow your waistline to angle down toward the ground in front of you, with your lower back now slightly arched (your shoulders shouldn't move when doing this). Next, bend one knee slightly while keeping the other leg straight and then alternate this pattern back and forth between legs as you shift your hips side to side (this will resemble a quirky little dance move in place). Now, crunch your bellow button up toward your chin to take away the anterior pelvic tilt. Your waistline should now be level with no arch in your back. From this corrected position, alternate slightly bending your knees again. Notice your hips don't move as much from side-to-side.[21] You are now aware of the implications of proper posture when running, as well as proper form during ST. This standing posture should also be one's running posture. The reminder is to roll the

---

21. This is a good teaching point made by Danny Dreyer in *Chi Running*.

hips up to a level position by "crunching the belly button up toward the chin." Try it sideways in front of the mirror so that you can see your waistline and lower back change positions. Basically, the goal is to remove the arch/sway from the lower back, similar to planks and push-ups. Another way to phrase this is to say that neither the butt nor the ribs should be sticking out while running. This correction only requires a subtle movement (crunching). If you're tightening, squeezing, or flexing your abs, like a body builder posing, then you're putting too much energy and force into this correction.

(Incorrect pelvic tilt on the left. Correct hip posture on the right)

Regarding a "total body lean," it must be differentiated from bending at the waist. Leaning and bending (two different actions) both put the chest forward, but *bending* will compromise proper pelvic tilt and hip alignment, as described above. Here is a separate drill to help learn what the proper lean should feel like. Stand barefoot with your toes just behind a straight line and the feet hips-width apart and. Lean forward, like you're aiming to fall flat on your face. The goal is to have a straight line from your heels to the back of your head. The amount of lean over your feet that you can hold without falling over is dependent upon core strength and ankle flexibility. It's not a contest; don't be too competitive during this drill. Your ideal (proper) lean is that which you can hold without your toes digging into the ground, without your calves flexing, and without your butt sticking out. This is the total body lean we're seeking when we run. Now, in super slow motion, ease back to your normal standing position and note that you were actually leaning farther than you thought!

Repeat the drill and pay attention to your pelvic tilt. The waistline and chin should both be level with the chin back. The lower back should not be arching. If the back is arching, then you will end up bending more than leaning, similar to what happens when running with a heel strike and/or fatigued. When you get it right, you'll notice that your feet are holding your balance in the midfoot (just behind the ball of the foot), which is essentially where you want to land when running. Also note the distribution of your weight into your feet (inside vs. outside). It should be even, like they teach in yoga. If you find you are placing significantly more weight on the inside of the feet, then you either have flat feet and/or need to strengthen your arches.[22] Do not expect to lean dramatically as in the Michael Jackson *Smooth Criminal* video; the lean is subtle.

We typically end up on the midfoot when we do faster workouts and this may be helping the forward lean, or the forward lean may be helping the foot strike. Both causal relationships work and each can be a new focal point. My college hurdle coach explained to me that running posture is like being pulled forward by a cord that is attached to the sternum. This

---

22. This is where orthotics/inserts can offer relief from shin splints.

would cause a total body lean over the feet (not a bend at the waist), which would help the feet land under the center of mass as gravity pulls the body forward. This should resemble the mechanics and teachings of downhill running. Therefore, another possible focal point is to run as if you're running down a gradual hill. As a coach, I rarely (if ever) tell a runner to lean because it is admittedly difficult to *feel*. It will happen naturally as the pace quickens and/or with a midfoot strike.[23]

Those runners who can maintain proper pelvic tilt and natural total body lean are better able to land midfoot. In turn, the braking action is reduced, the strains to the calves and shins are reduced, and contact time with the ground is reduced (cadence increases). Furthermore, both speed and endurance improve, recovery improves, and more training can be done. The extra, resultant training might be the difference in a few minutes over the course of a half-marathon.

We hear the expression "run tall," but it may be better to run "proud." The latter is a better reminder to keep the head up, chest forward, and the shoulders down and back.[24] Look 10 - 20 feet at the ground in front of you. The eyes can be down, but the head should still be level. I frequently spot runners from across the track with their heads pressed forward and/or tilted too far down, like they're still looking at their computer screens. Therefore, better posture at work will help form good habits. The eyes will naturally go down to see hazards and to help equilibrium, but that can still be done with a level chin, or the chin *slightly* down.

---

23. When many runners attempt to intentionally run with a forward lean, they end up merely angling their shoulders (and hips) downward and sticking their butts out, yet they are absolutely convinced they are leaning. It reminds me of the sailing scene from the comedy *What About Bob?* In this scene, a schizophrenic patient named Bob (played by Bill Murray) has been tied-up with ropes to the mast of a sail boat (coincidentally with a perfect total body lean) by his friends. While the boat full of friends cruises along the lake, Bob repeatedly exclaims ever-so-proudly, "I'm sailing! I'm sailing!" Clearly, he wasn't sailing, nor should runners think, "I'm leaning!" when they run with their butts sticking out.

24. When coaching youth athletes, I sometimes tell them to picture themselves as Superman or Superwoman, or their favorite Marvel Comic Hero, as I explain this proud/strong posture.

(The lean drill)

TREADMILLS

A major goal of my coaching is to permanently kick runners off the treadmill, albeit with some outstanding circumstances. Not only does running outdoors help acclimation to the elements, but run mechanics can be adversely impacted while on a treadmill. Specifically, many (but not all) people are likely to develop a heel strike on a treadmill, even if they are normally a midfoot runner. This means that if I work with someone to improve his/her form, which is always done outside, running on a treadmill soon thereafter can sabotage the ability of the new form to be fully engrained. The reason for this change in mechanics might be due to the fact that the treadmill is a moving floor and the brain senses greater safety in gripping the moving floor (right away) with the heel and maintaining that grip as the floor continues to roll underneath the foot. Alternatively, treadmill running can involve bobbing up and down, which is not the desired motion. Moreover, when running outside and having to move forward, the body has to work harder (in a good way). Therefore, oxygen uptake is increased when running outside, which increases the training effect.

FULL SPEED SPRINTING

Many folks I coach are training for a military or law enforcement Physical Fitness Test that has a sprint component. Even if I didn't coach such individuals, I would still need to see how runners look when doing a full sprint. As articulated previously, I believe (and witness) that runners have better form the faster they run. Do we have to go all the way to a full sprint to realize this? No, and that is where 4th gear workouts, like Repetition-pace (R-pace) and striders, can be placed into a program to help. Fartlek runs are also a great time to hit 5th gear for a short burst. Because full sprinting stresses the hamstrings exponentially more than T-pace and I-pace, I also ease some people into full sprints with Accelerator workouts.[25]

I once observed an 800m Olympic qualifier runner at a track doing full 100m sprints as part of her taper process. She had perfect form and was running them fast! She wasn't built like a sprinter, but I could tell she was training seriously. You'll occasionally hear about pro runners, at

---

25. All of these types of workouts are all explained in Chapter 8, *Understanding the Workouts.*

all distances, doing full sprints in a workout, anywhere from 20 meters to 400m. I would be surprised if any champion marathoner didn't do full sprints at various points in the year. So why don't I prescribe full sprints to all the runners I coach if they are beneficial workouts? I'll resort to a default answer: It depends. There's a time and place for everything, but because of the added stress on the hamstring during full sprints, I cap most of my athletes at R-pace or hill repeats. However, they can always do a dosage of sprinting in their fartlek runs. Even if it's not a *full* sprint, 4th gear is still close enough to achieve the main benefit being sought for amateur runners—improved form via improved stride length and foot strike.

Ideally (i.e., with proper running form), running in 5th gear would place the stress mostly on the glutes and hamstrings. However, for a heel striker, additional parts of the body become overused, so that's another reason I am hesitant to prescribe full sprints. Similarly, I hold off on these workouts for beginners and anyone returning from an injury. This is one way I, as a running coach, differ from many personal trainers, who swear by full sprint workouts without weighing some of these variables. A final take-home message is that unlike professional runners, the energy system trained during full sprinting doesn't apply to the goals of most of the runners whom I coach. However, there is a time and place for everything in that full sprints can be a way to change a routine and add some "fun" to the program.

ARM SWING

I teach proper arm mechanics the same way I teach the leg mechanics, which is to learn how to have good sprint mechanics first and then water it down into jogging. The *general* mechanics of arm swing do not change as a runner quickens or slows his/her pace, nor is there a different type of arm swing used for running uphill or downhill. The only specific change (based on either pace or terrain) is the *range of motion* of those mechanics. Using the same simple analogy that we have five gears like a car, the arm swing basically remains unchanged for gears 1, 2 and 3, which for most runners means long run pace through tempo/10k pace. Although stride length increases as runners move faster from gear to gear (stride rate is essentially steady), the arm swing is relatively relaxed from 1st gear through 3rd gear. A runner doesn't need to begin "pumping the arms" until 4th gear. A phrase to bear in mind when running in gears 1 - 3 is to "keep your wrists by your ribs." This ensures that the arm swing is not too great.

In a full sprint (5th gear), one hand will travel up toward the cheek (below the chin) and one hand toward the hip, or slightly past the hip. This is what sprint coaches typically refer to as the "hip-and-cheek" position. This puts both arms at approximately 90-degree angles. As a runner's pace slows from 5th to 4th gear, the amount of arm motion would be cut in half. Slowing down to gears 1, 2 and 3 means the arm swing is now a quarter of what it was in 5th gear. It's intuitive to think that the faster we run, the more arm swing that is needed, but there shouldn't be any wasted energy in "pumping the arms" if the arms aren't needed. Basically, the arm motion in gears 1 - 3 is still a version of the hip-and-cheek positions, although obviously a smaller motion.

In gears 1 - 3, moving the arms more than is needed does not yield any additional benefits because it doesn't help the runner move any faster at that point (this is related to the general notion of conserving energy in the entire upper body). Once we lengthen our stride beyond 3rd gear, the hips will want to rotate more, which should be prevented. So with the increased range of motion of the arms, the arms become levers to help prevent excessive hip rotation. Studies done with runners typically show that the runners with minimal hip rotation/movement are the more efficient, dominant runners. Also, the increased arm swing at the faster paces helps to balance the runner as the legs begin to move through a greater range of motion.

(Hip-and-cheek arm positioning for 5ᵗʰ gear)

At any speed, the arms will be held at approximately 90-degree angles, give or take a few degrees. The angle of the arm doesn't change much as speed changes. The exception to this rule would be evident in true sprinting (Olympians, professionals, top college sprinters). Because the average reader is an average runner not training in true sprint events, I won't delineate further.

We know that shorter levers (i.e., arms forming a smaller angle) can move faster and use less energy than longer levers. Meaning, arms forming a 60- to 90-degree angle can move faster than arms that are only slightly bent. Because the arms and legs are always in sync, running with longer, slower arms would either cause the stride rate to be limited, or the shoulder muscles would have to work harder to move the arms at the same rate as the legs.

(The more compact version of the hip-and-cheek arm swing for gears 1 - 3)

A common error in the semantics of describing arm swing is the expression, "move the arms forward and backward." Although this is generally correct, this phrase is often misinterpreted and runners move their forearms in a straight line forward and backward, which puts extra work on the shoulder muscles in order to keep this alignment. This can then create tension in the neck muscles.[26] Instead, the forearms should move in a slight diagonal as they come forward, which puts less work on the shoulders; however, the arms should not swing across the centerline of the body.

If the forearms are moving at a slight diagonal, then the elbows should end up away from the body as they swing backward; however, this should not be confused with "running with the elbows out," which would be

---

26. Getting rid of unwanted tension in the upper body is the reason I am not a proponent of running with a water bottle or iPod in hand.

excessive. Keeping the arms *relatively* close to the body will help prevent any excessive horizontal arm motion, but the arms should not be held "tight to the body," which is a classic misinterpretation of what is being taught about running form. There should be a gap between the upper arm and the body during all phases of the arm swing. When runners "tuck" their arms against their body, then the lack of upper-arm movement will cause excessive upper-body rotation in order to compensate.

(Above: The typical arm positioning of someone running with "long arms")

To repeat, the elbows are held *relatively* close to the body when running, but it can also be said that the elbows are held *relatively* wide too (as opposed to having them held tight against the body). If the upper arm is being held more than a 45-degree angle from the body ("elbows out"), then this could be a sign that the runner is subtly attempting to balance, similar to how a tightrope walker uses an elongated bar to balance herself. Glute strength can usually help improve balance, so that is a good first step toward bringing the arms/elbows relatively closer to the body. Runners whose arms are very wide also tend to have their shoulders hunched; therefore, keeping the shoulders down and relaxed is another way to prevent the arms from being carried too wide.

The palms should be facing inward, which is the same as their natural resting position. Runners who run with one or both palms facing downward typically display more of an unnecessary side-to-side arm swing. This error is often made because a runner misinterpreted, or exaggerated, the proper cue to "run with relaxed hands."

(Above: The typical arm positioning of someone running with the arms too close to the body and/or moving the arms incorrectly in a straight forward-and-backward motion)

(Above: The typical arm positioning of someone running with the arms too wide)

(Above: A side-to-side arm swing caused by the palms facing down)

ASYMMETRIES IN RUNNING FORM

There are three asymmetries I observe in runners' mechanics. The first case carries over from the last section and is usually more noticeable—that is an arm swing where one arm moves in a different motion than the other, or is held in a different position. This could be a coordination issue, a muscular issue (tightness on one side), or related to how one's body healed from a past injury. A coordination issue would be related to the runner simply never being made aware of this asymmetry before, which is the case 50% of the time and is therefore an easy correction. Sometimes in sports, athletes can simply focus on a technical correction and the correction is made. This would be true for tasks that are more related to pure hand-eye coordination. However, in most endurance sports, the technical flaws are often due to an underlying muscular or neuromuscular issue, as in tightness or injury. The coordination issue is often related to a runner being accustomed to running with a water bottle and/or Garmin watch on the same hand all the time, so that arm is trained to be more motionless (this is more common than you think!). It's easier to run with a relatively heavy water bottle when its being held in place, and it's also easier to (frequently) check one's watch with the wrist is held still.

In the case of underlying muscular issues, I've seen many runners get rid of an asymmetrical arm swing just by receiving a professional massage that loosened up the knotty soft tissue that forced the one arm into an unnatural (compensating) motion. In the long-term, overlooking this constant tension and tightness can cause one to adapt their shoulder posture a certain way, even while standing and sitting. Becoming aware of the arm swing and some type of muscle manipulation therapy will both help resolve this issue. An asymmetrical arm swing isn't as an important factor for leisurely runners compared to more serious runners who are adding consistent speed work and high mileage. For the latter group, the overcompensation in the shoulders and/or arm swing can eventually funnel its way into the neck, back, and hips when the training load is increased. To further clarify this point, just remember the old tune that says, "The knee bone is connected to the thigh bone…" Having one arm move farther forward or across the body could be the result of one side of the body having tightness in the hip(s), obliques or back. In other words, a restricted arm movement could be the result of tightness somewhere else. This is good food for thought for anyone experiencing any extra fatigue or tension in the upper body when running fast and/or far.

The second and third asymmetries are related to each other and observed in ~10% of runners with whom I meet. One is in the foot strike, where one foot lands midfoot and the other on the heel, and the other is the stride length, which is observable in the height each foot travels during the recovery phase of the stride. The foot strike issue is less often an issue of coordination and more so either an asymmetry in ankle or calf flexibility, or a weakness in hip flexibility and/or glute strength on the side that heel strikes. The role of hip flexibility and glute strength in determining stride length and foot strike was described in previous sections. Briefly, the leg with the shorter stride and/or the foot that travels lower to the ground (due to hip inflexibility or a lack of glute engagement) is more likely to land on the heel. A runner can focus on leveling out the stride length on each side, but the correction in that case is forced and potentially not really doing the runner justice. "Thinking about it" will only have minimal benefits until the runner remedies the underlying functional asymmetry of the muscles and joints.

STRENGTH TRAINING AND RUNNING FORM

If we're going to spend time doing run-specific ST, then we need to put it into action when it's time to run. I encourage you to *feel* the ST when running. What this means is that during a run, an athlete can focus on the muscles that have been strengthened from ST. Do you feel your hips and gluteus medius (upper-outer butt muscle) preventing your hips from shooting out laterally when your feet hit the ground? Do you feel flexible in the hip extensors during the recovery phase of the stride? Do you feel strong in the abs, mid-back, and upper-back as you focus on posture? These focal points are why ST should be run-specific. This also helps to bridge the gap, mentally, between ST and running. In other words, when ST is functional, progressive, and dynamic, as it should be, then it's easier to see the carryover effects of ST. When focusing on (imagining) the ST exercises while running, this awareness can help running form in some specific way. Therefore, this is a way to put your money where your mouth is—if you believe that ST can help prevent nagging injuries and/or improve running form, then put the ST to good, practical use. *Visualize* it and *feel* it when running.

Similarly, when doing a particular ST exercise, focus on *all* the muscle groups that are being strengthened. ST exercises will typically strengthen more than one muscle at a time, especially as ST becomes more functional, progressive, and dynamic. For example, when doing push-ups (there are many modifications for those who claim they can't do them), rather than focusing simply on the chest muscles, you can focus on the muscles in the back, shoulders, triceps, and most importantly, the abs. Becoming very in tune with the body and truly feeling all of the muscles working in a particular exercise will help ST motivation because the benefits are perceived *in the moment*. Eventually, the benefits are also perceived while running. If someone thinks about ST while running, I bet he will notice at least one benefit to his form.

During 1-on-1 ST sessions, I try to remind athletes when/how a particular exercise relates to running form or race performance. "Hey Mike, I want to feel strong at the end of _____ race." Great, I want you to as well, but it doesn't happen by *hoping* it happens. I'm not a fan of hoping. So do your run-specific ST and *make* it happen. If athletes invest in me to help motivate them, then this section offers much in the way of motivation. This ST approach of mine also explains why I appear to be so focused and technical during 1-on-1 sessions. I'm personable and comedic, but during a paid ST session I'd rather talk about how to correct one's form than chitchat too much.

BREATHING

One of the most frequent reminders I give to runners during track work-outs and pre-race emails is to be in control of their breathing. This doesn't mean remembering to breathe; if a runner has to do this, then that spells trouble! All it means is learning to control the breathing at all times, which means inhale when you want to inhale, exhale when you want to exhale, as opposed to having an erratic breathing pattern. A good place to start is to exhale upon every other left foot strike (a "2-2 pattern"), which means taking two steps for the inhale (left-right) and two steps for the ex-hale (left-right). This should work for any distance or pace. After a week or two, it'll become automatic. If running on a route/course that does not have mile markers, a runner should eventually be able to accurately guess the pace simply based on the rate and depth of breathing.

I agree with Dr. Jack Daniels that a 2-2 pattern should be practiced during *all* runs in order to establish consistency and familiarity. Knowing the breathing patterns will set up success on race day by keeping a runner calm on tougher courses and/or with non-ideal weather. Stride rate and breathing rate being synced creates a very peaceful mind during training and racing. Therefore, breathing patterns during a race should greatly mimic breathing patterns during training. Consistency equals confi-dence. It's wonderful to know that stride rate and breathing rate don't have to change (for the most part); however, a runner may notice that he/she will eventually have to breathe more frequently during maximum efforts because the muscles require more oxygen at faster paces. This typically only applies to workouts that are faster than tempo pace and/or at the end of a short-distance race where the intensity is higher than nor-mal. The alternative during these faster workouts would be to take longer, deeper breaths, but that would make the breathing laborious and is not preferred. Depending on the moment of the race (or terrain), the pattern may quicken to a 2-1 or 1-2 pattern (as in alternating feet on the exhales). Eventually, the patterns will work themselves out naturally and a runner can simply focus on other aspects of the race.

After researching breathing patterns for runners, the good news is that breathing in/out through the mouth is fine and perhaps preferred, so there's no need to breathe through the nose if it's not comfortable. By all means, a runner should do what works best for him/her. *Rhythmic* breathing is most important and that refers to the timing of exhales. There is a theory that exhaling on the left foot strike is preferred in order to help prevent side stitches. It's related to the anatomy of internal organs. Experimentation is fine, but it's not always feasible to exhale on every left foot strike, especially with faster paces (i.e., a 1-2 or 2-1 pattern in that case).

When a cramp is experienced while running, there are a few ways to remedy the situation. First, slow the pace to regain control of the breathing pattern. Second, do the "seal stretch" while standing—lean back, suck in the stomach ("hollow and tall") and use two fingertips to massage the cramp away. While allowing some time for the cramp to subside, re-evaluate what you ate beforehand, although that may not be the problem. Evaluate posture, too, as in checking to see if the hips are tilting forward. The cramp could be attributable to weak glutes which compromises the posture of the runner, forcing other muscles in the lumbar/abdominal region to work overtime. A stronger core will obviously lead to better posture. Finally, can the cramp be endured by continuing to run, and if so, for how long?

Other than a runner simply running too fast for what his/her body can handle, another theory explaining why cramps occur is that there is a build-up of fluid between the tissues in the abdominal area due to a repeated movement, so a change in terrain and stretching the abdominal muscles over the span of a run might help move the fluid around. Nonetheless, it's difficult at this time to point to a single cause for stomach cramps.

Uphill Running

A commonly asked question is, "When running uphill or downhill, should my form change?" The simple answer in either instance is "no," not unless there is an increase in effort. In order for any aspect of run mechanics to change when going up or down a hill, the runner must be running fast and/or the hill has to be considered steep, either of which would cause an increase in effort. The obvious first point here is that *fast* and *steep* are certainly terms that will be relative to the individual. To be more specific, if the speed isn't faster than tempo pace, and if the hill is not significantly challenging, then form will stay the same. It's tough to pick an exact gradient to determine whether a hill is steep or not because that will most likely depend on the fitness of the individual. However, if I'm forced to pick a gradient, then I'll say steeper than 5% (either up or down) would be when running form might change. But again, the main factor becomes whether or not effort increases while trying to maintain the same pace. If the hill doesn't capture your attention, or if you have to give pause and think about whether or not a hill is steep, then it's probably not steep enough to change your mechanics.

So what changes if either of these criteria is met (speed and/or steepness)? First, when going uphill, foot strike changes to more of a *forefoot* landing, which normally is avoided, as explained above in the *Foot Strike* section. If runners are ever going to intentionally run on the balls of their feet, then it's going to be when going up a hill that is relatively steep and/or when running faster than tempo pace on an incline. This adapted forefoot landing should also feel more natural at this time due to the foot coming into contact with the ground sooner than when running on a flat surface. In other words, due to the increased angle of the running surface, the leg has less time (even if technically miniscule) to complete the swing phase of the stride (the leg moving from behind the body to in front of the body), so landing higher near the forefoot makes it is easier to adapt to this small yet significant difference in timing. This shorter stride thereby makes it easier for the brain to "trust" a forefoot landing (as explained in the final paragraphs of the *Foot Strike* section).

Concurrent with this slightly shorter stride, the stride rate (cadence) may increase slightly, which is analogous to cycling uphill and selecting an easier gear while increasing the cadence/RPMs. In addition, the other aspect of run form that changes in this instance is that there should be a more pronounced total body lean into the hill. Because of this total body lean, it is also more natural for the feet to land more directly under the center of mass, or slightly behind the runner's center of mass in cases when the hill is tremendously steep. An increase in cadence will feel more natural when the stride length is reduced by the demands of a hill.[27]

To reiterate, remember that there must be an increase in effort moving up a hill for the runner to simultaneously change foot strike and body lean—the runner must be moving at a fast pace and/or moving up a steep hill. Otherwise, to lean into a hill without either of these conditions might mean running with incorrect posture, with the butt sticking out and an incorrect pelvic alignment (explained in the *Posture, Pelvic Tilt & Leaning* section). To state these main points another way, if the pace is relatively relaxed (tempo pace or slower) and/or the incline is insignificant (no change in effort) then keep running as you normally would.

When the foot strike and body lean change when going up a hill, then there may sometimes be an associated increase in arm swing, but this is also going to be an individual preference based on the speed of the runner at that moment. The final pointer is to make sure that the head does not hang down/low as the body lean increases.

DOWNHILL RUNNING

For downhill running at a fast pace and/or on a steep hill, the foot strike actually changes to a heel strike and the posture will change to a *backward* lean, in order to have more stability and perhaps more safety.

---

27. To expound upon a main point from the sections on *Stride Length, Stride Rate* and *Foot Strike*, many runners are instructed to *always* run with "a shorter stride and higher cadence;" however, to end the instructions there is often the cause of a heel strike. The key word missing from these instructions that I have strongly emphasized is the word *relatively*. Running with short strides per se is *not* the answer to better form.

This is typically not ideal running form, but then again, long, steep downhills are not the norm either. Otherwise, the natural total body lean will remain the same or increase slightly when running downhill, but, as always, I don't recommend making total body lean a focal point for runners.

Because of gravity, everyone would technically run faster on a downhill compared to a flat surface. However, issues arise when a runner is not strong enough and/or light enough to support the increased force from an increased pace. In other words, to run downhill at tempo pace or faster while maintaining a midfoot strike may cause the runner to become unbalanced and out of control. The best way to adjust for this increased force is to lean backward (even slightly) and land with the foot in front of the body (as heel strikers do) to cause a "braking action" with the legs.

Rather than *resisting* the urge to go faster on a downhill, a runner can usually go with the flow and speed up, but it's imperative to maintain good balance by adapting a heel strike (it's an exception to the rule), especially as the length of the downhill increases. With that in mind, a runner could maintain a midfoot strike on a steep downhill if it is a relatively short duration (a few seconds). Individual body weight and leg strength will be the determining variables, but *all* runners will be heel striking (braking) on the toughest downhills in order to stay under control. The stride can also shorten a bit on downhills, but if it's not a significantly steep downhill and the steps become choppy (by any definition), then this may be a sign that the hips and quads need to be strengthened. Strong hips and quads allow a runner to absorb the extra stress on downhill courses.

In other downhill instances, rather than speeding up, the pace may stay the same, or even slow down, as in the case of significant gradients. A steep gradient only reinforces the need to lean back and "put on the brakes." The reason this adapted heel strike does not pose much of a problem in terms of additional (unnecessary) fatigue is that most race courses don't consist of multiple steep downhills in order for this problem to accumulate. Anyone who has raced such a course was no doubt sorer than expected, and possibly had a slower finish time than the terrain would have predicted. Having said that, not all downhill courses guarantee a PR, but such a course is usually an exception to the downhill-PR rule, with the Boston course being the most notable of these exceptions.

The runners who are able to maintain a midfoot strike on down-hills and/or handle these courses the best are those runners who are lightweight and/or possess a very high strength-to-body-weight ratio (something that is improved through ST and plyos). Otherwise, what is typically seen in runners when they run downhill at fast paces without enough leg strength and/or run down a steep hill is that their arms flail wide to help them balance, or they appear out of control. In sum, in order to maintain a midfoot strike going downhill, the pace needs to be relatively slow (slower than tempo pace), the gradient needs to be insig-nificant to the runner, the strength-to-body-weight ratio must be high, and/or the duration of the descent needs to be short. This means that the stronger a runner becomes through ST, then the hills won't appear as steep; therefore, the more a runner can capitalize on downhill courses without a need to put on the brakes.

Closing Thoughts on Running Form

Long-distance running (1st gear) should resemble a "slow sprint." Not only does this phrase serve as a healthy reminder about proper mechanics (there shouldn't be a drastic difference in form from 1st to 5th gear or vice versa), but it also helps foster a mentality of being a "fast" runner. When the pace becomes too slow then the mechanics will reflect that, and there may be some resultant self-talk that reminds the runner that he is "plod-ding along." On the hottest, most humid days I can see how that might happen and I would withhold judgment. However, when mechanics do not break down into a shuffle of some sort, and the jog becomes a "slow sprint" (regardless of actual pace), then a runner may develop the mentality that he's having a good run based on the feedback the mind is receiving from the body. As described in the *Understanding the Workouts* chapter, Fast Finish runs and post-workout striders can help this mentality become more consistent.

I have much success in changing heel strikers into midfoot runners. Not every runner gets it down pat in the first Running 101 session, but typically by the end of 60 minutes, nine out of ten runners are "cured" of their heel striking. I say that the success of future runs is mixed because it depends on the runner's willingness to temporarily reduce his/her RV in order to have higher quality run sessions and accelerate the learning curve. You cannot, in my opinion, carry the new running form into a high-volume running routine without regressing into old habits (due to fatigue) or making new injuries likely. I admit that the more athletic runners will have quicker success and are more apt to get the midfoot strike to stick. And by "athletic" I mean hand-eye coordination and/or some background in another team/ball sport. This finding is true because in remedying someone's mechanics, there has to be a degree of treatment acceptability, for which athletic individuals typically have past experience learning new skills (mechanics) and/or picking up on cue words more quickly.

If all this seems like much to remember, then it probably is, don't think *too* much when running. These are just things to monitor every now and then. Watch other runners. You will notice their posture and form, and that is an immediate reminder about what you might look like (or not look like) when running. I've seen many fast runners at races over the years, some of them with unusual looking strides. Former marathon world record holder Haile Gebrselassie pronates at the ankles more than anyone has ever seen. Biomechanical studies on the Olympic runners in Beijing in 2008 produced an array of mechanics when viewed in detail. There is no correct way to run; we're all like individual snowflakes, but keep the basic principles in mind—relaxed upper body, proud posture, midfoot strike, relatively long stride, and rhythmic breathing.

The final advice in this department is something that is not always politically correct in the running world: Be more competitive! Related to my philosophy in getting more people to train like *athletes* and not *exercisers* or *runners*, if someone is more competitive with his/her running, then perhaps he/she will become more likely to develop a "natural" running stride due to faster paces. Upon hearing this approach, many folks say, "But I'll get tired more easily and won't be able to run as far." I agree 100% with this observation, thus my reasoning that not everyone is cut out for longer distance events right away. Many runners don't want to put themselves in a competitive environment and/or don't want to push themselves to run hard, so they jog at a very relaxed pace and say, "I just want to enjoy the run." I do agree with this mantra and coach many runners who I don't push to be competitive. However, for many runners, it's the mentality of running slowly (in order to enjoy the run) that puts them into unnatural running form. I show lots of patience with my runners and I also ask them to be patient at times. For instance, I sometimes encourage a runner not to sign up for a marathon because he doesn't quite have the full-body strength needed to maintain a solid pace (a.k.a. good run mechanics) at the longer distances. This is where I jokingly dub myself "the crusher of hopes and dreams," but I know this moniker is worth it in the long haul. My runners will be more successful at the longer distances when they're patient because they'll have better mechanics and therefore fewer injuries. They'll even be faster, and it's fun to be fast! To the runners who are correctly changing their stride, yet experiencing shortness of breath and suddenly feeling out of shape again, I say, "Don't sweat it. You're now running correctly and naturally, and your cadence, stride length and pace have all improved. You can now safely *build* toward the longer distances again."

TRAINING PROGRAMS & RUNNING FORM

As it relates to the training programs, a beginning runner's first goal is to make sure he/she can handle the given distance on race day, so increasing the mileage is first priority, regardless of any goal time. However, training volume depends on the foot strike. A midfoot runner will be able to handle both higher run mileage and speed work (within reason) with no foreseeable problems. Beyond that, it's up to a runner as to which approach to maximize. For instance, if a runner has a goal time or wants to be competitive in the race field, then more than one speed workout per week on occasion is a good idea. On the other hand, if a runner just wants to finish a given race and his/her love for running through Rock Creek Park in DC is the main motivator, then there's no need to be hard-pressed for speed work. Furthermore, if the runner in question is a heel striker or forefoot runner, then it's probably (but not always) worth it to correct the form anyway, so that he/she can better enjoy the training by being injury-free (a healthy runner is a happy runner). In the case of the latter, I would cap the mileage as needed until the form is corrected. Running shorter and slightly faster helps to correct form more quickly because it negates the longer, slower runs, which inevitably resort back to running in 1st gear and a likelihood for heel striking.

To reiterate, the reason for capping RV is so that a runner can have a more natural running stride while running at slightly faster speeds. Therefore, the goal of early-season speed workouts is to work on running form, specifically, increasing stride length with the goal of strengthening the glutes and hamstrings, better enabling a runner to land midfoot.

WARMING-UP & STRETCHING

There are basically two types of stretching, dynamic and static. There are of course further breakdowns of these categories, but we'll keep the headings simple. Static stretching is the common mode everyone is familiar with, like pulling the foot to the butt to stretch the quad or the butterfly stretch. These can be done with a partner as well (e.g., passive-active resistance stretching, or PNF stretching). Dynamic stretching involves movement of the joint/muscles, as the name implies, such as arm circles, leg swings, skipping, and high knees. Dynamic stretching should not be confused with ballistic stretching, which involves getting into a static stretch position and rocking or bouncing the body in that position, as in flapping the legs while doing the butterfly stretch (I have not seen ballistic stretching promoted much). Review studies conclude that dynamic stretching is superior to static stretching as a warm-up prior to exercise, whether it is running, ST or anything else. Compared to a control group whose protocol is not to warm-up or stretch at all, these studies show that static stretching prior to training actually reduces strength, sprint speed, endurance, and power. Dynamic stretching is typically shown to have the opposite effect, with improvements in performance.

Contrary to popular belief, stretching and flexibility have not been shown to prevent injuries to a significant degree, but if done properly, they can improve performance. The purpose of a warm-up is exactly that—to warm the muscles by increasing the temperature of the body via an increase in blood flow to the working muscles. Therefore, it is the increased blood flow that warms the body. Static stretching, by its nature of little or no movement, cannot do this. The fact that static stretching has often been shown to reduce strength, speed, endurance, and power is related to a reduction in the stiffness of the contractile units in the muscle (less tension produces less force) because the prolonged state of the muscle contractions fatigues the muscle fibers. Occasionally a PT will prescribe specific static stretches for pre-workout and these are an exception to the rule, whereas static stretching in these instances might benefit performance or keep an injury at bay.

Perusing the start line area of a local 5k will surely give a glimpse of the many warm-up routines adopted by runners. However, keeping a closer eye on the race favorites will reveal some interesting looking running drills; and these would appropriately be dynamic stretches. Dynamic stretches also offer lessons in running form because they foster improvements in flexibility, balance, and coordination, all of which improve athleticism.

Because the muscle fibers used during an easy jog are different than those used when running at faster paces, a more specific warm-up is needed prior to speed workouts and races. Easy distance runs admittedly don't require much of a warm-up since the muscles will not go through a great range of motion and the intensity is low. Before a long, slow run, a runner could simply do leg swings (using a fence/wall) and a light dynamic warm-up for the upper body to rid tension and prevent wasted energy. However, prior to the higher-intensity workouts, additional drills should be added to target specific muscle groups. When a runner I coach has a sub-par race or reports to me that she "didn't feel right" during a race, I bypass most of the analyses and simply ask, "Did you do a thorough dynamic warm-up beforehand?" A lack of a thorough dynamic warm-up accounts for most of the variance in a race or speed workout.

After exercise, dynamic stretching such as leg swings, or cool-down laps, is once again superior to static stretching. However, in all reality, static stretching is probably most preferred at this point because it allows one to sit down and rest, plus it guarantees that this element of training is incorporated during the week, as static stretching should not be avoided altogether. It is a basic method to maintain the range of motion of a joint and/or muscle group, which can aid performance for those who have flexibility limitations.[28] Performing a few static stretches before an activity is allowable if one is so inclined (if muscle tightness is more than usual), but ideally the static stretching would be done about 30 - 45 minutes before the activity (and before the dynamic stretching). A stretch only needs to be held for 10 - 30 seconds if flexibility is not an issue, as there doesn't appear to be additional benefits in holding a stretch longer than 30 seconds unless one is extremely inflexible.[29]

Below is a condensed list of dynamic drills and a suggested order to perform them, given that a dynamic warm-up should progress from

---

28. Static stretching was discussed further in the *Massage* section in Chapter 2.
29. There is *Recovery Runs & Cool-downs* section later in this book, as well as a *Race Prep & Warming-Up* section.

general to specific, and from slow to fast. There should be about 5 - 7 minutes from the end of the warm-up to the beginning of the workout/ race so that the HR is still slightly elevated at the start line:

- easy skipping (similar to marching, no emphasis on height or knee drive) - 20 meters
- A-skips (emphasis on a high, fast knee lift past 90-degrees) - 10 meters
- Ins-and-Outs (similar to A-skips, but moving the leg to the outside as well) - 10m
- Loosy Goosy (a side shuffle while crossing the arms above/below the head) - 30m
- Carioca (sideways crossover steps) - 30m
- walking lunges (both legs at right angles) - 4 on each leg
- power skips (driving off the ground for maximum height) - 10m
- back pedals (lower the hips and lean forward for balance) - 30m
- butt kicks/ heel flicks (fast turnover, fast arms) - 5m
- high knees (fast turnover, fast arms) - 10m x2
- striders at race pace - 50 to 100m x 2 - 4

6

TECHNOLOGY & PSYCHOLOGY

PACE VS. INTENSITY (GARMIN VS. ZEN)

THIS TOPIC SURFACES a good deal when I discuss proper goal setting and pacing in the weekly replies to my athletes. There is a crucial distinction between pace and intensity, with intensity being more important due to the myriad factors and extraneous variables that can affect pace. Many runners love numbers and data, which means they love *pace*. However, trying to maintain a given pace without accounting for variables like temperature, humidity, dew point, terrain, wind, hydration status, energy levels, clothing selection (ability to sweat), and experience may do a runner more harm than good. When the variables are favorable, then it's very possible that holding a given intensity will lead to the goal-pace (or vice versa), but the aforementioned variables and the body's real-time status should be considered first. This may sound like common sense, but why then are so many runners not at peace with their finish times? Perhaps it's because a runner's craving for data is too strong. So let's hear about Garmin watches.

The same personality trait that wants to buy the Garmin in the first place is perhaps the same personality that has the potential to *overanalyze* data mid-race or post-race. Obviously, this does not describe all

Garmin runners, but in my experience as a coach, a Garmin watch often ends up being detrimental because it tells a runner that he, technically speaking, could have run faster, which often leads him to think that he was "slow." Either of these thoughts can lead to a dose (great or small) of feeling unsuccessful. As much as a Garmin runner may say, "It's a hilly course; I'll just run based on feel," I find that he will forget all about that idea once the starting gun goes off and when he takes that first peek down at his watch and mutters, "Gee, I'm way slower than my PR pace." Post-race, that same runner might say, "I was pretty slow on the hills...not a good race for me." If the hills were supposed to affect pacing, then why would the runner use the phrases "pretty slow" and "not a good race"? How can we address this mentality before the race or workout even begins?

Using data to help guide training is perfectly fine; it's natural. However, my conjecture is that a personality that adores data and numbers is more attracted to faster paces on the watch, so *those* numbers (faster numbers) become the dominant thoughts mid-race and post-race. In turn, this data analysis may create an unwillingness to accept the slower paces that are actually predictable based on race conditions (i.e., terrain and weather). Ultimately, a runner is prone to feel slow or less likely to feel successful. I too frequently see this distinction between the runners I coach who use a Garmin versus those who have a simpler watch using only elapsed minutes and seconds. With this in mind, you can imagine the extra processing that takes place midrace if the GPS signal cuts out.

I can recall a particular Time Trial I coached on the track when some runners were bamboozled when their Garmins told them the distance of the TT had elapsed when there was still a half a lap to go. A regulation track is 400m, so the track is never wrong. Keep it simple when using the track; set the watch to timer mode and just peek at the watch every 200m or 400m to check splits (elapsed time). Other times during races, Garmin watches have signaled that a mile has surpassed some distance before or after the course mile markers. Rarely does a runner finish a race with an accurate GPS readout according to the official race distance. This discrepancy is due to GPS/satellite interference, as well as the fact that it's not always feasible to run the course exactly the way it was measured by a race official. I attempt to convince runners to ditch their Garmins more regularly, which has positive effects on race day, especially in the long-term.

The idea of running based on perceived exertion (intensity) is new to everyone at some point in his/her running career. Some runners are more experienced in this way and may not even own a watch. Eventually, it should be easy to pace well on a trail without mile markers or to know the exact pace 20 seconds after a race starts. Garmins will not always be proper guides in a race setting. We need to know our limits and what we're capable of achieving based on how the body feels and what it's saying. In this regard, it can be more useful to monitor heart rate (HR) as opposed to pace, but more on that in a moment. Garmins should not be telling us how fast to run during the middle of a race; rather, they should merely be satisfying our curiosity. Knowing how the body is reacting in real-time is more important than the actual pace maintained. For instance, becoming very in tune to rhythmic breathing and stride length during training will enable one to know what kind of effort can be sustained during a race. Moreover, sometimes the weather for a weekend run is too perfect to get caught up with numbers, and this falls in line with Zen running—race day can be a part of this practice, too.

I once attended a collegiate baseball game and hung out by the field before the game started. I listened to a pitching coach, a former two-time NCAA World Series MVP and MLB player, as he was coaching a freshman pitcher during pre-game warm-ups. In order to coach the pitcher how to throw pitches to targets *everywhere* in the strike zone, the coach emphasized the point of focusing on how the pitch delivery *felt*. The coach repeated, "Stop *aiming* it and just throw it!" He even positioned the catcher ten feet outside the strike zone, just to teach the young pitcher that he should have the ability to throw to *any* target by knowing what it *feels* like to hit a target. I feel the same about learning different running paces. A runner should be able to hit ten different speeds in a run with relative ease, without a Garmin or HR monitor as a guide. To paraphrase the pitching coach, "Stop aiming with your Garmin and just *run* it!"

Personally, I typically run without a watch and can therefore easily convince myself after any run that it was the fastest I've run a particular route. Without anything/one to tell me otherwise, I've been riding a PR-high for over 10 years, which doesn't allow for many gaps in my confidence. If, on the other hand, my track splits were off the mark and my race times remained stagnant, then I could say that I'm not running hard enough during my weekly jogs, but as long as my track data continues to be on par, then it's a good system for me and a good mental tactic to incorporate into training. The main coaching service I offer is not the training programs (on paper); rather, it's the *mental* approach to training and racing. I haven't had a "slow run" in over 10 years of training, unless selective amnesia is doing its job (a marker of elite athletics), and I don't think I'll ever feel "slow." That mentality builds tremendous confidence. I can't open a lid on a runner's head and dump confidence into his brain, but this tactic just described is a great way for a runner to increase confidence himself.

Using Perceived Exertion in Races

Consistent pacing is related to the phrase "staying in your element." Your element is your stride, posture, breathing, the amount of tension in your body, the nature of your thoughts and so on, which are all of the things we hopefully tune into frequently during training. Suppose you start the first few miles ahead of PR pace, how do you know if you can *maintain* that pace, rather than thinking you blew it and went out too fast? If the intensity and perceived exertion during a race are mimicking a similar feeling experienced while training at that pace or distance, then you're most likely right on par (you are in your element). Understanding intensity is important for race day; therefore, like racing, relocating speed workouts off the track at some point in the year is crucial in learning proper intensities. Specificity of training implies that this move is vital for success on race day.

Staying in tune with the body during training will give confidence for when a Garmin signal cuts out or when mile markers aren't always accurate, like in some smaller, low-key races. This can be stressful for some runners, who use these markers to help them pace, but if a runner can determine pace based on perceived exertion then peace of mind is granted. A runner should always be able to know the pace *before* the one-mile marker (there shouldn't be any surprises). Unless it's a high-caliber race, don't always expect the mile markers to be precise, nor for each mile to be marked. Therefore, be prepared to use rhythmic breathing and stride length to guide the pacing and to know whether it can be sustained.

During the races at the peak of my running fitness, I noticed that I was rarely passed after the first half-mile or so, regardless of the distance. I chalk this up to picking the right pace from the starting gun. Is it also possible that I start out too slow and therefore it's easy for me to pass others from behind? I like to think this is not the case, given the accuracy of my finish times versus predicted times, and the fact that I usually end up beating the runners who were around me at the halfway point. However, most importantly, I also notice the people I pass are often getting slower, a sign that perhaps they went out too fast, so it's not always a matter of me speeding up.

HEART RATE MONITORS

HR monitors offer an advantage for training in that they let a runner know when the intensity is too high or low. They offer specific, immediate feedback, just like breathing patterns. They can help a runner adjust the depth or rhythm of his/her breathing for a target HR zone and to help with pacing. For instance, tempo pace (~10k pace) is approximately

88 - 92% of maximum HR, or 83 - 88% of VO$_2$ max.[30], [31] Not to sound contradictory, but I'm not a proponent for *racing* with HR monitors. The day before the 2008 Boston Marathon, I chatted briefly with Peter Reid (a legend in endurance sports) about HR monitors and he said what I thought he would—he didn't wear one while racing because it's better to race based on perceived effort, not numbers. However, an athlete can only afford to do that if he is totally dialed in to the body (perceived effort) during actual training. Then, an athlete can leave the HR monitor at home on race day so it does not distract or limit him.

My advice is to initially use a HR monitor retrospectively, meaning do the workout and check the HR data *afterward*, as opposed to saying "I'm going to do this workout at a HR of ___." The latter can come after you've learned the appropriate HR zone for a given distance or workout. To reiterate, I believe nailing down the pacing on the track using even splits (and rhythmic breathing) should come first and then that can be crosschecked with the HR data. Once the track splits are consistent, then one can run off-track and use HR as a guide. It's also worthy to note that HR will naturally increase over the duration of an endurance activity even as pace stays the same. This increase in HR is known as *cardiac drift*. Meaning, a runner has to work harder on last few reps or miles just to maintain the same pace. This phenomenon is the result of water in the blood being lost when sweating. Over time, the cumulative water loss reduces the amount of oxygen being carried in the blood, hence a higher HR needed to allow the body to produce the same output (pace).

There are many variables that affect HR, such as temperature, hydration status, mood (anxiety and adrenaline), clothing selection, and cardiac drift (just to name a few).[32] Therefore, similar to my view on Garmins, don't rely on HR monitors exclusively on race day, nor as set data points

---

30. A new proposed formula for calculating estimated maxHR is [206.9 − (age x .67)].

31. The relationship between maxHR and VO$_2$max isn't an exact correlation; it's something to the effect that 80% maxHR = 75% VO$_2$max.

32. Indoor workouts (e.g., treadmills, spin classes) can result in a higher HR due to lack of air circulation.

to always guide training. When it comes to racing, it is best to be able to push hard and not be limited by a beeping device. For instance, a runner may want to pick up the intensity on a downhill section without thinking, "Oh no, my watch is telling me I've hit my limit." HR monitors can be good for athletes with health problems, preventing these folks from pushing too hard into a danger zone, but as long as we are racing within our limits, we should be free to race at will.

PACE CALCULATORS

The foundation of how I calculate goal times for workouts and races is based upon the detailed chart in the book *Daniel's Running Formula*, along with a dash of the art of coaching. The Daniel's Formula is a trusted source, and the art of coaching that I sometimes (not always) insert is based on other factors that the chart does not consider, most importantly the specificity of training, though Daniels writes well on this topic in his book. The main caveat here relates to marathon goals. With other race distances, we can usually assume the chart is accurate because a runner's general training volume will bring her to the start line in good shape for 5k through a half marathon (a "Half"). However, because marathons and races one mile or shorter require the greatest specificity of training, they usually have the greatest fluctuation in predicted times, as you might predict. There are more variables to consider in marathons that don't show up on the radar at shorter distances. For instance, if you ran 1:40:00 in a Half, then your predicted marathon time would be ~3:28:00; however, this assumes you are "marathon ready." If your longest training run has only been 10 miles and you don't do much run-specific ST, then I wouldn't predict you to finish near 3:28:00 at your upcoming marathon, regardless of your recent Half performance. Specificity of training must be very high for pace calculators to work for the marathon distance, which means doing long runs at goal pace, along with higher-volume training at specific points in the year.

There are several factors I consider in giving any goal time, which are often intangible factors that remind us just how slippery pace calculators can be. Most world records and local course records are typically set in overcast conditions with little to no wind, and temperatures in the 60's (or down to the mid-50's for the marathon and up to low 70's for shorter races). This is the weather most conducive to lower sweat rates, yet not so cold that it restricts blood flow to the muscles. It is difficult for experienced and advanced runners to hit PRs in the summertime due to the adverse effects of heat, humidity, and dew point. Therefore, for someone racing and training consistently for several years, expect PRs to occur in the spring or fall, especially for those living in the Mid-Atlantic region, where summer weather is not advantageous. However, beginning runners, by definition, have limited race experience and have not yet tapped their full potential, so they could be expected to set a PR in non-ideal race conditions.

Laying out the correct goals is part of a positive mental approach to running in which there is recognition of what is challenging, yet *realistic*. Veteran athletes possess the wisdom to know how to account for variables such as hills and weather. To overlook these variables in calculating predicted marathon times would be cause for a coach to pull an athlete back onto the learning curve. Don't get caught up thinking every race should be a PR or that you should be getting faster and faster every week; it's not always possible given conditions outside of your control. If the conditions are under your control, then do everything you can to maximize that potential!

FOCUS & COMPOSURE

Focus and composure are similar terms, but not the same. Focus is the ability to block out task-irrelevant cues during the right moments. Composure is the ability to maintain that focus over an extended period of time. Anyone can be focused for the first two minutes of a race, but how long does that focus last? How long can you keep your cool? Focus and composure can be learned; they are skills. Based on prior life experiences, as in professional roles or experiences in other sports, some runners are already equipped with these skills. I strive to teach these proper focal points during the track workouts I coach. The ability not to space out too much by the end of a workout or race is called composure. Focus and composure can be viewed as the ability to concentrate on the elements of a race that are in one's control (e.g., stride length or breathing), as opposed to giving attention to task-*irrelevant* cues, such as the crowd.

Elite athletics teaches us that race day doesn't require much more than showing up and doing what we've been training to do. *Extra* effort isn't required on race day. Physically, extra effort would imply a pace that is too fast. Mentally, extra effort often has the opposite, undesired effect. Part of showing up and feeling ready to go is making sure there are no distractions, and that both mind and body (through their reciprocal relationship) are in the proper state of arousal. For this reason, going out too fast in a race is often due to not being in the right mode, either mentally or physically, which explains some of the variance in race performance. The importance of dynamic warm-up drills is apparent in this regard. Therefore, a dynamic warm-up (a.k.a., routine) is part of proper preparation, though it is frequently overlooked when runners interpret their race results. In this way, dynamic warm-up drills ("track drills") are a part of what a textbook would call *Psychological Skills Training*. Imagery, muscle relaxation, goal setting, attention training, emotional regulation and breathing control are the primary examples.

Occasionally, race-day logistics get thrown off due to unforeseen circumstances or last-second changes that needed to be made by the race director. These conditions are always out of your control, so rather than worry about the who, what, when, where and why of unexpected events, stay in your own element and focus on those factors within your control, like rhythmic breathing and stride length in the opening segment of the race. Develop the ability to block out negative self-talk or emotions that might otherwise enter the picture. This composure should also be a regular part of one's personality in dealing with day-to-day tasks. Over the years, I've seen athletes I coach display composure during setbacks, whether it was a watch losing power mid-race, racing without mile markers, or missing the official start of the race. All of these examples listed were met with positive results.

Maintaining proper focus and positive self-talk are keys to success in running and should not be confused with mental toughness, for which there is a separate section in this chapter. When it comes time for race day, we don't want to have to rely on mental toughness. I use the terms focus and composure to mean something different than mental toughness. I don't agree with the sentiment, "running is 90% mental." It's supposed to be 90% *physical* without much mental energy needed at all. This point is reached when proper pacing (intensity) is learned in training and when form is flawless and automatic. The less we think the better off we are. That is true of all sports. Just ask any golfer, or watch Michael Jordan hit a foul shot with his eyes closed; running should not be much different in relation to expending relatively little mental energy, especially since its technical components are much easier than golf and basketball.

SELF-TALK

Part of self-coaching is the conversation an athlete has with him/herself while engaged in a workout or race. The in-the-moment words and phrases that enter an athlete's mind can tip the scales toward having a great race from start to finish or help to salvage a sub-par performance. The aim of this section is to provide the reader with a more detailed understanding of how self-talk benefits performance and how it can be done. In short, a self-coached runner needs to know how to give sound advice to herself *in the moment*, as if a coach were running there alongside her.

In 2009 I heard Ryan Hall speak at a charity fundraiser. After hearing his account of the NYC Marathon that took place a month prior, I noticed he alluded to positive vs. negative thoughts late in the race when he wasn't feeling great, battling a hip pain he never had before (he still finished 4th by only 90 seconds). I asked him to expound upon those remarks and he said his self-talk during races is simply the same thoughts he has during training and that is what allows him to keep the self-talk positive. When the going gets tough, he reminds himself that he is tired or not feeling 100%, "because he is working hard," as he phrased it.[33] He made a great point in stating it's all easier said than done, but during races, he also reminds himself of great training days he had leading up to the race. We can take this as one definition of confidence that I use: The feeling you've been there before. That's a common definition for public speakers, too.

Reaching new goals and uncharted territory takes hard work, and without a simultaneous positive outlook, motivation might suffer. Positive self-talk is usually only successful if practiced regularly. The good news is that practicing self-talk and focusing on the cues/tasks that are under *your control* (key phrase) are specific skills that can be developed virtually every run. When mastered, it lends itself to confidence. I'll share another quick story to illustrate this point further. One particular March, a runner I coached hit his marathon goal of cracking three hours. Yes, hard work pays off and he was well prepared to run under three hours, but the reason I use his race as an example is because the weather was rainy, windy, and a tad on the cold side, yet not enough to defeat his goal, given his fitness. These conditions were certainly adverse, but they are something that many runners experience all winter long. Rather than let the conditions turn any self-talk to the dark side, he kept his composure and reminded himself, "I've trained through these conditions all winter (I've been here before)." Positive language equates to positive mood and breeds confidence.

Does the weather affect our bodies and pacing? Yes, absolutely. The goal times I send my athletes typically reflect their upcoming race conditions. However, the difference is that the weather does not have to affect the *mind*. In the case of the runner from the above example, he (and most runners) had run in non-ideal conditions prior to the race and he reminded himself of that. That reminder is one method to keep the self-talk

---

33. I have written similar advice in the *Race Strategies* section.

positive. Could he have run a minute or two faster in better weather? Sure, maybe, probably. The weather can affect our pacing via its effect on the body, but keep it together upstairs (composure) and have positive mantras (self-talk) that are actually believable. You can't BS yourself! You can't just hope that self-talk is successful on race day; it doesn't work that way. Rather, positive self-talk is a skill that requires *practice* during training, just like any physical skill.

Many people can easily point to and understand the practical implications of variables such as wind, hills, and rain. However, the big difference lies in how they interpret it at the moment, which unfortunately is the not-so-easy part for many runners, meaning what exactly do you say to yourself at that moment? "It's windy...I'm slow" (period, that's it) vs. "My pace is off an ideal time because it is windy; I'm still running well." I believe that many runners adopt the former self-talk, instead of the latter. Soaking up all the positive results of a workout/race, while dismissing the negative aspects, is definitely a skill that great athletes practice. Knowledge is power in this regard. If you know why something is hard or why a workout is going a particular way, then that should eliminate any negative thoughts (anxiety, pressure, "I'm slow").

Self-talk should not be generic phrases that don't offer specific focal points. In other words, merely thinking, "be positive," might not do an athlete any good because it's not specific enough. Be positive about what exactly? *How* do you feel more uplifted during a tough run? Understanding proper goal setting, namely *process goals*, allows the thoughts to be focused on more relevant, specific elements of the run.[34] As previously mentioned, a runner needs the ability to focus on elements of the run in his/her control, like rhythmic breathing, stride length, and pacing. Having said this, the phrase *positive self-talk* doesn't always imply thinking positively per se, nor is it feasible to have these types of thoughts 100% of the time during a workout or race. It's best to turn the mind off as frequently as possible, so in that regard I remind my runners that the thoughts can also be "neutral" or even non-existent. Cue words and process goals are often synonymous

---

34. There are more details on proper goal setting in Chapters 7 and 10.

and are ways to keep the thoughts on neutral, without feeling the need to have to be "positive."

Putting innate instinct on the back burner for a moment, thoughts and feelings can stem from the language used when interpreting a situation. Subsequently, one's mood is a result of these thoughts and internal dialogue. Moods are therefore very transient; they can come and go based on the thoughts or language relevant to the interpretation of a situation. Because we generally encounter dozens of different situations on a daily basis, we strive to maintain a fairly stable mood throughout the course of the day, week, month, etc. If we want to maintain a positive mood during the situations involving training and racing, then we need to understand the importance of the specific language we use. *Practicing* the cue words/phrases in certain situations thereby helps to understand *how* positive self-talk is a skill. This same psychological pathology occurs in many phobias. For example, the exact phrases a person says to himself when entering a crowded subway car are crucial in whether or not he begins to feel "boxed in." Anxiety can be habit forming, like Pavlov's dogs and classical conditioning. The coaching point here is for athletes or those with a phobia to develop a small set of *specific* cue words/phrases that lead to desirable thoughts and moods.

If a runner begins thinking negatively mid-race, then it can adversely affect how the body feels, and in the worst cases it spirals downhill in a reciprocal way. If in fact a runner did have a bad start to a race and began beating himself up mentally and losing composure, then the effects of the non-ideal start become magnified. The finish time may then be much slower than it would/could have been if he had at least kept his composure the rest of the race. What this means to me as a coach is that a runner spiraling downhill mid-race makes the race invalid. A race like that offers little meaningful feedback and there's not a chance in heck I'll look at that race as a "measure of fitness" the same way the runner might. The important distinction is how the runner and I will interpret the end result (finish time) differently. Whereas the runner might look at the finish time as "all he could muster that day," I know this isn't the case. I know that once he started thinking negatively during the race, he simultaneously sabotaged his fitness and the physical aspect of the race. Therefore, I don't interpret the result as valid. In my eyes the final x-amount of the race wasn't a test of fitness at all because the worry/negativity masked what could have been accomplished. Have you done this to yourself? Learning how to snap out of a mid-race funk is not as important as learning how to prevent it in the first place.

To follow-up on the last point, feeling good physically allows one to feel good mentally. This is certainly a reciprocal relationship, in that confidence and relaxation during the race can ease muscular tension, but I do favor the first causal direction stated. Positive self-talk is easier when the body feels better (when the pacing is appropriate and the body is fueled correctly). A runner can physically push harder when the muscles feel good, and there's also more confidence in the ability to keep pushing the pace. On the contrary, feeling good mentally does not always make the pain go away or allow for a PR; therefore, I encourage runners to control their pacing in the beginning of a race so that they set themselves up for a good second half of the race. For instance, when the pacing is appropriate at the beginning of a race, then it's more likely that a runner will feel physically strong near the end. It's impressive, yet not surprising, how much this sensation of strength toward the end of a race contributes to positive self-talk, which in turn feeds the body more energy. Track workouts help establish this consistent pacing, teaching a runner how to stay in his/her element in order to set up a strong finish.

IMAGERY

Imagery is often called visualization. It can be a useful tool for runners; however, I acknowledge that it is not for everyone, nor is it a necessity. The premise of imagery is to visualize success during a race, which also includes the positive self-talk that will occur at given points on the course. Imagining a race while doing a workout is a chance to gain race experience, especially if the workout paces match race pace. Additionally, the start of every rep of a speed workout can be practice for the start line of a race. In other words, in the countdown before a workout begins, imagine a start line scenario for an upcoming race, including the sights, sounds, smells, tastes and feels. The best-case scenario for practicing imagery is on the course for which one is training for a peak race.

Here is a quick overview of the goal of imagery. Ultimately, the goal is to begin developing positive thoughts/themes during track workouts, so that the track reps can then be associated with racing. Each runner should come up with what is called a *cue word* or *cue phrase* that will serve as the origin/catalyst of this positive association. The word or phrase may be unique to the runner, her own language repeated in her own mind. The rhetorical question is this: How do you want to feel, both physically and mentally, in the moments *before* any workout or race, as well as *during* those instances or when crossing the finish line? When you answer that question, chop it down into a cue word or phrase. Once the imagery and muscle relaxation session is underway, that cue word or phrase is then repeated when a relaxed state is achieved, when the mind is in its correct state. Remember to think about how you want to feel (physically and mentally), as opposed to how you do *not* want to feel. There *is* a difference, as attempting to block out how you do not want to feel actually (technically) still puts those words/thoughts in your head (like a word on a page, it must be visible first before it can be deleted).

Don't use fluff words as cue words. Use very specific, pinpointed, meaningful words in order to have a more powerful effect on the mind and body. For instance, when a runner gets goose bumps before an event, that might signal that it's going to be a great day, so the runner might repeat the word "goose bumps" to get in the right frame of mind, even if that seems like a funny example. A runner might have a warm sensation move over his body when he feels ready before a competition; it may be that he competes at his best in these moments. This is also where routine, such as dynamic warm-up drills, enter the picture.

Entering peak race season, thoughts can shift much more to races and those specific goals in mind. There will be more key workouts on the program during a peak phase, and possibly a higher mileage, or at least an increase in high-intensity running. This is the goal for hitting a peak (recall the *Periodization* chapter). This also means that visualization sessions should now be more specific to the peak event. Instead of thinking in general terms, "I'm feeling good and running well," hone it down to "I'm going to feel smooth on that winding road cutting through the park at Mile 3." To reiterate, athletes should also start to peak *mentally* during race season.

A detail to imagery is that as you learn to associate the positive self-talk you're using in training with how you want to feel on race day, be careful not to treat your track workouts like "marathon day" because the intensity of training is often different than that of racing, so the carry-over effect isn't 100%. However, in a general sense, there is room to carry over general positives, like rhythmic breathing.

It's purposeful to do imagery sessions lying in bed at night or anywhere else that's relaxing. I recommend doing imagery prior to practicing self-talk, so that the visualizations allow the subsequent self-talk to have more validity. Because a relaxed mind is better able to visualize (focus) on the right cues, a muscle relaxation session, such as practicing breath control, typically precedes imagery.

RUNNING WITH MUSIC

If music is used to enhance performance prior to or during a run, then make sure it is suited to the distance and intensity of the race. Generally speaking, we don't want to be "pumped" or "hype" before an endurance event of 60 minutes or more. This is an individual preference of course, but consider the general rule of thumb that too much arousal in the brain and/or body can lead to extra muscular tension, which can lead to premature fatigue (recall the Fight or Flight Response from your

Psychology 101 class). This is the ultimate goal of muscle relaxation sessions, to put an athlete into the proper mental and physical state, or *arousal level* as it's called in the textbooks. The goal is to "feel right" prior to competition, so that a calm mind equates to a body in better control. However, a Beethoven symphony might cause too much relaxation, which isn't good because the nervous system needs to be awake and firing. At the other end of the spectrum, a Metallica song might cause too much excitement, which is related to the Fight or Flight Response. Choose the tunes wisely.

If it's desired to have the mid-race thoughts focused on one's own element and positive self-talk, then the degree that running with music might distract this process should be considered. Try not to wear the earphones during every run. I acknowledge that it is impossible or not even preferred to have one's thoughts limited exclusively to the act of running for the entirety of the run, but effectively monitoring the body is a skill, which is more than just hitting the pause button on the iPod here and there. The music should not interfere with the mental rehearsal of performance goals and race strategies (if there are any).

I believe that the music *can* distract runners from monitoring their stride, posture, and breathing, hindering a runner's ability to successfully master positive self-talk. You'll read later that although I believe mental toughness is *not* something we should have to use all the time, I am a firm believer in self-talk in order to assess performance and remain levelheaded when the going gets tough. If we don't have experience in how to cope with our own thoughts during harder efforts, then we're more likely to focus on the wrong cues on race day or think negatively. Nonetheless, I will note that *pre*-race music could be an exception to the rule. I recognize that warming-up with music can help an athlete get into the preferred mental zone before a race; however, once the race starts my opinion swings the other way and I prefer my athletes not have music in their ears at that time.

Related to safety, I once read a short newspaper article titled, "Death by iPod Accidents Cause Alarm." The article discussed the deaths of runners and cyclists who were listening to iPods when struck by vehicles, where the athletes were either crossing traffic lights without realizing it or didn't hear the vehicle coming. The article also discussed the hazards for joggers and pedestrians who could be more vulnerable to crime due to the auditory distraction.[35] We're all old enough to make our own decisions, but I offer the John Blaisman quote again, "Can you be alone with your own thoughts and enjoy the company you keep?"

On a related note, I once read an article by world champion endurance athlete Tim DeBoom regarding saying "hello" and/or waving to other runners and cyclists while crossing paths. His article inspired me to echo those thoughts. It's a privilege to be able to get out and enjoy the weather and be physically active, so I hope we can all be ambassadors of the lifestyle and give a friendly "hello" when we can. This is a plug for not running with earphones all the time because it can block out the world around you (unless that's your intent). I also find it difficult to cheer for racers wearing earphones. I remember my first year coaching high school XC and running alongside one of our seniors during a jog around DC. At one point we both waved to a runner coming toward us, to which there was no acknowledgment from this runner. The high school runner said to me, "That's how you can tell a runner from a non-runner—whether or not they wave or say hello." These were profound words from a young person. You can't say "hi" to everyone, especially on a popular trail, but consider that it can help ease the suffering a bit on a long, tough training day. Try to say "hi" or "thank you" to race volunteers on the course. It can sometimes make you forget you're racing and instead it can give you the sense you're out on a training run, which can bring a sense of familiarity. This familiarity boosts confidence, which in turn enhances performance.

---

35. Earphones are sometimes deemed illegal for road racing (most definitely for triathlons).

MENTAL TOUGHNESS

I believe mental toughness is overrated, which surprises people when I say that. Let me clarify. Although I think mental toughness is an important skill and that it separates levels of competition, I don't think it should define one's training and racing. Experiences that require mental toughness are draining. It's been said many times that mental toughness is when you have to "go to the well" or "dig deep." I agree. I also agree with the saying, "How many times can you go to the well before it dries up?" As with all matters of psychology, coming to a mutual understanding on a given concept can be based upon whether or not we are using the same definition. In my definition of mental toughness, there is significantly more mental self-talk and effort required to complete the task. There is a time and place for everything, but this is generally not a desirable mental state.

Attributing successes to mental toughness during endurance events is natural, but I don't want it to detract from confidence. It is better to have confidence in the physical abilities already possessed *before* the race starts, rather than becoming confident only when things get tough *during* the race. On one far end of the spectrum, if the legs are too tired to keep moving (in the truest sense of fatigue) then there is little effect the mind can have on the situation (picture someone crawling to a finish line even though his/her mind is saying, "get up"). In these instances, it's "matter over mind." There are several physiological mechanisms for muscle fatigue, none of which have anything to do with the central nervous system (mind). It's been said, "You can have all the heart in the world, but it doesn't mean anything if you don't have the legs." I believe the *everyday* examples of mental toughness lie in the decision-making processes used to maintain a consistent training routine even when tired or sore. This aspect of mental toughness is evident in making the decision to head out the door, but once the workout begins, *physical* toughness should be the goal, without having to rely on mental factors.

A lesson I've picked up from all the pro athletes I have known from various sports is to be physically tougher and fitter than the competition (via smart training) and then mental toughness rarely has to enter the picture. It's better to have a machine-like approach to training: "Eat, Drink, Sleep, Go Like Hell," than to have to put in *extra* mental effort on race day. An athlete doesn't need mental toughness to win a game/race when he/she can easily outmatch the opponent. Every now and then, we all have a day when we exceed our own expectations and capabilities to have the performance of a lifetime. That could be an instance when mental forces come into play. It could happen only once per year or once per lifetime, but we know it when it happens.

In order for an athlete to reach higher levels of performance, he/she must be selective in choosing to add mental components to the training or competition. In instances when an athlete is not motivated to do a particular workout, when he/she has to "push herself" to start it or complete it, my advice is to find ways to eliminate this mental component. Finding the motivation to do the workout can sometimes be filed under the mental toughness category, but it's a better long-term goal to embrace challenges and make that part of one's personality. As I've written in *Body Weight and Body Fat* section, "Becoming fit is hard; staying fit is easy." Embrace the challenge of becoming fit (get over that hump) and there may end up being a slightly downhill path ahead, with much less mental effort with each passing month.

Troy Jacobson, a renowned former triathlete and cyclist turned coach, once wrote:

Going to the well once too often is a phrase with 14-century origins and is essentially a warning against pushing one's luck. This phrase can be accurately applied to the athlete who schedules a demanding training and racing schedule with expectations of achieving a peak performance at each event. Many times, these highly motivated and focused athletes fall short of their goals, not realizing the root cause is that they have gone to the well too often and can't reach down deep again until they get recharged mentally and emotionally. Physiologically, an athlete can peak once or twice in a year, depending on the design of the training regimen. Similarly, from a psychological perspective, an athlete can only go to the well on a limited basis each year too. The key to having a successful season is to learn how far you can push yourself without going overboard.

Here is the moral of the story: Everyone obviously needs a break from training every now and then. Moreover, how many times can you rely on mental toughness to get you out of a tough (or painful) situation before it results in mental burnout? Burnout has been shown to weaken the immune and neuromuscular systems, in turn causing illness or injury. When something is perceived as stressful (mental or physical), hormones are released to regulate mood. Too much perceived stress and subsequent hormone release leads to a break down in the immune system. In other words, a suppressed immune system and the body's breakdown are due to the brain sensing increased mental stress, which can lead to mental fatigue (or burnout in the worst cases). The summation of all these points is to embrace the physical training and leave the mind at home.

MENTALITY OF A CHAMPION

When I took the public tour at the Olympic Training Center (OTC) in Boulder, CO, it began with a video to outline Olympic training and a theme I noticed is one which separates Olympians from other athletes—pain tolerance. This reminded me of an old interview with Simon Lessing (now retired), one of the most decorated triathletes in the history of the sport, across all distances. I also had a chance to talk with him briefly after the Escape From Alcatraz race in 2006. What I gathered from his interview and our short conversation was totally in line with what the OTC video portrayed: Top-level athletes not only have a higher pain threshold than everyone else (aided by long-term training), but they also *want* the pain. I would add that the confidence derived from the higher pain thresholds (physical toughness) is also what separates all levels of athletes.

I'm speaking here about muscle pain (fatigue/training), not joint/bone pain (injury).

"Train hard!" is how I sign my emails, but that phrase is always relative to the individual. We all can't train like Olympic athletes; however, we can all push our *own* boundaries. Over time, repeating this process allows the pain threshold (boundary) to be extended/elevated. Some people are naturally drawn to the higher levels of pain they inflict on their bodies (the nature of endurance sports), as well as the endorphins that come with the territory.[36] This attraction is a personality trait; it can be developed at any time. Developing the desire to push boundaries and bring to fruition all the cheesy T-shirt slogans is what it takes to reach the elite level. Is this mental toughness? Yes, it is. As I wrote above, I think mental toughness lies more in choosing to do hard workouts day-to-day, like the desire that Lessing had. However, having the ability to be on autopilot once the competition begins (when it counts) is what it means to leave the mind out of it.

How hard an athlete works toward his/her goals is ultimately self-determined, though certainly my role as a coach is to help athletes in this department. The coaching cornerstone of Bobby Knight is the question, "Are you enthused?" The term *fun* is a relative one, but if it's not fun in the end, we're missing the point. Fun takes on many definitions among individual runners. Track workouts are fun to some runners (due to the variety and challenge they offer), but dreadful to others (for various reasons). Some people need two or three speed workouts per week to get their kicks, while others are challenged and rewarded with only one speed workout per week. To each their own. Climbing the switchbacks up Flagstaff Mountain on my bike in Boulder many years ago was fun for me; it was hard as hell, but it was fun. It was different and challenging. I enjoyed hearing my heart beat through my chest, and I enjoyed the view from the top when all was said and done. This message bears resemblance to the old "the journey is greater than the destination" spiel, and that's also

---

36. Technological advances in science and medicine have allowed us to determine that some people are born with higher pain thresholds than others, which is certainly a hereditary advantage in any sport.

a point of the last chapter of this book when I discuss the concept of flow. Hard work and training aren't always fun, but the lifestyle you choose surrounding training/exercise should at least be rewarding.

I was once talking with Coach Touey, my former college track coach at Widener University, when the parent of a high school runner approached us. The parent was casually inquiring about college scholarships for her son and his possibility of elite success. Coach Touey made an excellent point, "Keep your child enthused about running; that's the best thing you can do." Having coached grades 5 - 12, I thought that was great advice. Recalling conversations with pro athletes across various sports who told me how much fun they were having while training, I'm reminded that this is all supposed to be fun! Does that contradict the previous notion that "putting some level of pain into our bodies is needed for success?" No, absolutely not. Remember, it's all relative to *you*. We only need a simpler goal of being healthy (fit), not necessarily winning our age group. If pain is included in your definition of fun, then so be it.

Scott Tinley wrote a great opinion piece in which he reflected upon his roller coaster of thoughts during the final miles of the 1982 Hawaii Ironman, where he lost to Dave Scott by 33 seconds. He said that Dave simply "took his own body to a place that only a daring mind would allow." I mention positive self-talk frequently and Dave Scott was certainly a master, and this was also an instance where mental toughness entered the picture, as might be expected when racing the final miles of a world championship. World champions, especially those in endurance sports, are often said to have more will power than the rest of us, and more than the silver medalists, too. I post my pictures with Dave Scott, Peter Reid, and Michael Wardian to my website because I'm glad to have met them and caught a glimpse of what drives them.

In the midst of these comments about the mentality of a champion and inner drive, there is a strong point to be made about not attempting to mimic the training of the pros. We don't need to mimic their specific workouts, their training volume, or how fast they run. On the other hand, some elements of their training and racing *can* be mimicked such as using perceived exertion, stepping outside your boundaries more often, and picking the right times to be *less* calculated. Many of the world champions in endurance sports, including former marathon world record holder Haile Gebrselassie, don't rely on numbers or log data as much as people might think. Some of them don't know what workout they're going to do until they wake up that day.

AGGRESSIVE TRAINING

Aggressiveness isn't a word that finds its way into the world of endurance sports, but when it does, it has a positive connotation. What I mean by aggressiveness is a specific mental approach to peak races and the dedication to reaching goals. When peak race season ("running season") approaches, which typically starts in mid-September for those in the Mid-Atlantic region, I challenge some of my athletes to be more confident in their training and to take that confidence to the start line. In order for race day not to be seen as an extraordinary challenge, I need to challenge my athletes with harder, longer and/or faster workouts. Aggressive training will give athletes the confidence that everything done on race day is in some way, shape or form something they've already done in training (confidence is "the feeling that you've been there before").

This "aggressive" mentality will differ among individuals, and therein is a difference between beginners and seasoned veterans. When questioning how aggressive one's training might be, don't grade too harshly. Dedication to training (the program) and hitting all the workouts each week is certainly a viable definition of aggressiveness (or mental toughness). However, for some of the seasoned runners I coach, I may challenge them a bit more and/or remind them to be more confident in their abilities. A phrase I use frequently is, "There is a time and a place for everything." No matter where a runner sits in the spectrum of ability, this phrase is where my rationale comes from in challenging *everyone* at some point(s) in the year. If the periodization model of training theory makes senses, then the logic is apparent in when and where that time and place reside, as in implementing the more aggressive training during peak season.

RUNNER'S HIGH

Runners often cite runner's high (RH) as a reason for engaging in what might otherwise be considered a torturous or boring activity. It alludes to a "flooding" of endorphins into the brain during or after a run (or any aerobic activity). The original studies done in the 1980s supporting this RH theory were later refuted due to methodological issues. For many years, it was left as speculative (myself included) since research design could not isolate the variables needed to make a definitive answer. Rather than go into much detail on the topic, there now appears to be more recent research showing that RH is in fact a legitimate phenomenon resulting from increased endorphin activity in the brain.

We often feel great after a run, but don't get bogged down in the details of RH—it can get complicated. There are dozens of activities other than running that that can lead to the same benefits of RH, or the state of flow (sometimes called "being in the zone"), such as chess, playing music, and deep-sea diving. But as long as happiness can be derived from running, then keep at it. The relatively new field of positive psychology and its research has much to teach about attaining the sensation of the runner's high through other activities.

7

RACING

RACE SELECTION

ENCOURAGE RUNNERS to race relatively frequently at various distances from 5k to 10-miler (if the latter is within reason) in order to strengthen the connections between the theories and the training, and to create a larger frame of reference for any coaching pointers. Racing will make the speed workouts more relevant as the athlete is forced to make the connection between what happens on the track with stride length and rhythmic breathing and how that plays out on race day. Additionally, racing the shorter distances means that certain light bulbs will go off that are relevant to ST. Pushing the body to maximum exertion during a race, as should be done, means a potential revelation as to which muscles are in need of more strengthening, such that the core muscles will be tested more than usual. So that is the first major point of this chapter: Consider how frequently, or infrequently, you race the shorter distances and what can be learned from it, even if the peak race is a longer distance.

If races are a few months apart, then many pointers and tips won't resonate; there's no frame of reference. The majority of the knowledge a runner can gain about him/herself will happen on the track and during short-distance races. Because we do more speed workouts than races, the lessons from the track are sure to carry over to race day. Moreover, these learning effects need to have a reciprocal relationship, so that a lesson learned in a race improves the next track workout. To continue doing speed workouts without racing may cause a runner to lose sight of the bigger picture and forget the point of the workouts. The more one races, the more one can look forward to track work because the connections will be apparent. Racing is a great way to become faster and better prepared for future races. Race to learn, not just to be competitive or to be concerned with the finish time.

For the beginners who have never raced before or need some motivation to get that first race under their belt, some practical advice would be to sign-up for a 5k that's a few weeks away (assuming you can run 5k without stopping). This small, yet symbolic financial investment will enhance dedication to a program. In addition, there will then be a short-term goal with a definitive date in the foreground, which should be motivating. This is reasonable advice in crossing that first race off the to-do list, and eventually the training and racing progress for other valid reasons. For the race veterans, when selecting races for the upcoming season, I suggest repeating a race that was done the previous year so gains in fitness can be measured. Think of it as a time trial to measure fitness but in a more realistic setting; just be aware of any course changes.

Not counting some the local Jingle Bell 5k's that are hosted each year, the unofficial end of race season is the week of the local Turkey Trots. If a runner resides in a city that has rough winters, then racing in January and February should not be much of a concern. There aren't too many races on the calendar at that time and the weather is just as non-ideal as peak summer weather, so I typically don't even put a goal time on such races. If athletes are taking ST and XT seriously in the winter, then they're not going to have fresh legs for many winter weekends. That is not a bad situation; rather, it comes with the territory. Therefore, we don't need too much emotional stock in winter racing. If a runner does the same race each year in these months, so be it, and that makes the race goal simple enough, assuming the weather is not drastically different from year to year.

During the fall ("running season"), runners should do more racing compared to other months of the year, with both intensity and specificity of training being at their highest during this timeframe. With the exception of those training for a Half or marathon, a runner could race the shorter distances almost every weekend in the fall without it being a conflict. The closer we get to peak season, the fitter we are and the harder we can race. In turn, racing hard increases fitness. It's a vicious cycle that ideally leads to confidence. I agree with Mark Allen in that races should be a special day and the whole idea of race day is to race, or as he says, "Go Like Hell!" A true peak performance only comes at the end of a full training cycle. Allen said, "In short, it is just not possible to have high race frequency and peak racing performances." As he also once told Chris McCormack, whom he helped coach to his first Ironman World Championship, "Chris, the reason you're not winning that [championship] race is because you're trying to be in peak shape 52 weeks a year and that just can't happen." Therein lies the importance of recovery, embracing off-season goals and a phase of *de*conditioning. This does not contradict the fact that I promote autumn as race season and want everyone to race as frequently as possible at that time. The difference lies in the length of the peak race, the length of the other races, how we define "frequent racing," and a runner's fitness.

When it comes to marathons, I pick on some runners who *only* run marathons and/or half-marathons (Halves) without racing the shorter distances. From a coach's perspective, an issue with only doing marathons and Halves is that these distances don't always offer insight into one's actual fitness due to the extra variables associated with these distances, including the courses themselves. If a marathon or Half is the only way to measure success or improvement, then we're missing out on much![37] In order to measure the fitness gains from the longer-distance

---

37. More on this topic in the next section.

training, I strongly suggest doing a short-distance race on flat terrain a few weeks after recovering from the peak, long-distance race. Once fully recovered, sign up for something short and flat and put the pedal to the metal.[38]

Finally, when it comes to receiving advice from run colleagues about a course, or whether or not to register for a particular race, some common questions will come to mind like, "How hilly or difficult is that course?" Be very aware whom you are asking. People ask me if the Cherry Blossom and Army 10-milers in DC are hilly courses and I would immediately say "no." I also don't think the DC Rock-n-Roll course is tough, albeit one monstrous hill at mile six. That is just *me*—that is *my* opinion based on *my* level of fitness. Ask somebody else and you may receive a completely different answer. A less experienced runner or a slower runner (a difference between these two) may think these courses are brutal. A super-fit speedster from an area that doesn't have a hill anywhere in sight may struggle on a hilly course. I've also heard many people on race morning state how hot/cold it will be that day. Was it actually hot/cold? Again, it all depends on whom you ask. Our inner-scientist needs to know the source of the information, meaning the fitness and experience (bias) of those who give the advice. That is why I pride my coaching on objectiveness.

"MARATHONERS"

I was always hesitant to be labeled a "marathoner" or a "triathlete," but I let it slide 99% of the time, as it would be an awkward way to interject in a conversation. However, if the timing was right then I would explain my rationale, which is the same rationale I use when setting up training programs for runners, whom I prefer to call athletes. I've run marathons, but I'm not a marathoner. I'm not a runner; I'm "someone who runs." What's the difference and what does this have to do with a training

---

38. I rely on individual conversations to address the topic of balancing triathlon races and road races.

program? What does this have to do with the mental approach to training and racing?

Social psychology tells us that labels can have a positive influence on behavioral change, as noted by the terms self-concept, self-identity, self-schemata, etc. If a man is frequently describe by co-workers as "driven," "passionate," or "energetic," then he will eventually develop a self-concept of being a productive worker, which is wonderful. If you have a friend that is trying to get off the couch and start exercising, you can always remind her after each spin class that she is "turning into a pretty good cyclist." Labeling your friend as a cyclist over and over will help define her as an active person, which is very important in shaping new behaviors. But it can sometimes be a double-edged sword. The man in the first example may become a work-aholic; the work consumes him to the point of stress. Or your friend may feel irritable if she doesn't exercise or can't find any alternatives to cycling.

As it relates to "marathoners," they sometimes don't feel productive or like they accomplished anything unless they are training for the marathon distance, or worse, unless they set a PR each successive marathon. I see it often, where anything other than a marathon PR is accompanied by not feeling successful and all the subsequent damage control therein. I don't see this issue in runners training for shorter distances, or those who are yet to run a marathon. The self-identity as a marathoner can dictate everything about the mental approach to training and racing, which indirectly affects mood via the interpretation of progress. For instance, the weekend long run becomes the magic bean of the program and much emotional stock lies within that run each week. A marathoner insists he must run a marathon each year (or season) instead of possibly taking a year off from marathons in order to correct muscular imbalances and build speed at other distances. This is where I, as a coach, enter the picture.

The main service I offer is *the mental approach to training and racing.* This means that the exact type of workout the athlete does is always secondary to the reason he/she does it in the first place. For instance, the question may be posed, "Coach, what speed workouts would I be doing this winter to prepare for a spring marathon?" My rhetorical question in response, "Does the marathon conflict with any other training or racing goals?" If the athletes' answers are sensible, then we build the training to prepare for the marathon, and sure, goals are set easily enough. I use this anecdote because I find that when people/runners/athletes label themselves as marathoners they are more likely to lose sight of other short-term process goals.

Marathoners become a breed of runner that can put too much emotional stock into one race, putting all their emotional eggs into one basket. It consumes them and their training. To some people, this behavior actually seems positive because it's interpreted as being motivated, but what gets lost in the shuffle are the important short-term goals, like rest days, running form, strength training, and PT. Therefore, the obstacles that arise are the unwillingness to take rest days, an inability to refrain from signing up for longer races at the wrong time, passing on an off-season that prioritizes ST, and an inability to correct running form because of constant high-mileage training.

I attempt to shift my clientele, specifically the beginners, away from "running as exercise," and into feeling like a runner. From there, I want them to feel like an athlete. The latter leaves much more room for interpretation and is less likely to trap the individual into a smaller role/identity (entrapment theory). I teach athletes to recognize short-distance racing as important for myriad reasons. Again (cover your ears), this can mean not running a marathon one particular year. Hearing that phrase stings if you're a *marathoner*. If you're an *athlete*, then you have other goals in which to focus and you're okay. Professional runners are a different breed whose bodily limits have a higher threshold compared to amateurs. Therefore, a training program, and more importantly, the mental approach to training, needs to reflect this difference.

In sum, think of yourself as an athlete and the doors of perception will be opened to many more aspects of training and racing. I can very easily identify marathoners from their first email or phone call to me. I know exactly why they feel unsuccessful and I already know before I ask that they haven't run a 5k in six or seven years. Change the way you think about who you are and what you do and your progress will sky rocket, your running form can change (due to lower volume training) and you'll feel more successful more frequently.

Is There Enough Time to Train for This Race?

Pink Floyd's song "Time" has been my favorite song since I was a teenager. The lyrics are timeless and apply to everyone at some time in his/her life. Time is a very peculiar concept, a concept made all the more mind-boggling given the notion that it's an expression of distance/movement and might not exist otherwise. Would it even exist without the universe's existence? I don't mind engaging in a deep conversation on such a topic; I enjoy a good mind melt. On a more casual basis, we can all agree that time is relative. For example, how quickly is your next big race approaching, like the first race of the season, your spring Half, or the Boston Marathon? Is two months a long amount of time or a short amount of time? Well, it depends because time is relative. Relative to what? At this point I'll chime in (pun intended) and say it's relative to the degree of confidence you have in your preparation, which is also a byproduct of how much emotional stock you have in the race.

If you're feeling confident in your abilities for an upcoming race, then the race can feel like a long time away. If you're not feeling confident, then you may feel like you're behind the 8-ball (not good). If you don't have much emotional stock in the race (maybe it's not an A-race or you're jogging it with friends), then once again the race has plenty of time to arrive, even if it's a few weeks away. Otherwise, if this race will be part of defining who you are as a runner and how you measure success (lots of emotional stock), then maybe a race six months away feels like it's coming up too soon. Catch my drift? As the song lyrics state, you either fritter and waste the hours in an off-hand way (lots of time, no perceived pressure or time crunch) or you're running and running to catch up with a sinking sun (not enough time).

I understand that personality can be a factor in this equation. Perhaps a worrisome self or type-A personality feels the impending race *looming* on the horizon, causing pressure, stress, and feelings of being under-trained and not up to par (behind the 8-ball). Therefore, there's a dreaded time crunch. On the contrary, perhaps a mellow self and type-B(uddha) personality views any race as having ample time to prepare. "Which is which, and who is who?" (I slipped in another Floyd lyric there).

This is a department where a coach can help. In knowing each athlete's personality, I know which elements of running, ST or XT can be emphasized accordingly to redirect one's focus away from the race date. It seems like merely a distraction, but the focus needs to be on the process goals anyway, not the race date. In this way, I offer assurance that we have enough time to work together and prepare. In essence, we're adjusting the *perceived* timelines. As with many aspects of athletics, the solution rests in proper goal setting. The more realistic and better managed the goals, the more confidence that exists, along with an increased likelihood to feel that there is ample time. As a quick aside, this is an easy "sports as a metaphor for life" analogy. Whichever personality-type you possess, do you carry this same approach into the workplace? Managing your own expectations and happiness in your career, with deadlines and a daily to-do list, is related to your mental approach. For instance, is it realistic that you'll accomplish all the tasks you've given yourself this week? If not, then here comes the stress and worry. Similarly, if the goals related to the task are too challenging (unrealistic), then that deadline will certainly feel much shorter than it actually is. Here comes more stress, less sleep, the sniffles, and a cough...

Getting back to running: I'm always going to try to help my runners become as fit as possible in the most efficient manner, yet when taking the science and physiology of the training into account (periodization) then yes, some goals take more time than others. This understanding reminds us, "Knowledge is power." Knowledge becomes the building blocks of attitudes, whereas the knowledge about the timeline of our goals shapes our attitude (mental approach) as to what is realistic. Physical therapists should be operating under this same principle—giving athletes knowledge about the timelines for strength gains and/or recovery from injuries so that there is more confidence in the rehab process. In turn, the rehab won't be derailed by a perception of a time crunch.

My goal is to have athletes thinking that life is long and that there is plenty of time to achieve their race goals for the entire year. Many of the folks I've coached have shared their longer-term goals with me, and all of them have demonstrated much patience and maturity in adjusting their goals on the fly mid-season, which adds to the overall feeling of success. That last point is a hallmark of champion athletes. Take it day-to-day or week-to-week, and don't put the cart before the horse. Enjoy training in the present day, live in the present, and the races will get here when they get here. I know that's sometimes easier said than done. If it feels like the big event can't get here fast enough and you're chomping at the bit, and even a few days before the race can feel like an eternity, then remind yourself that there's nothing you can do to change the clocks. You can also remind yourself that this eagerness probably means you are ready!

The take-home message is to mentally push these races back so that you can feel confident that there is enough time to prepare, as well as to enjoy life in the present. Does this mean that we adapt a lax, passive attitude toward training and life? No! It means that you don't need to put a sense of urgency on your training. If you struggle to do this, then what can you do to reconfigure your mental approach to training and racing?

RACING AS A "TRAINING RUN"?

I don't recommend using races as "training runs." Throughout of all my coaching years, runners have a very low batting average when it comes to actually using a race appropriately as a training run, which is why I rarely (if ever) suggest the idea. If you're registered for a race, it's not training, it's a race! Are races the best way to boost fitness? Yes, they usually are, but that assumes the race was given 100% effort. The central point is that "using the race as a training run" can take the athlete out of the proper race-day mindset that should be developed for the peak race(s).

I'd rather coach a runner to always run hard on race day, versus backing off on race day because it's been labeled as a training run. Anecdotal evidence suggests that a struggle exists between telling oneself "this race is just a training run" and actually being able to do the race without being concerned with the finish time. In the end, a runner will inevitably run harder than intended that day. The runner's race recap in this instance usually includes a negative outlook on how the race went, which is surprising if it was only supposed to be a "training run," right? Our competitive spirit is primarily a positive thing and it's usually present, so I'd rather cater to that competitive spirit, avoiding any gray area altogether.

A half-marathon leading into a peak marathon is an surefire way to boost fitness if it's *raced,* and I'd expect a runner to run hard that day. When runners say they're "just going to run it as a training run," it rarely happens. Instead, "race mode" kicks in and because the proper mental approach was lacking in the preceding days and/or on race morning, a non-focused race is completed and is reported to me as an "unsuccessful" training run. How tragic. I suggest either racing hard or doing a regular weekend run instead. I'd rather have race day be viewed as something special, like an opportunity to push boundaries and test limits. Otherwise, save the training runs for training. If you're thinking, "I can do this race and get a good workout," then I agree, but the devil is in the semantics. If getting a good workout is the goal of the race, then *race*(!) and go hard, but eliminate the phrase, "this is for training." Otherwise, your goals may be blurred and you'll have more questions than answers on the commute home.[39]

---

39. There are certainly a few exceptions to this rule. For example, there are usually low-key races at the longer distances that can be viewed as large group

An Introduction to Setting Race Goals

First, there is a *Pace Calculators* section in the *Technology & Psychology* chapter, which relates to this section, and there is also a longer, more detailed section on *Goal Setting* in the final chapter. Amateur running counts as a sport, and it's never too late to show your competitive side, even if you're just competing against yourself. Once an individual gets past the "I just want to finish" point of his/her running career, then goal times are the next step. I don't always give goal times because sometimes it's not in the cards, as in a first-time marathoner, adverse race conditions, a long layoff from racing, or bouncing back from some setback. However, generally speaking, once track work becomes a regular part of a routine and harder efforts become a familiar feeling, then goal times will enter the picture and will also become more accurate with each race.

Briefly, there are three types of goals. *Outcome* goals (e.g., winning, overall placing, rank) are not in our direct control, so we need *performance* goals (e.g., pacing, mile splits, points scored) and *process* goals (e.g., technique, focal points, strategy) in order to improve the chances of hitting outcome goals. It's beneficial to be able to set goals mid-race, such as adjusting for race conditions and altering the goal time. For example, there may be A, B, and C goals for a race. If the race conditions don't allow for a PR, or if the A-game isn't there by mid-race, then it's best to adjust on the fly and resort to other meaningful goals to stay engaged and feel successful.

Hope, Luck & Confidence

In conversations with many runners (either those who I coach or those outside my own client base) who are getting ready for big events, I hear

---

training runs for marathoners, where talking to running buddies during the race is the norm.

a few words routinely pop up, such as nervous, worried, hope, lucky, and maybe. As a coach, when I hear these words I know the runner is either under-prepared, not well-schooled in proper goal setting and/or not interpreting a small dose of nervousness as a positive sign.

The word that I want to hear more often is *confident*. I define confidence as "the lack of uncertainty." It's the feeling of getting to the start line and knowing exactly what will happen after the starting gun (or when the first whistle blows in other sports). If the goals are clear, there's no room for uncertainty, and therefore no room for worry or anxiety. Conversely, if the runner has trained properly, then the goals should be clear with therefore no need for luck.

We all know that goals should be specific, objective, and measurable, but what is often overlooked is *how* the athletes will reach these objective, numerical goals. In other words, qualifying for Boston and/or setting a PR are fabulous goals (*performance goals*); however, runners too often leave it at that. They don't have the *process goals* laid out. To take a step in the right direction, a runner should hone in on the required pace per mile, but even that focal point is shy of the real beef of what gives athletes confidence, namely, process goals. For example, *how* do you run an 8:00/mile? *How* do you run sub-3:10:00? The numbers themselves don't really give the actual focal points for when one is out there on the course, in-the-moment.

The process goals are breathing patterns, stride length, posture, fueling strategies, frequent reminders to not get caught up in a random pack of runners, and so on. Hopefully, these are all the things receiving attention during weekly workouts (at least the key workouts). Focusing on these process goals is why I often persuade the runners I coach to do less training with the Garmin technology. Focusing too much on pace during training can leave a runner empty handed on race day, when present-moment variables enter the equation. This is not a rant on being anti-tech, but that last point is very much related to confidence on race day. When someone is able to hone in on the *process* of running certain intensities, then the brain has an easier job, thereby increasing confidence. As more training and racing take place, it becomes easier to hit the goal intensity (and therefore goal pace), which allows the process goals to be kept simple because the mind is operating on autopilot. When the goals are simple, then there is a quieter mind, which is preferred. In this sense, although the mind is at work during races, it is very simple work (ideally), so this is why I say running is only 10% mental (if goal setting is done correctly). When goals are incorrectly set, then there is much more mental energy required to make adjustments mid-race.[40]

Thinking during a race is sometimes beneficial, and other times it is counter-productive, and this is the heart of the debate as to whether "running is a mental sport." It depends on what the thoughts are. Typically, we don't want the mind working too much when competing, as the mind can get in the way of letting the body function in a state of automaticity, which is usually the goal for the coach/athlete. Like driving a car, racing should be done on autopilot. We don't have to think too much about the actual process of driving a car because of its simplicity. To actually think about the act of driving a car while driving would be dangerous since it would break the state of automaticity. This is what is meant by *paralysis by analysis*. In other words, naturally occurring movements would be interrupted. For this reason, overly cautious drivers can be hazardous on the road due to too much mental activity.[41] When a task is perceived to be easy, then the brain has less work to do, the perception of pressure is diminished, and there is less tension in the muscles and therefore no *premature* muscle fatigue. In turn, the brain *remains* quiet because there is no additional, unnecessary feedback coming from the body. This is why running should *not* be 90% mental.

K.I.S.S. is an acronym that is used frequently by coaches and sport psychologists. It stands for Keep It Simple and Stupid, and is a reminder for athletes to avoid paralysis by analysis and helps to reduce anxiety. What *is* anxiety? It's uncertainty about what will happen next. Too much brain activity and too much self-talk only compound this problem. When

---

40. I discuss this premise in more detail in the *Mental Toughness* section.

41. Candid conversations I've had with driver's education instructors only confirms the truth in this statement. They state, "The kids who think too much are the worst drivers."

an athlete has too many goals or if the goals are not clear, then there is too much left-brain activity, lots of processing, and very little room to "Just Do It." Great athletes don't engage in much analytical thinking when they compete. If an athlete is engaging in analytical thinking then perhaps the goals may not be specific enough, not simple enough, or the focus is on the outcome instead of the process. Confident athletes are masters of proper goal setting. From this logic it can be reasoned that simple process goals alleviate much doubt and nervousness, but perhaps not *all* nervousness.

A small dose of nervousness is allowable and also natural. I would even distinguish it from anxiety or worry. Being slightly nervous shows that you value your performance and that your leisure time activity isn't a waste of your time and energy. The people who aren't nervous before a marathon might be those whose goal is simply to finish the race alongside their co-workers, or those who are *extremely* confident in their goals, the latter of which explains the perceived "arrogance" of so many professional athletes. Nervousness is a sign that the body is alert and therefore prepared, versus not having a care in the world about the outcome. Having butterflies in the stomach is fine; it's just a matter of getting them to fly in formation. There are relatively few athletes in the world who are not nervous before an event, and you can spot them every so often because they might paint their shoes gold before the race to show that there's not a doubt in their minds that they'll win the gold medal.[42] Anytime you have a good race despite a dose of nervousness beforehand, file that away for future reference. All is not as bleak as it seems with a *dose* of nervousness (it can be good energy).

What I offer to the reader is that if you know you have *too much* nervousness before a race, if you're *hoping* you hit your goal time, or looking to catch a *lucky* break, or think *maybe* you'll have a good race, then it's time to restructure how your goals are phrased on paper and in your brain. Make sure you are focusing on specific tasks in your control. When a college basketball player makes the sign of the cross before he takes his foul shots, the announcer Dick Vitale will exclaim, "No confidence, baby!" So don't look

42. American sprinter Michael Johnson donned a custom-designed pair of golden-colored racing spikes during the 1996 Summer Olympics on his way to winning the gold medal in the 200m and 400m. Confidence to the max!

for divine intervention on race day and don't hope to get lucky. Control your own destiny and plan to know exactly what will unfold when the starting gun fires.

RACE PREP & WARMING-UP

I typically schedule the day prior to the race as "open" for the athlete to do any routine he/she likes (within reason, of course). However, the week leading up to the race may contain an OFF day, a break from ST, putting the speed work on a different day, or a different type of speed workout. There is good rhyme and reason as to how I schedule the week before a bigger race compared to other run-of-the-mill races. Typically, the speed workouts during the week of a peak race are done at race pace and with a relatively low volume. This allows the athlete to get in tune with their goal pace a few more times, like a dress rehearsal, but also avoids zapping the legs before the race. The mental approach to racing as well as understanding how the body responds to workouts will come into play here, both of which should be touched upon regularly conversations so that coach and athlete are on the same page when race week arrives.

A common question is this: Should I do anything differently on race morning to get ready? The answer would be "probably not." Outside of the actual logistics of the race, treat the race as any other key workout, especially in terms of warming up. Obviously, the race distance, fitness level, and competitiveness against the age-group (or the overall race field) all play a factor, but generally speaking, a pre-race warm-up routine should be exactly what is done before higher-intensity workouts. This consistency creates both physical and mental readiness. Routine is a wonderful thing. The dynamic drills (not just leg swings) and race-pace striders bring a runner to the start line physiologically prepared. Much variance between the predicted finish time and actual race performance can be explained by lack of a proper pre-race warm-up.

Warming up before races follows a simple model: The shorter the duration and therefore the higher the intensity, the more intense and longer the warm-up should be. For example, a 5k warm-up needs to be longer and more intense than a marathon warm-up. In any case, end the warm-up with some race-pace striders, as in a few 15- to 30-second runs at predicted pace, or the pace in which the runner intends to start (consider it a final dress rehearsal). A pre-race warm-up for races 10k and shorter should end five to seven minutes before the race. Longer races require a less intense warm-up and can therefore end ten to twenty minutes prior to the start. In any case, avoid idling for too long in the minutes before the race and do not get caught up in what other people are doing to warm-up; just focus on you.

A warm-up should not leave a runner exhausted for the race or track workout. The warm-up jog can be a half-mile or two miles or more; it depends on a runner's fitness. The number of race-pace striders to do before the start also depends on fitness. Answer these questions in training, before race day.

Here is a sample pre-race warm-up routine:

Beginner

# of minutes before the race:

:15 - :20	3 - 4 minutes easy jog (avoid hills) + general dynamic warm-up
:10 - :15	track warm-up drills (find an open space)
:05 - :07	2 x 50 - 100m striders
:01 - :05	rehydrate and get to the start line (keep the legs moving if race is delayed)

Experienced

# of minutes before the race:

:25 - :20	5 - 10 minutes easy jog (avoid hills) + general dynamic warm-up
:15 - :20	track warm-up drills (find an open space)
:10 - :07	2 x 50 - 100m striders
:05 - :07	1 - 2 minutes total at race pace (break-up into sets)
:01 - :05	rehydrate and get to the start line (keep the legs moving if race is delayed)

I'm aware many people don't want to do the dynamic drills at a race or track workout because they'd be the only one doing them and they feel a tad awkward about that. This is something a runner has to get past if he/she values performance. The overwhelming majority of runners simply aren't well schooled in what is meant by a sport-specific dynamic warm-up and that is why they're not doing it. Trust the training, be confident, and stick to the drills.[43]

The start and finish lines are the typically the same, or in the same area, but the warm-up jog should include trotting over to the finish area (or final portion of the course) to locate a landmark for where the final sprint to the finish line can begin. Always know where the finish line is. This sounds like an oversimplified tip, but it only takes one time to make this oversight that can sour your race or mood.

GENERAL RACE STRATEGIES

First, regardless of the race distance, remember that running is meant to be a very simple sport. From the perspective of a sport psychologist, I will repeat the best strategy for any sport: Keep It Simple and Stupid (K.I.S.S.). "Paralysis by analysis" hampers even the best runners. These tips below assume you are *racing*. If you're simply trying to beat the clock or finish without walking, don't think too much about the specific tips I offer below. Instead, you can either race against your goal time, or you can race the person you've been running next to for the majority of the race. Either way, there is nothing wrong with being competitive at a competition!

Regarding starting positions, I would rarely (if ever) encourage anyone to begin in the very back. Many negative race recaps begin there. The result is usually the same—there's much frustration in the opening mile (or two) due to excessive weaving around walkers and very slow runners. With the exception of a premier event, like the Boston Marathon, which tries to bar runners from leaving designated corrals, I suggest

---

43. There is a *Warming Up & Stretching* section in Chapter 5.

starting as close to the front as possible. Self-seeding based on predicted pace is the general etiquette, but it's not set in stone; therefore, moving closer to the front of the pack is less of an issue than you might think. What about blocking the faster runners? As long as you're not in the front lines, most local races aren't big enough for that to be a factor. Move up as far as you're comfortable so you have more space to operate when the starting gun fires. As long as you're in tune with your own pacing and are cool, calm, and collect then you'll be able to resist pacing with the faster runners around you. The point is that your finish time and, more importantly, your rhythm, is greatly disrupted having to shuffle around people.

The goal of any race is to begin under control. If anything "bad" would happen during a race, it will usually be the result of going out too fast in the first *two* minutes or so; that's all it takes to sabotage a race. To put that into more specific language, focus on *your* stride length and *your* breathing for the first two minutes of a race. *Listen* to your breathing. If it's not rhythmic like it is in training, then you're running too fast. However, most times your breathing will feel fine in the opening mile, even if you are running entirely too fast, so it's better for the primary focal point to be stride length. In other words, in the first two minutes of a race you could pretty much run as fast as you want and the breathing would still be rhythmic, perhaps not even heavier than usual. This is simply due to the fact that only a fraction of the race has surpassed and you still have a full tank of energy. Therefore, get in tune with your stride length in training (at all paces). We've all gone out of the gates once or twice with a crowd that was too fast for us (our parents warned us), yet we felt like we could handle it. Before you suffer by making this mistake again, remember to check your stride length out of the gates.

With the exception of the 5k distance or shorter, the best pacing strategy is to run "even splits," as in attempting to run the same pace each mile. Once you factor in weather, wind, terrain, etc, you discover that steady *effort* (intensity) is actually the better term to use (not *pace*). For instance, many races start or end with a hill, so it's difficult to hold the same pace for each mile, hence, the emphasis on consistent effort and consistent breathing patterns.

Here's a tip on breathing and stride length taken from a flat 8k I ran, a race won by National Champion runner Michael Wardian. A young collegiate runner virtually fell to pieces after the first half-mile of race while trying to stick with Wardian's blistering pace; I knew better than to keep up with Wardian. I also knew the young runner had gone out too fast because when I eventually caught up to this runner after he fell off Wardian's pace, I could hear his breathing and he was exhaling almost every step, clearly breathing too quickly/shallow (a sign of too much effort in the beginning of an 8k race). So that is the tip: Figure out how the other runners around you are feeling by listening to their breathing and watching their strides. Feel stronger when you know they're fading. I can usually tell who is going to fade down the road based on the sound of their breathing early in the race. On the other hand, for the longer races, if a runner looks and feels strong, then try running alongside him/her to help each other hold the pace (see the *Forming an Ally* section below). How do you know whom to resist chasing vs. who could help you pace? If you run with someone for ~200m and find you are in unfamiliar territory relative to the race distance (i.e., your stride is too long or breathing is too labored), then back off (not much brain work required in that decision).

The course for the aforementioned 8k was straight out-and-back, and as we approached the turn-around cone I was in 2nd place and all by myself. I saw Wardian go by me in the other direction and he was hauling butt! I knew he had picked up the pace a bit because I was constantly noting our gap the whole race and watching his stride. He either quickened his pace because that's his general strategy for a race of that distance, or it was simply an attempt by him to make sure I knew not to try to catch him; it was a strategy on his part to defeat me mentally. Little did he know, I had a snowball's chance of hell of catching him anyway (he's speedy!). His acceleration was probably instinct for him, like it is with me, since I used the same strategy against the 3rd place runner (that same younger runner, who was suffering a great deal at this point). Surge at the turnaround points to open a gap on the pack with whom you've been running. It may wear them out physically and/or defeat them mentally. This is a good time to embrace fartlek runs as race-specific training, getting used to pushing hard for any amount of time to open/close a gap and then feeling comfortable settling back into the previous pace.

When you pass runners, do so with a purpose. It's usually better to pass on downhills early in the race rather than uphills near the end.[44] Also, if a pass is made to potentially mentally defeat the competition, then also realize that when you get passed, someone may be using this same tactic against you. During a particular 5k, I noted the difference in passing technique between the 2nd place runner and me. I led comfortably through mile one; he passed me shortly thereafter, but he only ran 5 meters in front of me for the entire next mile. So was he really faster than me, or did he simply go around me at that one point? If he were faster, he would have continued to pull away little by little. Because he didn't, I knew he wasn't any fitter than I was (unless he was baiting me in), so I decided that rather than catch up to him and run side-by-side, I'll *surge* by him and open up a more substantial lead before settling in to my previous pace. It takes a bit more effort and positive self-talk, but it usually works. Without increasing my pace the last mile, the gap grew. Maybe he went out too fast and paid the price regardless of any of my strategies being employed. In any case, the point of this strategy remains unchanged.

To recap some of these tips, keep an eye on any runner who passes you the next time you're in a competitive situation. If the gap remains constant, then it's likely that someone just put a quick move on you. You have from that moment until the finish line to return the favor—choose wisely (fartlek runs make excellent practice sessions). However, if the gap grows then it's usually best to let him/her go. Be true to thy self and stay within thy element. You can also listen to the other runner's breathing as he/she goes by you and determine how hard he/she is working. Finally, remember that passing is a two-way street in that someone you pass may be keeping an eye on you for a few moments.

---

44. Consider for a moment why that might be.

This is also a plug to run relaxed, which most runners misinterpret as "slow down." The key to running hard is to not make it look like the end of the world is coming. It's classic Body Language 101: Mask your own level of effort; yet try to note it in the faces of your competitors. A common reason elite athletes wear shades (even at night or when it's cloudy) is to hide their eyes and face, which is where we reveal our emotions and pain.

Have a plan for the aid stations. There is less congestion for the faster runners at the front of the field, but I've been at enough races to see the scrum that forms when many runners arrive at the stations at the same time. It's preferred to keep running when taking cups, unless walk breaks are planned into the race. Learn to drink on the go—pinch the opening of the cup slightly, open-wide, and remember there are no points for cleanliness. Get in and get out! I offer this tip, and this is especially true for marathons, because if you come to a full stop late in the race, not only does it disrupt your flow/pacing, but also it may cause leg cramps. This cramping is due to the change in blood flow when stopping after a few hours of movement. In this case, the blood moves from the legs back to the gastrointestinal system. The bigger races might have aid stations staggered on both sides of the street; check the race website in advance to give yourself peace of mind. Dumping liquids onto the head to keep cool is an acceptable practice, even if it's something other than water (beggars can't be choosers). If it's wet and liquid then it will do. Regarding fuel belts, I generally remind runners *not* to race with them. Utilize the aid stations and enjoy not having to carry around the extra pound or three from the water bottles. If it's a longer race that requires fueling, then I recommend shorts with pockets, triathlon shorts, or a SPIbelt.

Runners often ask me, "How hard of a sprint should I have at the finish line?" I respond by saying, "probably not your best." If you can outsprint 20 people in the last 50 meters of a race, then you either have a great running stride, or perhaps you didn't push yourself as much as you could have prior to the finishing sprint—perhaps you had too much energy left in the tank. My intention here is not to cause doubt about each time a runner had a great sprint to the finish line. I'm simply suggesting that it's better to spread your energy over the entire course than save it for 10 seconds of glory at the very end. Again, that's not to say a runner can't (or won't) run hard at the end of a race because it's assumed that everybody will finish as strong as they can (that's human nature). Push harder and pass more people before the finish line comes into view. In sum, a sprint to the finish line should require more effort than usual due to an increase in effort over the majority of the course, not just the final stretch. Often, the folks with miraculous sprints to the finish are usually jogging the first 99% of the race, so don't let them discourage you in any way.

Long Hills Don't Exist

This section offers a mental strategy for running up long inclines.[45] There are surely some inclines that *all* runners would agree are tougher than others, but those are the exceptions, not the rule. The steepness of an incline and its duration are always relative. For instance, the faster the pace, the shorter the hill lasts, so subjectively speaking, a faster runner may not perceive a particular hill to be significant because it doesn't take him/her too long to ascend it.

If an incline is long enough (let's say a minute or longer), then it may be possible to convince oneself that the hill isn't there. How so? At some point on that hill a runner would settle into a steady effort, or at least I hope so. With that in mind, the runner has the ability to do what is always done (or should be done) on every run—to focus on *intensity* instead of pace. When the intensity (perceived exertion) begins to level off soon after starting the incline (which is advantageous), a runner may feel as though he's running on a flat stretch of pavement. Don't believe me? That's okay right now as you read this, but give it a shot next time you're

---

45. Because we think in terms of language, and one's word usage affects one's beliefs, calling it an "incline" may serve more good than calling it a "hill."

out there. This strategy is made easier if the thoughts are positive or even focused on something other than the hill itself, the latter of which often tends to happen naturally anyway.

When I'm halfway up a long stretch of incline I honestly forget sometimes that I'm even running uphill. Because I'm focusing on perceived exertion (intensity), and as long as I feel like I did when I was on the flat portions, then in my mind, I'm merely running—nothing more, nothing less. Try it and see if you can't convince yourself that the rhythm of your feet and the rhythm of your breathing are just the same as running a flat stretch, and once you're on the hill long enough you become desensitized to the hill.[46] It's no longer a "dreaded hill that won't end."

Contrary to popular belief, and related to one of the more common questions from my athletes' race reports, training does *not* have to be done on hills in order to improve hill running during races. If you find that you are able to tolerate hills in a race in such a way that they don't cause any *premature* fatigue, then that is the result of three factors, namely proper pacing on each hill, speed training, and quality long runs (aerobic fitness). Having said that, *fitness* is the best buffer against the effects of hills. Stated another way, fitness in general will allow an individual who is not even a runner to run a hilly course at a steady effort. Moreover, fit runners from the flatlands of Florida or Delaware can kick butt on a hilly course as long as they are improving their general run fitness. Long runs (90 minutes or more) help all runners become better at running hills because the long-term effect of long runs is a more efficient cardiovascular system that keeps the breathing at a sustainable rhythm and depth (due to a stronger heart with a lower HR).[47] With that said, don't allow one monster hill on a course (an outlier) to be the sole cause for any special (erroneous) post-race thoughts related to hills. It's like trying to throw a basketball the entire length of the court, missing that shot, and then saying, "I need to get better at 3-pointers." Hill repeats are certainly a great

46. Changes to running form when going uphill or downhill are discussed in Chapter 5.
47. This training effect is described briefly in Chapter 2 on *Periodization*.

place to learn how to pace hills properly and they are good speed workouts for anyone at any time, but similar to any workout, don't view them as a magic bean.

SHORT-DISTANCE RACING

As a reference point, for the average runner, tempo pace (tempo workouts; T-pace) is equivalent to 8k or 10k pace, or roughly a 6:00 - 8:30/mile tempo pace.[48] So the goal in a 10k is to run six tempo miles in a row. This may sound like a daunting task; however, it's always easier to push yourself in a race setting because of the other runners around you (misery loves company). Faster runners (sub-6:00 tempo pace) are able to hold T-pace for a 10-miler. Pros can hold tempo pace for a Half. For runners whose T-pace is between 8:30 - 10:00, they'll be able to sustain tempo pace for a 5k or 4-miler.[49]

As stated previously, most runners attempt to hold a steady effort/intensity for the duration of a race ("even splitting") regardless of the distance, and this is generally the best practice. However, for experienced runners in a 5k, even splitting isn't the goal. Instead, at the 5k distance, these runners will go out of the gates relatively hard and hold on to that pace/intensity for as long as they can, so the second mile usually ends up being slightly slower (and the slowest mile of the three), with the pace of the 3rd mile being somewhere in between due to a strong finish. This general 5k strategy is a good exception to the rule of even splitting and it applies to virtually any runner who has begun structured speed workouts. For those who might struggle to complete a 30-min run without stopping, the goal for a 5k is to treat it like a regular run.

At the 2009 Bastille Day 4-miler, which I have chalked up as the hardest I've ever run in my life, I was not in a happy place *physically* during the

---

48. Workout descriptions are given in Chapter 8.
49. I highly recommend using the *Daniels' Running Formula* charts for predicted/goal race times.

second half of that race because of the sustained intensity. However, I was calm *mentally* because of one of the two definitions I use for confidence, "the feeling you've been there before." A 5k I won a few weeks beforehand was also in a similar fashion—opening a wide margin off the start and holding on for the win. The tip I offer here is to ask yourself at any one point in a race, "Have any races or speed workouts mimicked this feeling/experience before?" Hopefully the answer is yes, especially if you compete against yourself (the clock) often in your track workouts or Fast Finish runs (described in the next chapter). The same self-talk and imagery used in training should be applied to racing. Having a reminder of a similar barrier that was overcome in training should be a nice jolt of confidence.

10-MILERS & HALF-MARATHONS

Beginning runners at these distances will most likely be treating these as long runs, sometimes without a goal time. For elite runners and top amateurs, their tempo pace will be relatively close to their goal pace for these two distances. The last 5k of a 10-miler or Half may feel harder even though the pace hasn't changed. This is due to cardiac drift.[50] In essence, this means Halves and 10-milers can feel like Fast Finish (FF) workouts, and for that reason you can schedule shorter FF workouts in the week or two before such a race.

"How do I know how to pace myself for a Half or 10M if the pace of my track workouts has been much faster?" The answer to this question is laced throughout this book—monitor your stride length and breathing during workouts. The key is to know what it feels like to run *x*-amount of seconds slower per mile than tempo pace. For example, if tempo pace is 7:30 per mile and your goal for a Half is 7:50 per mile, then what does 20-seconds per mile slower *feel* like? Experience certainly helps answer these types of questions, but structured speed workouts also help a great deal. Knowing what pace you can handle (based on perceived

---

50. Described in the *Heart Rate Monitors* section in Chapter 6.

exertion) in a Half or 10M is also why I never want long runs to be *too* slow. Occasionally pushing the pace on long runs will help to stay confident on race day.

If you're going to make a wristband with goal-splits for a long-distance race, make it spot on for your goal pace the whole way through. In other words, even though I recognize that the goal of hitting the marks precisely on the dot will be difficult for any race, design the wristband under the false premise of having perfect splits and simply view it as a reference guide, knowing that each mile will vary based on hills, wind, etc.

MARATHONS

For the marathon distance, there are a variety of pacing strategies to be employed. These are based on one's level of fitness, the consistency of the RV (mileage), and the quality of the long runs. In general terms, for the experienced runners, the most recommended strategy is the most logical one, to run the same intensity for all 26 miles. This strategy is the common theme for racing, except for 5k's (as previously outlined). For beginning runners and those who don't anticipate being able to run the entire marathon non-stop, I recommend adding 20 - 60 minutes of walking into several long training runs, even if done at the very end. Assuming one has proper running form, walking and running use different muscles, so the walking muscles should be trained too. Coincidentally, any walk breaks can be timed to coincide with fueling, for ease of digestion. Walking at the end of training runs also serves to extend the total time of the workouts to let the body adapt to prolonged durations of work, and also to help answer the questions about quantity and timing of fueling for race day.

Mile 20 is usually when runners are said to encounter "the wall," but from my coaching standpoint, "The Wall" is merely the greatest music album of all time. Running a marathon (or longer) can bring with it an ebb and flow or energy levels, with an accompanying emotional roller coaster. So it's certainly valid to plan for a period of mental toughness, as a bit more self-talk during the race is certainly warranted. However, even though running hard for 2.5 hours or more can start to take its toll *physically*, there is no rule that states runners have to cave *mentally* around mile 19 - 21. Due to health safety concerns on the marathon course, running publications will always print articles and tips related to "the marathon wall" (a.k.a., "bonking"), and these articles are certainly helpful from a physiology and fueling standpoint. I would only add that there are more people being forced to walk and/or drop out of a marathon due to some joint/ligament pain than due to bonking (low energy). Besides, proper pacing and proper fueling usually negate any wall.

As it relates to bonking, there is a psychological phenomenon known as ironic processes of mental control, also known as suppressive imagery. To describe it in detail would take its own section, but in short, when you hear the phrase, "Don't think of a pink elephant," you will inevitably think of that pink elephant, even if just for a moment. As stress, worry, and/or pressure increase, there is an increased likelihood of focusing on the very thought you are trying to ignore. The ironic aspect of this process is that you end up focusing on the very thought you are trying to block. What do you think happens when golfers repeatedly say to themselves, "Don't hit the ball into the sand, don't hit it into the sand..."? The ball might end up in the sand, especially if a sense of worry is in the equation. What might happen when a runner repeats to him/herself, "Don't hit the wall, don't hit the wall"? The take-home message is that rather than tell yourself what *not* to do (i.e., "don't bonk"), tell yourself what you want you *want* to do (i.e., "keep the intensity under control and hit the aid stations"). This tactic makes a difference under conditions of stress and is a part of both proper goal setting and effective communicate styles for leaders.

Experienced runners are usually focused on process goals and task-relevant cues, which allows them to ignore any unnecessary negative thoughts. Experienced runners also probably have their fueling strategies nailed down, which is the best defense against hitting the wall. Based on anecdotal evidence from runners I've coached, I can attest to the statement that marathon experience helps map out good fueling strategies. A fueling strategy properly employed allows the athlete to feel good physically. In turn, self-talk remains positive and there's a good chance of avoiding any such wall, or negativity. In this regard, I agree that it takes a few marathons to finally get the feel of it. Success in this regard is partly knowing how to fuel and partly believing that the wall only exists if you want it to. Relatively speaking, everyone hurts the last 10k of a marathon regardless (hey, it's a marathon right!?). When your body starts to fatigue, keep up with the positive self-talk by reassuring yourself that you've been in a similar condition before, even if you have to stretch the truth a bit.

I once attended a running seminar where the guest speaker, a professional runner, said that only one out of six marathons is a "good one," where everything goes according to plan. Why so few? Simply said, a great deal can happen in 26.2 miles, or three to five hours. One out of six sounds like a low percentage. I would prefer to say one out of three, but the definition of "good" can vary. There is certainly a *feel* to running the marathon correctly. How do we know how to hold a steady pace for 26 miles (which can be such a long time)? Training runs certainly help, but marathon day can be a little different with all the people and excitement around. The more we run, the more we learn, and the more we have the *feel* for these kinds of races. If only one marathon is run per year, then it's harder to get in tune with the marathon feel, unlike running 5k's at any point. In the end, be patient with marathon training; there are many variables involved. I'm always reminded of a picture of former marathon record holder Haile Gebrselassie holding up a sign that reads, "You have good days, and you have bad days...Today was a good day, 2:04:26." Keep that in mind.

FORMING AN ALLY

It can be easier to stick to your pace when running with others, especially in the longer distances. This is one major point I used to hammer home to my young 7th/8th grade XC teams in telling them how much easier it is to figure out the pacing when running alongside teammates (strength in numbers). If you're an adult runner without actual teammates, then the best thing you can do to get a runner to work with you is to make them feel like your teammate. Take a second to look at him/her and say, "good job." That's it; it's that simple. That phrase can diminish his/her defense mechanisms in a flash (if their guard was up in the first place) and allows him/her to see you as someone to help push the pace, rather than being too competitive against you.

"But how do I know if a total stranger is my pace, or if they went out too fast/slow?" Great question, easy answer: You shouldn't plan on finding your ally early in a race, which we'll consider the first two miles of any distance over 5k, because there are too many variables to consider in the beginning of the race. Little by little, you discover whose stride and breathing mimics your own. Discipline is vital. In a marathon, you can generally assume that the people around you at miles 15 - 18 are the ones you should be running with, and in a Half you can pick them out at the 10k mark.

In determining who is a good ally, as I wrote previously, watch runners' strides and listen to their breathing, which helps in knowing who is a solid distance runner and who is laboring. At a Half I ran in 2010, I already knew by the 1st mile marker which of the runners around me had gone out too fast. I also knew which runners wouldn't be able to keep up with me in the last few miles, based on my observations of their stride— they would lack the stride length to keep up. What does this mean for you? It means it's easier to push with a pack, but choose wisely. Know *how* to choose wisely and at what point in the race to form your allies.[51]

At a competitive 5k one year, the top female finisher passed me a half-mile into the race and stayed just in front of me. I watched her form for a bit (I do not possess an internal "off switch" as a running coach concerned with form) and noticed she was pumping her arms too much from what I might expect, given our pace. Her arm swing was ~4th gear arm swing

---

51. Using pace groups is an individual choice; I can go either way on that decision.

(this will make sense assuming you've read the *Running Form* chapter). What did that tell me? Her arm swing informed me that she was working too hard at that moment, so I therefore knew her pace was too fast. Nobody should be "pumping" their arms in a 5k, not until the home stretch, when one decides to kick it into overdrive. Sure enough, she slowed down shortly thereafter, she knew she was running too hard; she faded and finished a good distance behind me. Knowledge is power (confidence). Having that information a few minutes into the race kept me cool, calm, and collect in knowing that my pacing was fine and it was *her* that went out too hard. Otherwise, couldn't I have easily assumed that the lead female runner is an experienced and knowledgeable runner? Keep an eye on the runners around you to assess who is working too hard, or not at all.

MENTAL POST-RACE STRATEGY

When it comes to coping with performance, races are often down-to-the-wire finishes against the clock, mainly because coaches and athletes try to do a good job of setting challenging, yet realistic individual goals. One thing you have to understand is that if you do not hit your goal time, there is no need to dwell negatively. Consider that the only reason you may feel disappointment is because you set a goal in the first place. If you hadn't set a goal, you certainly could have eliminated the possibility of having a "bad race," but you also potentially eliminate the possibility of having as an exhilarating experience crossing the finish line. In addition, without a goal to strive toward you may be less likely to test your boundaries in training. To each their own. It's a trade-off between specific training (fresh, exciting, and challenging) vs. generic training ("finishing" or simply "running" as its own feat). Hopefully, one of these is more appealing than the other. If runners I coach don't hit a goal time, then I'll still coach them and they'll still be good runners. I'm simply attempting to expose people to what it means to think of oneself as an athlete. It's an individual sport so have fun with it!

Don't Judge a Book by Its Cover

During an interview with *Competitor Magazine* I was asked for "the biggest mistakes runners make." One of my answers was the same point of this section, the misinterpretation of race results. Are we supposed to become faster with each race we run? Should every race be a PR? Are we supposed to PR at every distance during the same time of year? How do we know when to shoot for a PR and when to have other goals in mind? First, the short answer: You are not supposed to set a PR every race, so let's have a round of applause for *that* peace of mind. For a beginner it is easier to hit PRs with each successive race because the room for improvement seems almost endless. However, for experienced runners and/or as fitness increases the window for opportunity becomes increasingly smaller, which is known as the ceiling effect. Race day conditions and the runner's state of being that day also need to be factored *prior* to solidifying race goals. Unfortunately, not all runners engage in this foresight, so damage control becomes the name of their mental game, without realizing they set the wrong goals. This is one of the benefits of a coach—preventing the need for damage control in the first place by setting appropriate goals for each race (as well as help with race selection in general).

The human psyche is very good at making one feel better after a subpar performance (whether it was actually subpar or just perceived that way). It's what some researchers call *cognitive ease* or the *psychological immune system*. It goes like this: You finish a race, see your results, think you could have done better and feel more unsuccessful than you should, but then the psychological defense mechanisms (rationalization) turn on to make you feel better. In other words, after the race, some runners will begin to factor in the heat, humidity, hills, wind, etc., so that they feel better about the finish time. However, what if they were able to make all of those calculations and predictions *before* the race began?

The main point is that *foresight* is a more powerful tool than hindsight. Hindsight is always 20/20, but again, it deals with rationalization and damage control. What if there wasn't any damage at all? Meaning, what if your goals were properly adjusted ahead of time (and mid-race as well) so that you felt successful as soon as you crossed the finish line? Goal setting done properly is a wonderful tool for avoiding damage control. Factor in as many variables as possible before setting concrete goals.

The *Technology & Psychology* chapter relates to this section. When training is going well, yes, it is much easier to rip one PR after another, but as a runner becomes faster and keeps improving, there's a greater need to more closely weigh the conditions, both internal and external. If you're not improving every race, then relax, it may simply mean that you're getting closer to your full potential; this is not something to fear. If one race isn't a PR, it's okay; it's just one race. Don't judge a book by its cover.

8

UNDERSTANDING THE WORKOUTS

LONG RUNS

'M GOING TO define a long run as 90 minutes or more. My view on pacing the long runs is the same as most other running coaches I've chatted with, which is to say the pace should be the fastest pace that can be maintained for the entirety of the run without fading much at the end. I use that word *fastest* lightly, as I don't want every long run to feel like a "workout" that leaves the runner drained. The long run pace can be derived from the tempo pace in an unofficial way. If tempo pace is sub-8:00, then add a full minute per mile to the current tempo pace (e.g., a tempo pace of 7:30/mile would unofficially yield a long run pace of 8:30/mile). If tempo pace is between 8:00 - 9:00, then the long run pace can be 1:15 - 1:30/mile slower. Obviously, a long run in hilly, hot, and/or humid conditions changes the pacing.

A long run pace of 10:00/mile or slower can create problems related to foot strike. Even though it becomes more important to keep the pace well under control as RV increases, running *too* slowly can cause a breakdown in form, changing the mechanics to resemble a fast walk, as described in chapter 5 on *Running Form*. On the other side of the spectrum, there's no need to sprint to an imaginary finish at the end of longer runs because the consequences (muscle damage) could greatly outweigh the benefits. Save the sprint for race day. Not to sound contradictory, but every now and again a long run can be done at a pace much slower than usual, as in an extra 30 - 60 seconds per mile. Chapter 5 explains why it's not good to run too slowly on longer runs; however, if a runner is not a heel striker and/or not experiencing any nagging pains, then one can consider doing an occasional long run at this slower pace. It may be discovered that many questions are solved when heavier breathing and increased stride length are completely eliminated from the equation. I offer this tip only to those who are confident they will not slip into some unnatural running stride. Again, this unnatural running stride is the original rationale for kicking some runners out of 1st gear in the first place. If the conditions above are satisfied, then try a long run at a snail's pace. As I say often, there is a time and place for everything. Make very slow runs the exception, not the rule. If someone is only running two to three times per week at less than 45 minutes, then this tip doesn't apply because his/her RV is relatively low and therefore less problematic. In any case, don't *overanalyze* the pace of these runs. Use perceived exertion (intensity) as the guide and it'll have benefits on race days.

For beginners, adding walks of 20 - 30 minutes to the end of some long runs is a helpful way to prepare the body for longer training runs without adding additional stress from the impact of running. Finish the run, gather your composure for a moment, get a drink, do some light stretching, perhaps change clothes, and then begin the walk. It's also a good time to practice fueling.

Here are some questions to consider: Are you running the same routes every week, or do you vary the location? Does using the same route every week cause you to fall into a lull with pacing? This repetitiveness may hang a runner out to dry when racing a long-distance course for the first time. Break up the monotony, not just for the sake of variety, but also to learn about perceived exertion over varying terrain. How do you know how to handle rolling courses if all your runs are flat out-and-back runs or vice versa? This is also how running without a watch can help one to learn about intensity.

STRIDERS

Striders, or strider-pace, refers to running at ~85 - 90% of top speed. For simplicity sake it can be thought of as 4th gear. However, don't confuse it with sprinting: It is *not* sprinting. Striders typically conclude a dynamic warm-up session prior to a speed workout or race, and the goal therein is to focus on some specific element of running form, as in gathering last-second focal points before the workout/race.

A basic entry-level speed workout for beginners is to alternate 100 meters of strider pace with 100m of jogging. The runner would "stride" the straight-aways and jog slowly on the curves, which corresponds to striding 100m, jogging 100m, striding 100m, jogging 100m, and so on for five or six laps. The jog portions can be held to the same pace as warm-up laps so that the runner can catch his/her breath and so that the legs can recover (these are beneficial considerations for beginners). Strider workouts should be done without a stopwatch, as there isn't a need for them to be timed workout, yet another helpful consideration for anyone getting their feet wet with speed work. It's a chance to focus on running form and breathing patterns without having to worry about pacing.

Another common time that runners do striders is after a relatively long run, but the format is different in this case. The runner would finish his/her distance run, wait about a minute or two, and then do four 50 - 100m striders with a 10 - 15 second recovery between each. The point of these striders is to teach the runner to focus on good running form while relatively fatigued. Runners have better mechanics (ideally) when moving at higher speeds, such as striders. Focusing on good form when somewhat tired (i.e., the end of a run) is a good skill to take into racing. Possessing the mental capacity and physical energy to run properly when fatigued is a confidence booster in knowing that it's possible to snap out of a lull midrace.

TIME TRIAL (TT)

A TT is the best way to obtain a VDOT score, which is basically a fitness score (based upon estimated VO_2max) derived from charts in *Daniels' Running Formula*, a book grounded in science and written by Dr. Jack Daniels, one of the foremost distance coaches. As a reference point, most college distance runners have a VDOT in the 60s.

All of the specific paces for track workouts and races can be determined after a TT. Ideally, a VO_2max test (or TT) is between 10 - 15 minutes long, which is approximately two miles for many runners. Choose the day and location wisely for the TT so there aren't any confounding variables, like terrain or extreme weather. A track is ideal because the pacing can be checked each lap. The goal is to run even splits, which, for a 2-mile TT, means the pace for each mile is nearly the same. For example, if it were a two-mile TT, a 7:00 opening mile followed by a 7:10 is much better than running a 6:45 opening mile followed by a much slower 7:45 with lots of fatigue in the 2nd mile. The goal is obviously to run the two miles as fast as possible, but also trying to do it at a hard, steady pace, with just a bit of kick saved for the entire last lap. As a coach, I'm not anticipating perfectly even splits for both miles, but the main point should be well taken.

The TT is the most informative workout to be done all year. This fitness test is vital for a coach regardless of the athlete's current *perceived* fitness level. If everyone "waited until they were faster" to run the TT, which I hear often, then nobody would run it because theoretically they could always be getting faster in the meantime. We could then rationalize the TT to always be pushed back. Waiting until the athlete is in "better shape" defeats the purpose of the TT. Ideally, a TT is done every six months (spring and fall). I often allow a pancake flat 5k to take the place of a TT, but never the longer distances. A marathon or Half doesn't reveal a runner's true fitness because there are too many other variables involved. Additionally, the TT is meant to be a measure of maximum aerobic output, which by definition does not occur at the longer distances where much pacing is involved.

Because of the higher intensity at the shorter distances, I remind runners before a TT, "This is the hardest you will run all year." Weekly track workouts are not as intense as a TT, nor should they be.

General Thoughts on Track Workouts

First, for those who despise speed workouts, consider why that might be, other than "they're harder." Why do they always feel so difficult? Before labeling them too harshly, consider hydration status, pacing, and whether you are doing dynamic drills beforehand. If any of these three factors are off, then the speed workouts will feel harder than they should. I expect a runner to feel a little queasy on rare occasions following harder efforts, but neither speed workouts nor racing should be judged based on how one feels in the moments right afterward. It's not a valid assessment. Athletes should give themselves 15 - 20 minutes post-race to come back to Earth before they judge the overall nature of high-intensity running.

I host two weekly workouts throughout the year for any of my athletes to attend, but I have no qualms with a runner doing workouts with another group—we're all a running family anyway.[52] Similarly, most running clubs don't mind who joins them. Attendance at my group track workouts is optional and the runners do whatever track or speed workout is on their individualized schedule for that week (assuming there is one). It's an individualized workout performed in a group setting; everyone runs at his/her own pace. Frequently, a few people are doing the same type of workout, but the number of reps and/or the specific paces may be different. So it's not always feasible to run with someone else because being 5 - 15 seconds faster/slower per rep could sabotage the workout for someone and lead to training in a gray area (junk training).

---

52. The final group workout I coach each year is the week of the NYC Marathon in the first week of Nov. We then generally switch gears to off-season training/ goals and the track workouts pick up again mid-Feb. The group workouts in between that time (wintertime) are hill repeats.

The track is traditionally run in a counter-clockwise direction. However, reps should be run in the opposite direction (clockwise) when possible, which is usually when there is a relatively empty track. In any case, it's proper etiquette to use the outside lanes when doing any laps in the opposite direction, or when jogging slowly and/or walking. Allow the runners going in the correct direction to have the inside lanes, with general track etiquette typically granting lane 1 to the faster runners, keeping lane 2 open for passing. Track athletes and elite runners doing structured workouts should be allowed to use lanes 3 - 4 exclusively (if they so desire), but this isn't too common. I don't advise doing *distance* runs (of any duration) on a track on a regular basis for the same reason I prefer warm-up and cool-down laps to be done in the opposite direction. Meaning, we want to avoid too many turns with the same leg (left leg) on the inside. Doing reps in the opposite direction also helps control for windy conditions, which determines if fast/slow splits are the result of the wind of if it's the runner's pacing simply being erratic.

To help the learning curve, check lap splits for every lap for each rep. The goal is to run perfectly even splits. For example, if the goal pace for a mile on the track is 7:00, then the goal is to run each lap in 1:45, which equates to 1:45 after the first lap, 3:30 after 2 laps, 5:15 after 3 laps, finishing the 4th lap at 7:00 (4 laps in a mile, not counting the extra 9 meters).

I rarely (if ever) schedule a runner for a "pyramid" or "ladder" workout on the track. The design of these workouts is such that the duration of each successive rep becomes longer, up until a set distance (this would be the top of the pyramid/ladder). Then the reps are run in reverse order as the runner makes his way back down the pyramid/ladder. The pace for each rep is different so that it corresponds with the longer or shorter rep duration, and the rest between reps can vary. For example, a pyramid may be: 200m @ mile pace + 400m @ 2-mile pace + 800m @ 5k pace + 1600 @ 10k pace, and then back down in reverse order. Pyramids offer variety, but because amateur runners need more practice learning proper pacing/intensity, I don't see the benefit of changing the goal pace after each rep. I'd rather the runner learn proper pacing by giving her the chance to learn from her previous rep. Meaning, if a ladder workout is being done and the runner is 4 seconds off the opening 200m rep (equivalent to 32 seconds per mile, which is *extremely* off target), then why make her move on to a new distance and new pace if she didn't even get the first one correct? Practice makes perfect, so it's best to allow a runner to keep practicing the same distance and pace the entire workout, honing in on the proper pace/intensity of the workout until it's nailed down. The learning curve is faster without pyramid workouts, and the payoff is confidence.

The last rep of a track workout is usually another lesson in race experience, which ultimately means another confidence booster. Confidence (the lack of uncertainty) is the greatest predictor of success in athletics. How does that relate to track workouts? If a runner is disciplined about even splitting, then he/she will no doubt have to push a bit harder on the last rep just to maintain the same pace (cardiac drift). Track workouts can be an experience in racing the clock, which most runners are doing anyway in races in order to hit a PR or goal time. With that being the case, runners can experience (practice) the feeling of being in a race during the last rep, rounding the last 200m (or more) with a slightly increased effort to cross the finish line and hit a goal time.

It is better to do more reps (higher volume) on the track rather than running a faster pace. For instance, if two runners of equal fitness are given the same tempo workout of 6 - 8 x 800m @ 7:30 pace, then the runner who does 8 reps @ 7:30 will be derive more benefit from the workout than the runner who does 6 reps @ 7:20. Using this example, an extra 1600 meters at tempo pace offers a greater training effect than does knocking off 10 seconds per rep for fewer reps. The reason for a range of reps being listed for a given workout is so that a runner can account for bad weather or general fatigue that day. Additional reps (higher volume) can always be kept in mind as a goal for progressing the training, but for those runners new to structured speed work, I design the program so that the first few workouts are intentionally on the low-volume end. In this case, I cap the number of reps they do so that they don't feel spent by the end, or feel deterred from future track workouts. I want beginners to feel energetic and confident after their first few track workouts, as opposed to feeling deflated and defeated.

R-PACE (REPETITION RUNS)

R-pace (Reps) is a term derived from Daniels' book and refers to a fast pace (approximately mile race pace) with a focus on proper running form. R-pace workouts are typically done early in the training year in order to boost running efficiency, so that the longer intervals, like Tempo workouts, that come later will be less stressful to the body. The goal of Reps is not necessarily to build fitness per se; however, fitness is gained indirectly. The goal of Reps is to teach a runner *how* to run fast. Knowing how to run fast means better running form at all distances, even the longer distances, which then increases the pace of the long runs. That is the indirect way in which R-pace workouts increase fitness. Learning proper running form is typically aided by running faster, not slower, so it's important to know how to move the arms and legs at the faster speeds, as well as how to have proper foot strike to avoid nagging injuries. The faster pace of Repetition runs helps accelerate this learning.

R-pace workouts have a volume of ~3200m per workout, and can be done once per week for 5 - 6 weeks at a time. An example of R-pace would be running 8 x 400m at 80 seconds (400 meters = 1 lap), as opposed to running 6 x 400m like this: 73, 75, 79, 81, 86, 89. The former allows for 2 additional reps and is more evenly paced, which suggests that more will be learned from the workout. In the latter example, the runner most likely fades at the end due to the first few reps being run too fast, which leads to a lower volume workout with less learned about pacing and form. The full recovery that is associated with this workout is typically a ~2:1 rest:work ratio (e.g., a 90-second 400m rep would get a 3-minute recovery). The recovery can be a standing recovery, without the need for jogging between reps. The goal is to eventually cut down the rest, so that the goal pace remains the same while taking 15-30 seconds off the typical 2:1 rest:work recovery.

Even though Reps are *not* sprints (I use the term *sprint* exclusively for running at 100% of top speed), a main benefit associated with Reps is the strength development in the hamstrings and glutes from running at higher speeds. For this reason, I remind runners that they can sometimes ignore the splits for these workouts and just focus on the hamstring and glute strengthening that is taking place. In this manner I do consider Reps as ST for the hips, hamstrings, and glutes (if form is correct), and they are similar to hill repeats in this regard.

T-PACE (TEMPO RUNS)

Regardless of which distance is being trained for, the bread-and-butter workout for most runners will be tempo runs (T-pace). These are the workouts that runners use to get fitter and faster after a base building phase. T-pace is described as "moderately hard," or "comfortably hard," which usually equates to 8k or 10k race pace for the average runner, 10-mile pace for the more experienced runner, and Half pace for the pros. Tempo pace is 88 - 92% maxHR, which is just below the point when mechanical fatigue in the muscle fibers starts to become the limiting factor; therefore, it's also referred to as *threshold* pace. The volume for T-runs is typically between 5000m - 8000m (or more for elite runners).

Tempo workouts are more aerobic than anaerobic. One coach has described it as "you want to stop, but you don't have to." When T-pace is run correctly, a runner will find that the legs feel fine, but breathing (or HR) becomes the limiting factor and focal point. Daniels refers to tempo intervals as "cruise intervals," but I use the term *tempo* to keep the language simple, whereas Daniels technically reserves tempo runs for steady runs of 20 - 60 minutes.

T-pace may seem easy enough after the first rep/interval, but keep in mind that these workouts are hard because the rest between reps is typically only 1-minute, which is *not* full recovery. On that note, there is such as thing as *junk training*. For instance, there is a big difference between a 60-sec rest and 90-sec rest. Similarly, if you run faster than tempo pace and don't give yourself full recovery, then it's training in a gray area. In other words, you don't quite receive the full benefits from either end of the aerobic-anaerobic spectrum.

Some experienced runners will hit a tempo workout most weeks out of the year, whether done as intervals on the track or as steady runs with no rest. I tend to take them out of a runner's program during the winter and/ or also during most of the weeks when there's an R-pace, I-pace, or hill repeat workout on the schedule (this is a simple way for non-professional runners to avoid overtraining). I tend to alter tempo paces based on race results and/or witnessing first-hand how a runner handles the pace. I'm hesitant to speed up a runner's tempo pace too soon because the intensity of the workout must be considered. For instance, one may run very hard to improve tempo pace by 10 seconds in a 4 x mile workout, but if each rep concludes with the runner bent over his knees, or huffing and puffing, then the pace was too fast and perhaps to no extra benefit. This is why doing more reps on the track is always better than running a faster pace. A higher-volume track workout done at the appropriate pace is better than blazing the track for a lower-volume workout.

I use 1000m tempo repeats as the benchmark workout for my athletes. After a period away from tempo work, a runner can do 1000m repeats on the track for comparative reasons. I don't specify the goal pace for this particular comparative workout. The goal here is to run the first two reps at the previous T-pace and to adjust accordingly from there. Running the first two reps at the previous T-pace is intentional so that a runner can feel how much easier the pace has become (ideally), and that is the confidence boost to be gained from that particular workout. I do admit that weather may occasionally negate this effect, but the point should be clear. The remaining reps can be increased in speed accordingly.[53]

I-PACE (INTERVALS)

Whereas tempo pace is described as *comfortably* hard, Interval pace is simply *hard*. Interval pace is two-mile or 5k race pace (4 miles for the elite runners). The reps for I-pace workouts are typically broken down into 800m's and 1000m's (and 1200m's for the faster folks), which allows for the pace to be faster than tempo, yet with longer rest periods. Again, as with most workouts, the goal of even splitting applies here. Because I-pace workouts are more demanding than T-pace workouts, they are usually done after base mileage has been built and after running economy has been improved with R-pace and T-pace workouts. Because the aerobic system is taxed to its fullest with Intervals, these workouts are the best boost to overall fitness regardless of the race for which an athlete is training. However, the quality of these workouts can suffer if the runner dives in headfirst with a subpar aerobic base, or without a sense of how to pace properly.

The intensity for I-pace workouts is ~95% of maxHR. Running at 100% of your maxHR does not necessarily bring about any further physiological adaptations compared to running at 95% of max, so yes, it is possible to run too fast for these workouts and not reap any further benefits. Ideally, I-pace is run at the "slowest" pace possible that still yields a 95% HR. Again, this is where intensity differs from pace, but if a high number of reps can be run at a consistent pace, then we can usually agree the intensity was correct. Similar to T-pace workouts, I-pace workouts have a minimum of ~5000m per workout, and can be done once per week for 5 - 8 weeks at a time. A great complement to these workouts is to toss a

---

53. I discuss this topic in more detail below in the section titled *A Sense of Urgency & Running Too Fast*.

5k into the program so that it coincides with the middle or end of a round of I-pace training.

A Sense of Urgency & Running Too Fast

When you do your track workouts, do you run each rep with a feeling of pressure to hit the goal time, thereby causing a "sense of urgency"? In turn, does this cause a bit of anxiety/stress during the workout? Because I coach a full range of personalities, I know for some readers the answer to this question is a resounding "YES!"

In order to eliminate the sense of urgency, get rid of the mentality that you are in a competitive race against the clock or coach. Hitting the pace on the dot is the goal, but even a few seconds over the goal time is acceptable. Some of you would nod your head in agreement with this notion, but do you actually believe your own head nod? Do you put it into action on the track, or are you always running with some unspoken pressure or urgency? As a coach, I want my runners to strive for precision on the track so that they learn proper pacing and so that they know what the proper intensity feels like, but by no means is there a perfectionist attitude on my end. Additionally, there should be no additional pressure coming from within the athlete.

Treat track workouts like a game, and the game is to get close to the goal pace, though it doesn't have to be exact (it takes most runners a year of track workouts to get to that point). I use the term *game* intentionally as a reminder that this is supposed to be a fun endeavor, not a stressful one. Two seconds under and two seconds over are both two-second differentials; don't put more emotional stock on one versus the other. I hope this resonates well with the reader. This advice is a piece of the puzzle in trying to eliminate unnecessary worry from a runner's persona. I want to help train athletes to train themselves how to eliminate unnecessary self-talk on race day, for which track workouts are a good classroom setting.

I've had conversations with many runners about their fears, anxieties, frustrations, and disappointments when they are not under the goal time for workouts. What often unfolds is that either all the reps are run too fast to avoid "failure," or stress and disappointment set in if even a single rep is over the goal time. Neither of these mindsets is warranted. A message I repeat at track workouts is that I'd rather a rep is 3 seconds slow than 6 seconds fast. This relates to running the proper pace or intensity early in a race to set up a strong finish. The responsibility of doing workouts at the correct pace is shared 50-50 between the runner and the coach. I have to make sure I'm giving the right paces and the runner has to be able to do it. To bring it back to the central point, do not stress over track paces. Being two seconds over the time *can* be filed under the "successful rep" category (imagine that!).

To repeat, the goal of a speed workout is to hit the goal time on the mark, versus striving to *beat* the goal time as in a competition between the athlete and coach. The more successful athletes are the ones who show discipline and consistency in hitting the mark. Anyone can beat a goal time; that's often easy to do because all one has to do is run too fast. When we run mile splits too fast early in a race, we usually don't finish well, so hopefully the connection between track workouts and racing is apparent. It's more beneficial (and a sign of improved learning) to hit the mark accurately. The carry-over this has for race day is in learning the appropriate intensity that corresponds to proper pacing. This also means learning precisely how much harder the body has to work to maintain the same pace as the race goes continues (assuming a flat course).

Sometimes runners beat the goal time because they're fit enough (and I'll adjust goal times in those cases), but other times running too fast sabotages the learning process. Running too fast on the first rep might remove the ability to pace well on the final reps. For instance, it's often not a "lack of ability to pace properly" that causes a slower pace on the final reps; rather, the culprit is *premature fatigue* caused by going too fast on the first two reps.

If a runner is x-amount of seconds faster on the second rep compared to the first rep, then the runner has to know *when* the pace increased, *how* she ran faster, and *why*. Checking the watch every 200m usually answers these questions. If you see that you're ahead of pace, what do you do? What do you say to yourself at that moment? This is often my message at the track workouts before we begin. *How* do you slow yourself down or speed up? If you notice that you are ahead of pace, how do you process that information? Do you ignore it? What correction do you make with your legs? Typically the answer is in stride length and that goes for speeding up or slowing down. Perceived exertion (intensity) should also change at that time, so that the depth of breathing becomes another way to monitor the change in pace.

A reminder that I often give everyone halfway through a track workout is to "run relaxed without slowing down." I'm not implying here that the runner is moving too fast, rather, I'm trying to make the point that too often people make the terms *relax* and *slow down* synonymous, which is erroneous. The person who wins the Boston Marathon each year will be running fast as hell, but he/she will be relaxed while doing so. Most likely, he/she is not running with a sense of urgency (unless the race boils down to a sprint to the finish). Run fast, or run the goal time, but do it while being mentally relaxed.

To think of it another way, the person who wins the next Olympic gold medal in the squat competition might be very mentally relaxed even though they are physically exerting a great deal of effort while squatting that 900 pounds. You will feel better physically once you train yourself mentally to stay cool, calm, and collect even during high-intensity efforts. Halfway through a track workout, a runner should begin making this distinction between physical toughness and mental toughness. For instance, how hard are you (mentally) interpreting the workout to be? Can you reduce the workout to only the physical aspect and leave the mental components out of it? This skill is a hallmark of champion athletes; they learn how to leave the mind at home and "Just Do It."

TLT RUNS (TEMPO – LONG – TEMPO)

This is a speed workout and long run in combination. This is a tough workout to do alone, similar to the progression runs that may appear in a program. The goal of the TLT runs is to run ~16 - 20 miles total, with almost half of those miles done at tempo pace. I suggest a very short warm-up jog (2 - 3 min) before doing dynamic drills.

Here is the workout: 2 - 3 miles easy + 2-3 x 2 mile @ T w/ 2 minute rests between reps + 6 - 8 miles easy + 2 miles steady @ T + 2 - 3 miles easy = 16 - 20 miles total.

If doing the workout based on time and not distance, it would look like this: 15 - 20 min easy jog + 2-3 x 15-20 min @ T w/ 2 minute rests between reps + 45 - 90 min easy + 15 min steady @ T + 15 - 20 min easy = 2 - 3 hours total (45 - 75 min @ T).

FAST FINISH (FF)

A Fast Finish run earns its name because the goal is to quicken the pace, or at least increase the effort, at the end of the run. That amount of time is usually one-third of the total time of the run, so for a 45-minute FF run the last 15 minutes would be finished at a pace faster than the usual jog pace, as in treating the run like a 30-minute warm-up followed by a 15-minute tempo run. However, depending on how a runner feels that day, the run can be finished faster or slower than tempo pace. It is never a sprint at the end, just faster than typical jog pace—as fast, or not so fast, as desired. It is a purposeful workout designed to become accustomed to finishing a race with some added effort (remember the principle of cardiac drift). Therefore, FF runs are a great mental training day because if anyone ever has visions of closing hard during a race, then these are the workouts to put your money where your mouth is.

As counterintuitive as it may seem, when fatigued at the end of a run, it is sometimes easier to speed up rather than slow down. This certainly isn't the most common occurrence, but it happens enough times for it to have truth. Even by speeding up ~10 - 15 seconds per mile, a runner may be using muscles that weren't being used most of the run. Slowing down can make a runner feel better, but the same holds true for speeding up. I can't make someone believe this; they have to experience it first, so don't overlook this particular element of training. This strategy of speeding up when fatigued in order to "freshen up" the legs (and mind) is easier to apply on race day if it's been practiced. The practice (and confidence) are realized during FFs and post-run striders. On a related note, did you ever wonder how you or another runner felt a "2nd wind" mid-race? It's not always a Herculean mental effort that accomplishes this feat. Rather, it's simply changing gears slightly and therefore changing the stride (muscle usage) slightly. The take-home message is that rather than summoning the pity party, try speeding up ever so slightly and see if it doesn't snap you out of a funk. Hot, humid, and hilly conditions would obviously make this harder to accomplish.

I tend to schedule FF runs during a recovery week or any other week I want to give a runner a mental break from running circles on the track. I also schedule them as an occasional second speed workout during the week. As specificity of training starts to build throughout the year, I may schedule more FF runs to help those runners prepping for a peak 10k or 10-miler.

DESCENDING TEMPOS & PROGRESSION RUNS

The goal of these two workouts is to put a little more structure into the Fast Finish runs. There is a time and place for structured and unstructured workouts; embrace both. Descending tempos begin with a 60 - 80 minute jog, followed by the following intervals: 7 minutes of harder running at roughly half-marathon pace (~20 - 45 seconds slower than tempo pace), followed by 3.5 minutes of jogging recovery (half the total time spent running hard), then 6 minutes of faster running, followed by 3 minutes of jogging rest, then 5 minutes of hard running with 2.5 minutes rest, continuing that pattern with fast running for 4-, 3-, 2- and 1-minute intervals and corresponding rest breaks equal to half of the preceding rep (as just described). The pace should gradually get faster with each rep, so the first sets need to be under control. If it's the first time doing this workout, then start the intervals at 5 minutes of hard running (not 7), which will make it easier to complete. This workout can be done on the track at some point in the run (if a track is along the way of the route) to help calibrate pace; however, I don't recommend running more than 30 minutes on a track in the same direction.

A progression run is a common workout for folks training for a marathon. The run is usually 15 - 20 miles in distance, with the run broken up into 3 - 5 sections (or sets), increasing the speed each set (as determined by the coach or runner). An example of a progression run is to run 2.5-hours total, done as five 30-minute sections, with each section being paced 15 seconds per mile faster than the previous section. A runner could start at their usual long run pace (relatively slow), moving through goal marathon pace and eventually into a faster pace (perhaps tempo pace) for the final section. This type or workout mimics the increasing energy demands of a long-distance race without having to run the full marathon distance.[54]

HILL REPEATS

Hill repeats are the key workouts for many runners in the winter, due to the tracks being less accessible, but they can certainly be thrown in during any season. The intensity for hill repeats is similar to that of R-pace workouts, with the same goal: Go as hard as possible for each rep without fading for the remainders—the fastest speed that can be *maintained*. Hill repeats are not performed as full sprints, but if the intensity of a hill rep doesn't feel harder than a tempo workout, then it's not being run hard enough. These are high HR workouts; hill repeats are definitely a speed workout. For this reason, dynamic warm-up drills should still be done. An ideal hill is between 150 and 400 meters long (30 seconds to 2 minutes) with an incline of an approximately 3 - 9 degree grade, which means it

---

54. I would not equate these two types of workouts with pyramid/ladder workouts.

could be a long and gradual climb, or short and steep. The number of reps is between 6 - 10, but if the hill is less than 30 seconds long then add a few extra reps. Occasionally, tackle a hill that is 3 - 4 minutes in duration, as it may help you to advantageously alter your definition of the word "hilly" so that shorter/gentler hills won't appear as daunting on subsequent runs.

The recovery time between reps is the time is takes to slowly jog back to the bottom of the hill, before immediately going up again. This equates to a 2:1 rest:work ratio (or a bit less), similar to R-pace workouts. This means the rest twice as long as the work, in terms of time (not distance). A 60-sec hill receives a 120-sec recovery.

Similar to track workouts, once two or three of these workouts have been completed and a runner has the hang of it, then I (ideally) want zero time differential between all reps. A runner shouldn't be fried after the first rep, nor should a runner save energy for a miraculous sprint on the last rep (something I term "the hero factor"). There's an element of sub-jectivity to this workout in keeping the quality of the reps high.

If possible, use different hills until scheduled to go back and duplicate a hill workout for comparative reasons. Variety in this regard refers to the du-ration of the ascent, the gradient, and the neighborhood. Explore and experi-ment. Similar to selecting different routes for long runs, changing the hill location allows new insight to be gained, even if it's just one new data point.

When it comes to scheduling, I'd prefer that hills not be done on the treadmill. If it's bad weather, move it to another day in the week; however, if hills can't be done outside for a given week, then the treadmill can be used. Set the treadmill gradient up to 3 - 9% and lower it to zero for the recovery jog between reps. Don't keep it set on the inclined gradient the entire workout in order to jump on/off (a safety concern).

DOWNHILL REPEATS

The point of these workouts is to learn how to run downhill at a pace faster than a jog without feeling unbalanced or needing to brake excessively with the quads. There is a section titled *Downhill Running* in Chapter 5, but to repeat one point from that section: The steepness of a decline will typically be a subjective matter based upon muscular strength and running experience. A key component in determining if the decline selected for downhill repeats is appropriate is whether or not normal running mechanics can be maintained while running at tempo pace. I do not recommend running faster than tempo pace (3rd gear) for downhill repeats. The recovery run back to the top of the hill is done at a leisurely pace.

MARATHON PACE (MP)

These are mental dress rehearsals, not true "workouts," and are added to the program in the final phase of training leading up to a peak marathon. The duration of a MP workout is open-ended, as long as consideration is given to the expected timeframe to recover from a long MP workout and/or the number of days prior to the marathon. Even though non-professional runners end up a bit slower at the end of a marathon, MP is typically selected as the average goal marathon pace, or target pace, even though the actual splits on race day may vary a great deal. There is usually a drop off in VDOT at the marathon distance when compared to distances from 5k through Half (marathons contain more variables), so I typically prescribe a MP that corresponds to a few numbers below a runner's current VDOT.[55]

FARTLEK RUNS

Fartlek is the Swedish term for "speed play" and refers to an *unstructured* workout where pacing and gears are varied throughout the run for as long and as often as the runner wants. A runner can choose to vary the pacing

---

55. There is a *Pace Calculators* section in chapter 6.

within a fartlek at his/her own desire, and to use landmarks instead of using a watch (e.g., from street A to street B). These are great for winter workouts since most track workouts are on hiatus. As a coach, I like fartleks because they add an element of freedom into the program. I essentially let the runners do whatever they want within these workouts, and similar to FF runs, I schedule them during weeks a runner can't access a track, or as an occasional second speed workout during the week.

Fartlek runs can be like classroom sessions, such as using them to practice how to regain composure after surging during a race. Use these workouts to either try something new or to improve a weakness. If hilly courses seem to be a weak spot, then attack all the uphills or downhills on the next fartlek run. A runner could also choose to work on how to change gears during a race by altering stride length and arm swing (this is where athleticism helps). If a runner has a habit of going out too fast in races and/or the opening reps on the track, then fartlek runs can be used to practice coming off the starting line. For example, begin the run at a given race pace for a few minutes, then stop completely in order to normalize the HR, and repeat 10 - 20 times, which equates to 10 - 20 starting line practice sessions in one workout.

ACCELERATORS

Accelerators are a type of sprint workout where the athlete smoothly accelerates from start to finish, as in accelerating from 1st to 5th gear over a 100m distance. The distance for each gear would be evenly distributed (i.e., ~20m per gear in a 100m accelerator). Accelerators help a runner progress into sprint workouts (if the program eventually calls for sprints, as in training for a military or law enforcement physical fitness test). Breaking up the gears/paces into more manageable distances allows the runner to remain focused on running form as the intensity of the pace is gradually increased. Because other sprint workouts done over a full 100m - 400m will place more stress on the hamstrings, accelerators are a good starting point to gradually bring the hamstrings up to the required strength for longer sprint workouts.

"OFF-TRACK" WORKOUTS

As the fall race season nears, a runner should be very in tune with pacing. For my experienced runners, I might schedule them exclusively for "off-track" speed workouts each fall. Some runners are an exception to this rule based on where they are in a training cycle, as I'd rather they continue to learn proper pacing on the track (if needed). Otherwise, the goal is to follow the principle of specificity of training by doing workouts on the trails and open road, where races take place. An off-track workout can include rolling terrain, mimicking a race course. This is where attention to breathing, stride, and perceived exertion is beneficial in keeping the effort consistent. I don't promote the use of Garmin watches at these workouts (we only use the elapsed time setting) because using them would defeat the purpose of the workout location. This is what it means to be a Zen runner, or a wise runner, so patience is needed with this particular learning curve.

RECOVERY RUNS & COOL-DOWNS

I think recovery jogs can be a great tool; however, I don't think every runner should do extra "recovery mileage" because it's not always necessary, especially if the runner has improper running form. The goal of recovery jogs and "maintenance runs" is to promote greater adaptations in the body so that fuel will be processed more efficiently and so that the muscular-skeletal system becomes stronger. However, this is not the only event occurring in the body on these runs; we wish it were that simple.

Recovery runs assume the body can handle the additional stress of said runs. Why can many pros run more than 100 miles in a given week? One major difference between them and mortal runners is running form. The reason pros can run all these additional miles, regardless of pace, has much to do with the fact that few of their runs cause *extra* stress on the body. Assuming they stick to good data points spelled out in their program, they can run as much as they want without destroying themselves. Sure, it helps that the pro runners have usually been running many years and typically carry a low body weight, but it also helps that they hit the ground with zero *additional* stress (out of the ordinary) with each foot strike. If you don't have proper foot strike, there is nothing recovery-like about a recovery run. Rather, you're still putting more stress on the body. That is the difference running form makes in building a training program. How many miles per week can you run? It depends on your running form. Better runners can run more miles. It has nothing to do with motivation; rather, it has everything to do with posture and foot strike. As I mentioned in the *Foot Strike* section, running too slowly on a recovery run will do more harm than good because form breaks down when the pace is *too* slow. For that reason, I don't put much stock on pace during midweek runs, as long as it's not slower than a regular jog pace and the foot strike is kept ideal.

Additionally, most runners are not doing enough weekly miles to have to incorporate recovery runs/miles. When someone runs 80 or more miles per week, then yes, it's a no-brainer that many of those miles will be done at a very relaxed pace. That is where recovery runs would enter the picture. However, if a runner *only* (I use that term loosely) runs 30 - 40 miles per week (or three to five times per week), then how slow does he/she really want to go? It's better to run a bit faster (or at least at one's "normal" jogging pace) to gain some fitness/benefits from each run. Let's be honest, for most runners, there is nothing recovery-like about a 5-mile run if it comes the day after an 18-miler. I'd rather see an athlete stay off his/her feet in that instance to let the body recover for an extra day.

In a similar vein, doing cool-down laps after a track workout isn't necessary and is somewhat overrated. Those who attend my track workouts know I rarely encourage such laps, and I'm yet to have a runner become injured as a result. I emphasize this point more in the summer when there's more heat and humidity. In those instances, doing extra running really isn't necessary; the body may already be overheated. Therefore, depending on who the athlete is, there are times I'd rather not have the additional stress on the body. The walk to the car/subway can be the cool-down. Put the energy into the workout. I wouldn't want to have a runner tell me he didn't do the full reps in the workout, yet did a mile cool-down. There are many other activities that give the same benefits as cool-down laps, such as icing, massage, and leg swings. In closing, under ideal conditions, I would encourage cool-down laps, but I've talked to enough elite athletes to sense that cool-down laps are an individualized choice, not a necessity.

AQUA RUNNING

Injuries can be a bit of a downer, which shows that an athlete values his/her performance, but there are always ways to remain active. When compared to swimming and cycling, aqua running has been shown to maintain more run-specific fitness during a layoff from run training. This finding is logical due to the principle of specificity of training. Therefore, when doing aqua running, maintain a normal stride with the legs, as opposed to an up-and-down high-knee motion. If one finds that the density of the water makes it difficult to sense a "running stride," then it's helpful to instead imagine oneself using an elliptical machine. Either way, the goal is to engage the hamstrings via the swing phase of the stride. Otherwise, merely using a high-knee motion will only train the hip flexors and the carryover effects are lost. The research is pretty stacked in stating that *high-intensity* aqua running is required to reap benefits, meaning it has to be done as *intervals*, versus merely jogging in the water. I'd almost rather that someone swim laps rather than do low-intensity aqua running, since the former may actually be better for fitness.

Aqua running is synonymous with deep-water running, as opposed to using the shallow end of the pool where the feet can touch the bottom. The latter is permissible depending on the nature of the injury. There are several types of specialty water-running flotation belts on the market now. An advantage to aqua running is that there is no stress on the legs whatsoever from any ground contact. Zero-gravity treadmills are the latest innovation in this department.

TREADMILL RUNNING

A coaching goal of mine is to have everyone running outside year-round, never using the treadmill (or at least only minimally).[56] Some people elect to do track workouts on the treadmill when they can't get to a track, but rather than have the treadmill be the 2nd option, just run anywhere else outside instead, running for the rep's designated amount of time and leaving the treadmill as the very last resort. Assuming a runner is in tune (familiar) with the appropriate intensity, there is no need to worry about exact distance covered.

Because treadmill running is relatively easier, increase the workout paces slightly in these instances and/or raise the incline to a 1-degree setting. I agree that there is a time and place for treadmill running, but with the exception of safety, extreme weather, or doctor's orders, head outside. On a humorous note, if you remember the movie *Rocky IV*, Rocky's opponent trained on treadmill while Rocky ran up mountains, and we all know who won by having more endurance at the end of the fight!

COMPARING WORKOUTS

Occasionally in a runner's program, I'll schedule a workout he/she has done previously within the 3-month phase, or in the prior phase. I know

---

56. The *Treadmills* section in Chapter 5 is related to changes in running form when using a treadmill.

the conditions and weather aren't always the same, but it's an attempt to get a glimpse of how much a runner has improved on paper and/or how much easier the same workout felt the second time around, which is all the more reason to keep score at home, at least for the speed workouts and long runs. It's uplifting to compare some of the same workouts from the previous phase or year. As stated in the opening chapter, race day should not be the only way that success is measured.

There needs to be a healthy balance as to how often the data is analyzed and how often workouts are compared. I don't encourage runners to compare their workouts week to week, and the reason is very simply rooted in that the physiology of training doesn't allow for significant changes week to week. Too many runners are "disappointed" in when comparing their performances week to week. Such feelings are not warranted. Look for improvements over a greater timescale as in three months apart or even year-to-year. On a shorter timescale, expect improvements no sooner than about every 6 weeks, which is in line with the physiology of the training. Improvements seen within a one-month time span are usually attributable to significantly different weather or to "learning effects," meaning the improvements are due to runner having a better understanding of how to do the workout, not necessarily improved fitness. Garmin runners usually have a tougher time resisting weekly comparisons. If you get caught in the trap of constantly seeking improvement, then it can lead you to feeling unsuccessful, unnecessarily.

BREAKTHROUGH PERFORMANCES

In a nutshell, a breakthrough performance is a workout or race that exceeds an athlete's own expectations and is usually an invigorating experience that changes the mental approach to training/racing. These only happen every once in a while, hence the term. However, it's possible to increase the likelihood of a breakthrough performance depending on how the program is planned. Every now and then I encourage a runner to find a flat course so that she can really put the pedal to the metal without hills becoming a factor. For instance, when was the last time you did an entire long run on totally flat terrain? Long, flat paths allow a runner to feel fitter after several weeks on rolling courses. In turn, that may be the breakthrough performance being sought. Similarly, after racing a flat 5k, a runner might think, "Wow, I had no idea I could run that fast!" After returning from a trip to Boulder, CO (high altitude) one year, I would have been a fool not to race that next weekend. I had a great race, a huge 8k PR on a flat course and I rode that Rocky Mountain high the entire race season. There's no substitute for that kind of confidence boost. So if you haven't done so in a while, go long on a flat course and maybe you'll exceed your own expectations.

On a related note, when was the last time you trained somewhere new? Have you memorized every crack in the road on your routes? Have you ever run your favorite route in reverse? Are you using different options for hill repeats? Tried running on a different track or driving to a new course/trail? Changing paths or taking a new side street is something I encourage to help break out of a mental training rut and/or a physical plateau. If we are not overly concerned with the exact pace or exact miles for most of our distance runs, then we can break up the monotony and explore new grounds. Sometimes it will lead to a hillier route, which we shouldn't fear. This could also mean running at a different time of day. For example, if you always run at home after work, try jogging around the office neighborhood before work, at lunch, or afterward.

Having a route or track that consistently produces good results is a good idea when seeking a breakthrough performance. Everyone should have a go-to place for when they want to have a stellar workout. Call it a haven. Some people have a race they do every year for this reason because they always seem to race well there. Others only visit such grounds every now and then as to not abuse the privilege. I try to schedule my hardest track workout of the year for a weekend I know I can swing by my alma mater, and once per year I have my best workout on a track where I love to run. Some of you may now be thinking, "Shouldn't the goal be to replicate that feeling all the time…at every workout?" Correct! You're on to something. However, I will only point out that by definition, not every workout can achieve the status of "breakthrough." It's similar to the old adage, "If *everything* is special, then *nothing* is special." Although it can be a subjective experience, the take home message is that even as we have great workouts on a frequent basis, only a few can, by definition, be considered breakthrough performances.

ALTITUDE TRAINING

There's certainly more to this topic than what is written here, but since most of us don't venture into these territories often, I'll keep it short and sweet by offering a few key points, truncating from Daniels' book:

1) No changes in mileage are needed while running at *moderate* altitude (4900 - 8200 feet). The volume can be reduced at altitudes higher than this.
2) R-pace stays unchanged. T- and I-pace get slowed down to basically match the proper intensity of the workout (a general rule anyway when considering intensity vs. pace).
3) Early morning running is preferred at altitude.
4) More hydration is required.
5) Load up on iron-rich foods to build more red blood cells, which the body wants to do at altitude anyway.

9

WEATHER & RUNNING APPAREL

Coaching athletes in the Mid-Atlantic region means that it's inevitable that each fall I'll receive messages from runners telling me how much more motivated they are to train once the cooler temperatures arrive. Nonetheless, being one of the few people training outside on days with non-ideal weather should be a boost to the ego and enhance the sense of determination. Being dedicated to training in the face of non-ideal weather should give a dose of pride.

For the sport of running, every degree increase in temperature above ~ 60 degrees makes it a bit more difficult to perform optimally, to the tune of a 2 - 3% decrease in performance every 10 degrees above 60 (~3 - 6 minutes for a 3:30 marathoner). For this reason, PRs and world records are usually set in conditions with temperatures around 55 - 65 degrees (depending on the distance) with overcast skies to block out the sun's rays. The mark of a wise and mature athlete is one that can adjust goals to match the weather conditions and feel successful about the performance without being *overly* (key word) concerned with the final finish time.

Winter Weather

A firm understanding of the purpose of off-season training will allow an athlete to keep a healthy perspective on relatively low-volume running during the winter. So if/when winter weather puts a damper on run training, then it can be taken in stride, knowing that other elements of training are more important during that time. Above all else, at least *try* to run outside before making a judgment that it's too cold. A 30-degree temperature by itself isn't necessarily cold; it can be enjoyable winter weather if dressed properly. The wind is always the deciding factor. I'm known as saying, "If it's not windy, it's not cold." Before resorting to a treadmill, try some other strategies, like bumping the workout to another day with better weather (don't let your routine be too stringent) or doing the run later in the day when it's warmer.

At winter races, some runners wear only shorts and a singlet, with perhaps arm warmers, gloves, and/or wicking headgear. They aren't crazy; they're just fast (and experienced). The body warms quickly while running, but the reason the experienced runners can get away with wearing so little clothing is because they are also doing a thorough dynamic warm-up before the race. The pre-race warm-up and what is done in the starting corral are just as important as what is worn. Idling in place for too long pre-race is the worst enemy in a cold weather race. In colder weather, blood flow naturally increases to the vital organs to keep them warm (survival tactic), which means the extra blood has to be drawn from somewhere, like the extremities. Blood flow is reduced to the *outer* extremities, so the hands and ears will be the first body parts to get cold. We might think the same about the feet and calves, but they'll stay warm because they are receiving blood as working muscles (more than the arms). Therefore, gloves and something to cover the ears are a good investment.

For headwear, whether it's a skullcap or a headband I recommend mois-ture-wicking material, like polyester. The same material should be worn for the layers of clothing closest to the skin (shirts and socks), so that the sweat is pulled away from the body and evaporates more quickly. This will keep the body dryer and warmer. Use Chapstick and additional face balm to protect against the wind. When doing an out-and-back run on a windy day in colder weather, head into the wind on the way out, so it is a tailwind on the way home. This way, sweaty clothes will contribute less to feeling cold.

RUNNING IN THE SNOW

Personally, I don't mind running on snow and ice if I have to, but I cannot encourage anyone to get out there and do it (safety first). Proper running form is what ultimately allows for the ability to run on ice, as in landing midfoot (or with a "flat foot"). For runners who land on their heels (even slightly), it's easy to picture how they would slip, like cartoon characters slipping on banana peels, with the heel hitting the ice in front of the body, potentially causing the slippage. As a midfoot striker, I don't alter my stride when running over ice. I might slow down a hair, but otherwise I keep moving naturally. I once ran in a long-distance race that had much snow and ice on the asphalt course. Most racers in the top half of the field were able to keep on running over top of the ice, while most in the back half were walking on the ice or off to the side of the trail. There's no rule that says the faster you run the more likely you are to slip on snow/ice. The main difference, other than perhaps experience, is that faster runners are usually (not always) midfoot runners, while slower or beginning run-ners are likely to be heel strikers. Running on snow (and occasionally over ice) also requires athleticism, which is the combination of coordination and core strength, both of which help one to regain balance quickly and safely if needed. Herein is another strong plug to be more athletic, which is aided by dynamic ST.

Over the years I've received many emails from runners after they've had an enjoyable run through the snow. If we truly enjoy physical activity and Mother Nature's company, and possess a hardy personality defined by a willingness to accept challenges, then running in adverse conditions, like getting up the hills in the snow, can be fun. This is a part of motivation that is difficult for me to hand out; it must come from within. Regardless of the weather, I love running, I love being outside, and I thrive on challenges, so running in the snow is a perfect storm for me (no pun intended).

SUMMER WEATHER

Similar to what I wrote about snow-filled winters, at least try to run in the heat before dismissing it. Acclimation is the best safeguard against falling prey to the adverse effects of the heat. The reason fitter runners tend to have fewer issues with summer conditions is because fitter runners most likely have spent more time running outside, in terms of frequency and/or longer durations. Their increased exposure to the elements, and their fitness alone, make them better acclimated to the weather. To take a direct quote from a 2011 Runner's World article explaining this advantage:

> Because of blood plasma's important role in the cooling process, training alone provides a bit of adaptation, because a side effect of running is an increase in total plasma volume. This helps to explain why the fittest athletes (and likely those with the highest plasma volume) typically adapt more easily to heat. In addition to regular training, running in hot conditions results in changes that make it easier to maintain a faster pace and cause perceived exertion to drop, including a higher blood plasma volume, increased sweat rate, decrease in salt in sweat, reduced heart rate at a given pace and temperature, and a quicker onset of sweating.

When training outside in hot/humid conditions, the duration and intensity can obviously be reduced. The longer the race the more that heat and humidity become factors. Obviously, running in the early morning or the evening is preferred. As an aside, it's hotter in the evening, but more humid in the morning. The gain in mental toughness from doing a two-hour run between the hours of 11:00am - 5:00pm may not be worth the suffer fest. Every now and then an athlete can test his/her limits in these conditions, but if the training is geared toward a peak fall race that will have decent weather, then there's no need to force the training in conditions that do not mimic the race. It might be a bit hot on race day or even a bit humid; however, as long as there is some exposure to it on a regular basis, then all is not lost.

Even with the hot conditions, a runner should never have a "bad" run. What was your mental approach to the run that made it so horrible by the time you finished? Did you not adjust your goals based on the conditions? World champions typically have much more competitive goals than us, so if they rarely have a bad workout, then why should we? Great athletes have the ability to change goals at any time.

Serious athletes shooting for a big race in a hot and humid climate should avoid living in an air-conditioned (A/C) world for about two weeks before the race (and in general). An athlete serious about improving race performance who is looking for little advantages here and there can remember this one: Stop living in the A/C. We hear stories about people passing out (or worse) during hot and humid race conditions, but these are the exceptions, not the rule. Humans are adaptive. How do some people do it? We are animals primed for acclimation, so turn off the A/C at home (use fans), take lunch breaks outside and drive with the windows down in the car. This tip is more practical if racing is a high priority, so this tip is not for everyone.

There's a thin line between being tough and being foolish. There is a need to keep water in the muscles to keep them functioning optimally. Hydration has more to do with the state of your muscles (i.e., preventing premature fatigue) than whether or not there is cotton-mouth. Water bottle systems, like FuelBelt, are commonplace these days, especially for distance runs, but I am surprised at how few runners hydrate during track workouts. Heart rate is obviously higher here than on distance runs, so why not take extra steps to keep the HR down? The goal of every track workout is quality reps, so if dehydration sets in during a speed workout then low quality training might be around the corner. In other words, in order to race fast, you have to train fast; hydrate to stay fast. Contrary to theories stating that fluids closer to the body temperature are better for absorption than cold beverages, the results are equivocal depending on which studies you research. From my readings, it appears that beverages served cold are more easily digested and help absorb more nutrients than beverages served warm. Plus, it's only logical that colder fluids will help cool the core body temperature.

When considering a speed workouts on the track, the general alterations to the workout are to slow the pace anywhere from ~10 - 45 seconds per mile, take an extra 20 - 30 seconds rest between reps, cut the distance of the reps by 200 - 400 meters and reduce the number of reps. In some instances, all four precautions can be taken. The idea is to keep getting exposure to the elements without overheating and/or getting too far out of the training/HR zone.

Visors and hats are beneficial if sunglasses aren't used, but I am more partial to visors than hats for three reasons. First, visors aid the body's ability to let heat escape from the top of the head. Second, it's ensured that the cold water being dumped on the head to stay cool will make contact with the head and won't be absorbed by the hat. Third, visors are a tad lighter, and even though that may sound trivial, it's better for long runs. However, for those balding on top, then a hat is probably the better option.

Speaking of our heads, consider getting a shorter haircut. Contrary to popular belief, we don't lose more heat through our heads *compared to other areas of the body*, but we don't want to *trap* it there either (the same reason you wouldn't wear gloves on a summer run). If you're running with a FuelBelt (or similar), pouring water on the head can keep the body temperature down on a hot day due to the number of blood vessels near the scalp (brain), so consider getting a shorter haircut to let the water make it to the scalp. HR increases naturally on hotter days because in addition to blood being demanded by the exercising muscles, more blood must also be transferred to the skin to aid in sweating (the cooling process). A shorter haircut may help reduce the body's need to sweat by allowing the heat to escape. Consider it a summertime haircut and then unleash the hippie within and grow the hair out once the winter rolls around.

For males to run shirtless or females to run wearing sports bras are individual preferences. The benefit to these two options, even compared to wearing a lightweight singlet, is that less skin coverage is better in terms of sweat evaporation and cooling the body. However, if it's a relatively long run/race on a bright, sunny day, the direct rays against your skin will add to your core body temperature, so experiment and choose wisely. If it's anticipated that racing in hot/humid conditions is likely, then it's a good idea to do a training run in those exact clothes (hat/visor included, if applicable). Then it'll be known if the race clothes are comfortable enough. I can always be sympathetic in adverse conditions, but make sure nothing comes as a surprise on race day.

Finally, every now and again it's okay for a runner to try to maintain a decent pace during a summer run. I won't contradict my frequent messages of properly adjusting pace/intensity for the weather, but try not to let the pace and/or form slip into an abyss. Some runners find out the hard way that it's tough, or impossible, to maintain a "normal" pace during peak summer conditions. However, a runner should test herself every now and then and see what she has inside her, or at least how long she can stick to a regular intensity during a long run. Contrary to winter training, if conditions are windy in the summer, then keep the wind as a tailwind on the way out, so that it becomes a nice headwind on the way back to help with cooling.

SUMMER RACING

Racing in the heat is tough, especially at the longer distances. There aren't many summer marathons scheduled in hot regions for this reason. Some race directors are honest on their race websites about discouraging begin-ners from entering their marathons because of relevant safety concerns, like the 2012 Boston Marathon. During the summer, I recommend short-distance racing for the runners I coach and fortunately there are twilight races around.

Consider whether or not the capacity exists to change race goals in drastic weather. Stubborn athletes may end up feeling unsuccessful be-cause they only focused on the finish time or certain splits instead of keep-ing things in perspective and having multiple goals (e.g., process goals). One variable in determining how to adjust race goals in hot and humid conditions is the runner him/herself, as the heat does not affect everyone the same way (as briefly outlined in the previous section), but either way, Mother Nature *always* wins. Experienced runners know that the terrain and weather on race day will decide weather or not a PR is in the cards.

When the weather is accounted for, then post-race damage control can be avoided. This helps prevent the athlete from describing a race or work-out with words such as awful, slow, disappointed or saying, "I hated the race." If one runs the typical race pace (for that distance) or faster on a hot/humid day, then he/she will sweat more and the HR will increase too much, which leads to premature muscle fatigue. *Then* the mind has to enter the picture and do damage control in the middle of the race, and that's when things can spiral downward. Conversely, what if the paces and goals were adjusted before the race began? The pace would be slower, which is to say it would be a more appropriate pace. Then the runner would feel better physically, which means he/she would feel much better mentally, and there wouldn't be a need to think that it was a horrible race. Remember that goals can *always* be adjusted midrace, but the personality (stubbornness) of a runner can sometimes deny this possibility. It is my job to help runners with these adjustments, and it takes some time to get to know each runner's personality, which is why the weekly recaps are important. It's a process.

During the summer, I receive many messages from my runners ex-claiming, "What a difference a week makes!" as they note the significant difference in long run performances (or track performances) from one week to the next. Don't be surprised when you're running slower (objectively speaking) on the days with more heat and humidity and then feeling like lightning during a subsequent week when the weather becomes more favorable. The more important message here is to leave the emotions out of it when looking at the paces on a non-ideal weather day. My job as a coach is to be consistent in this emotional detachment. One week can make all the difference in the world and that's usually based on the weather. Do runners gain miraculous super human strength in just one week? No, because the training effects take longer than one week. In the event of non-ideal weather, check the emotions at the door, leave the exact numbers/pacing alone, and accept whatever Mother Nature dishes out that day. Many runners receive a large confidence boost in the fall as the summer training reveals itself, having been previously masked by summer weather. Be happy and confident with the feeling of improved fitness, but don't be surprised. Surprise can often be synonymous with uncertainty, which is the lack of confidence. If you're too surprised at something you did, then does that mean you didn't think you could do it in the first place? I'd rather someone have that confidence all along.

Rainy Weather

I will admit there is a bit of toughness that develops from training in the elements, but it does not (and should not) have to be a constant. In any case, during the summer, embrace the opportunity to run on a rainy days (not a thunderstorm, just rain) to enjoy a run in potentially cooler weather. Knowing that running in summer humidity each week can be difficult, running in the rain does make some sense. Plus, it could rain on race day and it's good to know ahead of time how it'll be handled. Don't let rain ruin any plans. If it's raining, but not a torrential downpour, then see it as a chance for a PR—many running records are set on overcast days. After the run, stuff the shoes with newspaper or paper towels and they should be dry the next morning.

COMPRESSION CLOTHING

There have been several references to clothing selection in this chapter, so let's continue with compression clothing. Not only does compression clothing keep the legs warm, but it also increases compression on the leg muscles. The theory is that this compression forces more blood flow to/from the legs, increasing VO_2max because more blood to the muscles equals more oxygen to the muscles. Increased blood flow from compression clothing can also aid in recovery via the removal of waste products, much how massage therapy functions. When compared to traditional tights/spandex or standard shorts, compression tights may increase performance over the longer distances due to less energy expenditure. The theory here is that compression clothing holds the muscles in place, so to speak, reducing the vibrations within the exercising muscles, which means less fatigue. Moreover, compression clothing (socks included) and Kinesio tape are becoming popular and you'll see them demonstrated more often at all the big race expos. Obviously one must consider the weather, as compression clothing may restrict the body's ability to sweat and cool itself. Some data supports the benefits of compression clothing on performance while other data refutes it.

When making the decision to wear compression clothing, make sure there is an objective means of measuring their effectiveness. Placebo effects are often welcome when it comes to recovery techniques, but it's always good to know if something truly does work. This means being weary of "one-shot case studies" when reading reviews of products. Set up your own situation for a better experimental design. This is similar to keeping a food journal or fueling log. If someone records his/her diet for a week, then another week, and another week, and only one or two things are tweaked, then it should be easier to hone specific elements of the diet.

On that note, therein lies the flawed rationale of trying to follow a celebrity's diet. One person doing one thing, one time means nothing (i.e., a one-shot case study). This is very prevalent in men's/women's health magazines. For example, a body builder might give his recommendation for a killer bicep workout, but until you know more about the individual and his/her other workouts and lifestyle, you can't put much emotional stock in that workout. Similarly, care should be taken when attempting to mimic professional athletes' training secrets. Will the same clothing or sneakers worn by last year's Boston Marathon winner make you faster? I don't know—maybe, maybe not. I'm sure that a top-notch training regiment has something to do with a champion runner's speed. Pro athletes often market products that are not related to their performance. With that in mind, every athlete should be his/her own test subject.

10

MOTIVATION, GOAL SETTING, CONFIDENCE & HAPPINESS

T HESE FOUR HEADINGS are grouped together for a reason—they are all interrelated, always functioning simultaneously. Below I will highlight the major points of these four headings as they apply to running and a healthy lifestyle.

MOTIVATION

Motivation, goal setting, confidence, and happiness can often be "fluff" words without much meaning attached, so they are misused and abused on a regular basis. Moreover, they are all too often not operationally defined; different people may be using varying definitions for each of these terms. Examples of other words that fall into this category are commitment, love, productivity, and success. With that in mind, let's establish a practical definition to be used for motivation: *The direction, intensity, and persistence of effort.* In other words, what are you going to do, how hard are you going to work at it, and for how long? Keeping this definition in mind makes it much easier to distinguish whether or not someone is motivated. This definition also reminds us that actions speak louder than words.

Each year around January 1st, millions of people are "motivated" to engage in an active, healthy lifestyle, but only those who actually begin the exercise routines are motivated. Stating the *intention* to run a 5k sounds like a good goal, but merely *stating* goals is not effortful. Exercising (training) at least three times per week for several months in a row is moving closer to being considered motivated because now there is measurable *persistence* involved. Additionally, people are more likely to be motivated toward actionable goals if the goals are written down, rather than only verbalized. Once goals are written down, it's an easy next step to jot down some shorter-term goals along the way. Short-term goals are the baby steps toward long-term goals as they help keep the long-term goals in view on the horizon. Crossing off a short-term goal every few days or weeks allows individuals to feel successful, and it's these frequent successes that make people feel good about what they're working toward. As a result, people are inclined to feel motivated as a result of the goal-setting process. Unfortunately, on the other hand, if the timeline for achieving a goal is too drawn out with no benchmarks in place, then motivation can suffer for what would otherwise be seemingly ambitious, healthy goals. It's commonsensical that frequently experiencing success (via short-term goals) boosts our confidence and maintains or enhances our motivation to stay on point. Therefore, motivation and goal setting are inseparable. If an athlete appears to be struggling with motivation, my first line of defense as a coach is to revisit the goals that were set (assuming it's not a case of mental burnout).

GOAL SETTING

Everyone can *think* about goals they want to achieve, but it is the ability to formulate action-plans and communicate these goals that separates success from failure (sounds cliché, but it's that simple). Saying, "I want to eat healthy," or "I want to start running this year," or "I want to look good" are psychologically useless goals doomed for failure. These goals, stated in this way, lack the key components needed for proper goal setting. Goals need to be specific, objective, measurable, challenging yet realistic, contain a short-term element, and have a deadline. What exactly is "eating healthy"? How *far* do you want to run? Why? How *much* weight do you want to lose? By when? How would you specifically define "looking good?" (That last goal in particular is a tough one to define, which is why it can become a gateway for psychologically-based eating disorders). If asked if goal setting is easy, the overwhelming majority of the population would respond "yes." However, not all data would support this resounding "yes." Many people fail to make their goals specific, objective, and measurable, as partially supported by the dramatically high dropout rate among exercisers (50% within six months) and the staggering numbers of adults who are sedentary or obese.

People sometimes choose goals that are too easy, which won't keep them motivated/active because the goal isn't stimulating enough. Other times, people choose goals that are very difficult with the rationale that "this will really push me to work hard." However, in the case of the latter, shortly after setting overly ambitious goals and upon realizing that the goals cannot be achieved, people will quit prematurely rather than have to deal with failure. The rationale is that it's much easier for one to stop trying and say the goal was never attained because one "didn't try" than it is to fail at trying to reach an unattainable goal and deal with the subsequent blow to one's self-esteem. Every now and then, seemingly impossible goals are achieved and an everyday person is revered in greatness as an athlete, writer, or citizen, but those instances aren't the norm. That is why we glorify people who overcome amazing odds. Most people are better served to set goals that are challenging yet *realistic*, at least in the short-term. I am always honest with the athletes I coach. Countless times I have said, "I have no doubts you will finish; it's just a matter of how fast." I stick by this. Most times, I am confident an athlete can finish any distance he wants, but I have to be realistic about how fast he can do it. I have on a few occasions said, "No, I don't think you should sign up for this specific race at this point." Now you know my logic.

To further this point, let's briefly consider a study performed with 5th grade boys, where each boy was asked to do a certain number of push-ups—5, 15, or 50. When considering who ended up working the hardest and rating themselves highest in ability, one might think that the boys who were asked to do 50 push-ups would get the highest marks because they were working toward the most challenging goal. On the contrary, because the goal of 50 push-ups was *too* far out of reach, these kids ended up doing fewer push-ups (quitting) and rating themselves lowest in ability and enjoyment when compared to the other two groups. Even though these were young boys, they demonstrated a facet of psychology that applies to adults too. I'll come back to this example later.

A runner should have multiple goals entering a race or workout, unless it's a "go out and run day" (there's a time and a place for everything). After a workout or race, a runner should be able to definitively say, "Yes (or no), I achieved the goal(s)." Athletes also need to have the capacity to change goals on the fly when conditions change, a concept I've addressed in multiple chapters. For example, if it rains on race morning and the winds pick up, can the athlete correctly adapt the goals to the conditions, and more importantly, can he/she be at peace with that?

As previously stated in the *Racing* chapter, there are three types of goals: outcome, performance, and process goals. *Outcome* goals (winning, finishing place) are not in our direct control, so we need *performance* goals (times, splits, points) and *process* goals (techniques, focal points, strategies) in order to improve the chances of hitting outcome goals.

Process goals are the bread and butter of athletics. Process goals are the *how* of the performance goals and outcome goals. For example, if the goal is to break an hour for a 10k (performance goal), then *how* will this runner break an hour? It could be by correctly pacing the first mile, proper hydration, or staying positive during the tough hill on the course (to name a few likely process goals). I sometimes don't give a runner any process goals before a race if I'm confident the runner is already equipped with knowing *how* to hit the performance or outcome goal. If the runner is training well enough where the performance goal will be achieved simply as a matter of fitness, then there's no need to overanalyze the race/strategy; there's no sense in "paralysis by analysis," and this implies that process goals are not always necessary. This approach of intentionally leaving out the process goals is typically related to the desire to *not* have too much going on in the brain on race day. The aforementioned acronym K.I.S.S. implies not to do too much thinking if it's not needed. "Less is more" (in the brain). However, coaches are nonetheless there to answer questions and to add more clarity to goals. Ask questions before the race because foresight is a more powerful too than hindsight.

AN ANECDOTE ON GOAL SETTING BY TWO LEGENDS

I read a story about a 3k race in 2011 in which professional runner Alan Webb apparently didn't have an A-race. The article included the reaction of his coach, past Olympic gold medalist Alberto Salazar.

Webb didn't want to talk post-race, but coach Alberto Salazar said:

"[The 3k] was just a race. I'm trying to get Alan to understand that he doesn't have to win every race or run spectacular times in every race. I feel that's been a problem for him in the past—the high expectations every time he races. What I'm trying to get across to him is that we can use races as building blocks for the season; use races as a training effort. Not that he isn't going to try to win, because he is. In this 3000m, he did everything he could to try to win. He positioned himself well but he just hasn't done the speed work yet, so he lost to guys who are faster. Yet he was leading with 150 meters to go. So he executed everything perfectly; he just didn't have the speed at the end."

Salazar said that it's hard to convince a runner as competitive as Webb—who had battled the flu and a sore hamstring earlier in that year—that it can be okay to lose a race:

> "I have told Alan, 'You're no different than any of my other runners.' We don't worry about losing some races. The goal is to compete well and win the big races. You love for athletes to be competitive, but as a coach you also want to control that and convince them that every experience is good. You want them to win, sure, but whether they're 1st or 5th, you also want them to be in range of their goal. For Alan in this 3000m, it was to run 7:50 and he was right there."

I agree with Salazar in that races should and can be used as training efforts. However, the runner's personality, molded by proper goal setting, is what ultimately determines his acceptance of the results and his mood following the race. In the case of Webb, it appears that he hadn't accepted the process goals set before the 3k race, so I think Salazar's response was logical.[57]

CONFIDENCE

Confidence is the one factor most highly correlated with success in athletics, and that is evident through both empirical and anecdotal evidence, especially when you consider at the elite level of most sports there is very little difference in the physical capabilities of each athlete. Therefore, as a coach, I preach about confidence frequently. I do so because I also know that once I can help an athlete understand what it means to feel confident, then his/her training will excel. As stated previously, confidence can be very motivating. When goals are phrased simply (K.I.S.S.) so that they are easily understood, then there is more confidence in knowing how to

---

57. I address this topic in more detail in the *Racing as a Training Run?* section in Chapter 7.

achieve them. Similarly, when goals are realistic, but not so easy as to the point of boredom, then confidence increases as a result of knowing that the goal will be achieved.

There are two practical definitions of confidence that I use: the feeling that you've been there before and the lack of uncertainty. I use the latter definition more often. Basically, confidence boils down to a sense of control (certainty) versus a perceived lack of control, and this is also a dichotomy that distinguishes those who are mentally healthy versus unhealthy, anxious, stressed, or worrisome. For example, many people with phobias, aside from a traumatic incident or neurological disorder, have such phobias because they sense unpredictability in a particular situation rather than certainty or control. In other words, they either don't know what's going to happen (uncertainty) or they assume the worst outcome. The same principle applies to athletics. Runners who have competitive anxiety and are nervous at the start line (to a detrimental degree) are uncertain what will happen when the race starts. At that instant, they don't perceive control over the race. Instances like this help to understand how imagery can play an integral role for some athletes to regain confidence before competition (i.e., visualizing themselves running the target pace). By that rationale, control versus uncertainty also helps us understand the mindsets of those who are successful in athletics versus the mindsets of those who are unsuccessful.

If an individual can control his/her breathing, knows how to put one foot in front of the other, and has control over his/her limbs, then there is control over the ability to run. Therefore, one can be confident in the ability to run well. Oversimplified example? Perhaps. But therein lies the opportunity for people to lack confidence—they don't believe they have control over their performances. Whenever I receive a recap of a race that went "poorly," whether from a 10th grader or a 35-year-old, I am almost immediately able to pick out little phrases and words that tell me they were not in control, and by that I mean they were distracted, focusing on the wrong cues. Athletes who focus on task-*irrelevant* cues in competition have many more obstacles to overcome; they constantly have to think and use their brains to get back on track and/or perform tasks that should be second nature. Therefore, *distracted* athletes are often forced to be mentally tough athletes. Does the *Mental Toughness* section make more sense now?

Michael Jordan, Joe Montana, Cal Ripken and Steve Prefontaine were great athletes because they knew exactly what was going to happen when the competition started. They had complete control over their bodies and their thoughts—they were very confident athletes because of this mindset. To them, any other external factors were meaningless because none of those factors mattered (task-irrelevant). Triathletes who swim well in adverse conditions could care less about the actual conditions. I learned that by chatting with Simon Lessing after the Alcatraz triathlon in 2006. For these swimmers, the currents, cold temperatures, strong wind, and choppy waves are all meaningless. To them, it's never anything more than, "stroke-stroke-breathe, stroke-stroke-breathe" (task-relevant cues), no matter the conditions. In that sense, all start lines can be perceived to be the same, and crunch-time situations can be perceived to be the same as any other situation. The crunch-time performances of the aforementioned athletes indicate that they had felt they had been in similar situations before. Therefore, they had confidence in moments when other athletes might have felt pressure or anxiety. This concept was taught to us at a very young age by our T-ball coaches, who reminded us often as we stepped up to bat, "C'mon on, *just like in practice!*" Keep it simple. Focusing on one or a few controllable process goals is what helps to keep it simple.

I've used the phrase "paralysis by analysis" several times already in this book. It's a phrase strongly correlated with poor performance. Whether it is making it to the elite level in a sport or hitting a personal PR, those who deviate from the state of *automaticity* (doing things naturally) and out-think themselves (too much mental effort) are hindering their performances. Michael Jordan was so automatic and so good at "not thinking" that he once made a foul shot in an NBA game with his eyes-closed. That's confidence! Steve Prefontaine ran himself into the ground every race and was very successful, but he was never nervous doing it because he knew ahead of time what he was going to do and how the race would unfold. There was no uncertainty. Even if he was proven wrong, he believed that he would succeed. Mark Allen's quote, "Eat right, gets lots of sleep, drink plenty of fluids, go like hell," helps us understand elite-level athletics and how to achieve the state of automaticity by keeping things simple. Practice makes perfect, and perfect practices makes confidence.

MORE ON MOTIVATION

Motivation can be divided into two main types, intrinsic motivation (doing an activity for its own sake) and extrinsic motivation (doing an activity in order to gain something external to the activity itself), referred to as IM and EM, respectively. It's important to note that IM and EM are not mutually exclusive because someone can rate highly in each category.

IM is engaging in an activity because of the inherent enjoyment derived from the activity, such as a teenager who is unable to put down his new guitar, playing it all day and night due to the novelty of the experience. IM has two major components, autonomy (self-determination) and competence (the ability to learn or demonstrate a skill). In other words, the teenager loves to play guitar because it's something he wants to do (let's assume the teen is not being forced to play) and he is talented and/or wants to improve. How does this relate to your motivation for running? Are you running because you enjoy it and genuinely want to do it (autonomy), or is it because you "have to in order to lose weight or look good." Additionally, does running become more enjoyable as you learn more about it and become fitter (competence)?

EM involves behavior in which something external to the activity is sought. An easy example is a child completing his chores to receive a weekly allowance or the teenager playing guitar strictly to achieve rock star status and the fortune that comes with it. The money, in either example, has nothing to do with actual process of performing the activity. EM is typically shown to undermine IM, as in rewarding a person for behavior that he would typically do on his own (the research is prevalent on this). This is why psychologists encourage parents to be careful about how and when a child's behavior is rewarded, especially if the parents want the child to continue to perform the behavior when the reward is absent. For example, parents should not reward kids for doing chores if they want the kids to appreciate the task in and of itself. Rather, have the kids choose to do it for other reasons. The same rationale holds true for not rewarding good grades.

Again, IM and EM are not mutually exclusive. For instance, a teenager may practice guitar frequently to gain notoriety (EM), but he may also practice frequently because music is his passion (IM). Both forms of motivation are operating simultaneously and serving a greater good. For many elite-level athletes, a high degree of EM is needed in order to make further gains, and this is also true for other realms of life. However, the difference lies in the individual's ability to *internalize* the external rewards and/or not be controlled by them. For instance, if someone receives a raise for a job well done, that *could* be detrimental to her IM, as the individual may become dependent on or expect some form of notoriety each time she performs the behavior, similar to a child doing chores *only* to get the allowance. This is also the heart of classical and operant conditioning (think of those old studies with rats in a cage or dogs salivating when hearing a dinner bell). If people are reminded that their *skills* allowed them to do their job, and if they still believe they have a *choice* in engaging in their behavior, then IM will persist, but many times this is not the case. For instance, collegiate scholarship athletes who eventually stay on the team *only* to retain the financial reimbursement and no longer have "the love for the game" report negative attitudes toward their involvement in the sport. Athletes who are paid but *don't* view the money as controlling of their behavior are less likely to have their IM undermined.

What does this mean for you as a non-professional runner? It means that you may absolutely set your goals to be whatever you want them to be, whether they are done for IM or EM reasons. You can do so with no worries, as long as your autonomy (having the freedom of choice to run) and perceived competence remain intact. I make this point because many times

I'll ask for someone's reasons for running and I sense that people are hesitant to admit to anything other than "to get faster" or "it's fun." Be honest with yourself and your coach. If you want to win your age group, reshape your body or be competitive in some other way, then let it be known. There's nothing wrong with any of these reasons, as long as proper goal setting is understood, as well as knowing how to internalize extrinsic rewards.

LINKS BETWEEN MOTIVATION & HAPPINESS

One of the most educational studies I've read was titled, *What Makes For a Good Day? Competence and Autonomy in the Day and in the Person* (Sheldon et al., 2006). In short, the researchers asked two questions: What types of people have more "good days" than other types of people, and regardless of the person, what factors determine if someone (anyone) will have a good day? The answer to these two questions was essentially the same, as the title of the study implies. People who perceive themselves as both competent and having a high degree of autonomy in their lives are more likely to have a good day, and they also have more good days than people without these qualities. Also, regardless of the person, when the activities on the day's agenda are autonomous (self-chosen), or at least perceived to be, and/or the activities allow the individual to demonstrate a skill or feel competent at a task then the day is more likely to be enjoyable.

These findings should sound very similar to the ideas related to IM and EM. When everything on your to-do list for a given day is something you'd rather not do, then you're less likely to enjoy that day. This is apparent in kids who *must* do something inherently unenjoyable because a parent says so. Are our activities autonomous? Do we choose them, or does something else force us to do them? Do the activities let us feel good about a skill or let us learn a skill? For running, the answer to both of these questions should be "yes." You should be running because you choose to run, while running faster and/or farther should make you feel competent about running. Therefore, theoretically, any day you exercise should be likely to contribute to a good day! The practical applications of this study are also related to the core of happiness.

In terms of personality characteristics, the people who tend to have more good days are those who generally sense autonomy in their lives and feel competent in their abilities to learn tasks or perform them well. At some point in the day, or as frequently as possible, you ought to be engaged in activities that are self-chosen and that allow you to feel like you accomplished something. As stated previously, feeling in control lends itself to confidence, but it now should be apparent that feeling in control also relates to motivation and happiness, as we can interpret control to mean a combination of autonomy and competence. The take-home message is *not* that one must become a "control freak" (that has other pathological connotations); rather, it simply means sensing self-determination and competence in life. Moreover, exercisers typically score more favorably on measures of mental health and vigor compared to non-exercisers because fitness provides the physical and mental energy to solve problems in life, which in turn means that there are then fewer problems to cause mental stress or unhappiness. Therefore, someone with a career that involves extensive problem solving should see exercise (fitness) as a necessity rather than interference, because it requires energy to solve problems.

I'm here to help my athletes go faster and/or farther, as well as to add some structure and accountability in the grand scheme of things, but I want to instill a sense of pride in my athletes to be active virtually every day ("Sweat once per day"). Regardless of whether you take the view that life is short, or the Jethro Tull view that "life is a long song," be proud about something you do in life. George Carlin taught us that pride should be attached to things we've worked to achieve and *not* to easily attach pride to conditions that were given to us, like being born half-Irish. Mom is wonderful, but I attach more pride to my athletic/running accomplishments than I do to being born half-Irish, as I had nothing to do with the latter. It's easy to be prideful about running because most people can't do it or won't do it (at least not in the U.S.). Phrased alternatively, most

U.S. adults can't adhere to a healthy lifestyle. Most Americans (66%) are sedentary, so there can also be pride attached to the dedicating oneself to an active, healthy lifestyle filled with goals.

Running as a leisure time activity truly sets the stage for a rewarding life. In terms of motivation, running fosters IM through autonomy and competence. In terms of goal setting, the possibilities are endless, as long as we adhere to the fundamental principles of goal setting mentioned previously. In terms of confidence, you will always have control over your decision to run, the goals you set, and how you perform, so there is little room for uncertainty. Therefore, running sets the stage to be happy both in the short-term and the long-term. One final point to consider is the state of flow.

THE STATE OF FLOW

Mihaly Csikszentmihalyi is a pioneering expert in the fields of life happiness and positive psychology. He's been studying these topics for nearly a lifetime and his work has been very influential across a spectrum of fields. One lesser known, but amusing example occurred during a Super Bowl victory locker room celebration with then Dallas Cowboys coach, Jimmy Johnson. During the celebration, Johnson held up one of Csikszentmihalyi's books about the concept flow and exclaimed, *"This... this* is how we did it...*this* is our Bible!"

Flow is the mental state in which a person is fully immersed in an activity through feelings of energized focus, full involvement, and success. Flow occurs when our mind and bodies are stretched to their limits in pursuit of some endeavor—when our skills are equally matched with the challenge in front of us. Many times we can equate the state of flow with the state of being "in the zone." When the flow state occurs, we lose sense of time, actions might even appear to happen in slow motion, and we are totally lost in the activity, almost unaware of what we are doing. The original research into the flow state was done with chess players, musicians, and spelunkers (those who explore underwater caves). Once you visualize a guitar virtuoso in mid-solo or an intense chess match and the focus of those involved, you really don't need much more of a definition.

Csikszentmihalyi's research has shown that humans, regardless of age, gender, country, ethnic background, or socio-economic status, will often describe their most rewarding experiences as those in which their participation in an activity was maximized, to the point they were extremely focused, not distracted by anything. Other times, there is no thought involved, but the body is pushed to its limits. Sometimes, it's both, as in an intense tennis rally. The key is to define the term flow as *rewarding* (the ultimate experience), as distinguished from fun, joy, or happiness. When we are in the flow state, we are not having fun, nor are we experiencing happiness. To become aware of our own emotions *during* the activity would interrupt the flow state. Think about the most rewarding experiences in your life or those times you would consider to be the peak of your existence. Chances are, you were lost in the moment, and whatever activity in which you were engaged was relatively long (this is related to the runner's high, in that the run typically has to be at least 20 minutes if not longer). Unfortunately, at times we only have a vague memory of the incident and the specific, detailed actions that occurred, yet we undoubtedly recall the feelings we had *afterward*. That is the point—the most rewarding experiences often aren't rewarding at that moment. It's not until afterward that we "come back to Earth" (so to speak) and experience the joy associated with the flow state. Getting a puppy is a wonderful experience, but it's not flow. Sure, the puppy brings joy, but joy and flow are different. Unless the physical act scratching the puppy behind the ears was deeply skillful and entrancing and it lasted over 20 minutes, then you did not experience flow; you experienced joy.

Running is a great way to achieve the flow state. When there are no distractions (e.g., trail running), total immersion in the activity (focused on the body, no earphones), a loss of the sense of time and space (leaving the watch and HR monitor at home), and when skills are equally matched to the challenge (the pace is appropriately matched for the distance), then there is a perfect setup for a flow-like experience. Perhaps you just never labeled it as such. If a runner's goal for her first 10k was to break an hour, and she crossed the line in 59:37, that was a perfect coupling between skills and challenge, which is the main requirement for flow. This event would no doubt be a joyous occasion *after* crossing the finish line (I've received race recaps describing moments exactly like this).

Recall the study mentioned previously with young boys who were asked to do a certain number of push-ups. Which group do you think did the most push-ups, had the most fun, and rated themselves highest? The answer is the group asked to do 15 push-ups because the boys' skills were matched to the challenge; their goal was challenging, yet realistic. For the group asked to do five push-ups, the boys experienced boredom because their skills were too great for the challenge. The group asked to do 50 push-ups, the boys experienced anxiety and failure, as their skills were too low for the challenge. A similar example is seen in a study with a group of "average" white-water rafters who noted their experiences were most enjoyable when they navigated the "average" course (course difficulty 3 out of 5). They were bored on the level 1 course and scared-to-death on the level 5 course, hardly a chance to experience flow. Some athletes continue to push the limits of human strength and endurance because that's how they attain their flow experiences. Most of the time, these pioneering athletes do not see the challenges in front of them as "crazy" (as we might label them) because their challenges are equally matched to their skills. That's why some people run 100 miles instead of 26.2, or choose do the Tour de France instead of just a Century ride, or climb Mount Everest, or train-surf atop the roof of a high-speed train. Anything less would not be testing their skills and they are merely seeking their ultimate experience, like the rest of us should be (albeit not atop a moving train!).

A quote with which we are all familiar further illustrates this point: "The journey is greater than the destination." I hope I've given a better understanding of why this expression makes sense. Arriving at the destination is not the reward; it's the journey itself. It's the goals and challenges along the way that make it worthwhile. For example, the act of receiving a diploma isn't what makes the recipient experience joy; rather, what makes him/her emotional is reflecting on all of the hard work and commitment along the way and the times when there was doubt in the face of some obstacle. After we find our paths with our careers and families, there needs to be more room for growth in terms of joy and happiness, and we instinctively search for these additional rewarding experiences, for which running as a sport offers that opportunity. This is not to say that our professional and family lives don't allow for these rewarding experiences to happen, nor does the flow state have to be achieved through running. However, happiness *can* be attained through running when we have the proper understanding of motivation, goal setting, and confidence. We can find a way to let athletics be a path to a truly rewarding experience. As I reflect upon what I have written in my Preface (and Mission Statement), perhaps this is what is meant by sports as "a metaphor for life."

RUNNING HAPPY

We should rarely experience failure in running and I like helping runners know *how* to feel successful all the time. It is my aim as a coach to have athletes feeling successful week after week—even in the face of a reality that says not every workout can be the best, nor will athletes have their A-game at every race. Given this reality, how or why should athletes feel successful each week? Well, first, I anticipate sub-par performances being few and far between. Athletes are allowed to have a bad day, but it's important how they weigh that one bad day against the overall upward trend of getting fitter and faster. I harp often about proper goal setting because I know it is vital in fostering feelings of success. Runners who are never satisfied with performances in workouts or races struggle to find the balance between being objective and subjective. When *both* are considered, I guarantee that feelings of success will become the norm.

If you don't feel you're making improvements, or they're not happening fast enough, what then are your benchmarks? How are you defining success or improvement? Are those definitions realistic, too far-fetched, too much of a "dream goal?" Running, in its simplest form, is meant to be an enjoyable leisure time activity. Signing up for races and being competitive is just icing on the cake because it's fun, or it helps goal setting. Everyone should feel fast because we generally get faster from year-to-year.

Remember that "fast" is a relative term. Running 10-minute miles is slow to some runners and fast to others. Some people think I am a fast marathoner, but in another reality, I'd have to run more than a minute faster *per mile* to even come close to Olympic Trials, so in that regard I am a slow marathoner. It all depends on the runner, distance, whether or not you're running through snow, and so on. But really, who cares? In the end, it doesn't really matter. We're all fast because we feel that way. Make a habit of comparing yourself to you. As I write this sentence, I haven't had a "bad run" in over a decade, and I'm 100% certain that streak will never end because I could never put that much emotional stock in any one run, nor would I be unable to find *something* positive and enjoyable about it. And this is coming from someone with pretty lofty goals and plenty of experience racing for 1st place, as well as having been sidelined by injury. Even if it didn't go exactly according to plan, every run or workout I've ever done was in some way enjoyable, productive, educational, or at the very least *completed*, but never "bad" or "slow." Perhaps this makes me lack empathy in understanding how running could negatively affect mood, but hopefully I just gave away my own secret.

I find little room for negativity in running; it should not be a stressful endeavor. Whether someone was 5 minutes slower than an educated-guess goal time at a race or merely 15 seconds slower, ultimately it should not affect one's mood the rest of the day. As they say, leave it on the field. This is regardless of your competitive side or even if you're only competing against yourself. If all an athlete could ever take from an "unsuccessful" workout or race is that he was behind the goal time, then his thoughts may be too shallow, and it's my job to help him discover the wealth of information that can be derived from any race/workout, such as, "*Why* were you behind the goal time?" Some of my runners send me their "take-home messages" following a peak race, which helps them put a positive spin on the race (and the training year) no matter the outcome. If someone isn't learning about running and him/herself following months of workouts, then he is less likely to see all the positive aspects of training. I don't want to hear that workouts are "going okay," I want to hear that they're "going great!"

Someone once asked me if I ever have days when I don't feel like running. Yes. One of those days was an uber-hot day in summer 2011. On paper, it may have been one of the slowest runs of my career, but it felt like a good run at that moment. How? I was outside; I like being outside. I finished the run for the allotted time, which was nice. I found a new street in DC I'd never been down before, which is always cool. And I had the next day scheduled as a rest day. There were lots of reasons it was a *good* run, despite the fact I really didn't want to start the run and despite the fact I ran slow as molasses. If you've suffered on a hot and humid day and felt crappy, then give yourself credit for slugging it out on a miserable day. Feel *successful* about that. I could go on, but hopefully the major points are getting across about how proper goal setting relates to happiness, which relates to positive mood and confidence at the start line.

As the saying goes, there are always greater tragedies in the world. Stay positive. Don't let a training program dictate your mood; don't ever let running get you down. There can be many turns in life that call for lots of mental energy and stress management; don't allow physical activity to become one of those events, especially as a non-professional athlete. I'm aware that many people use running as personal time to collect their thoughts before or after their workday. Balancing work, play, a social life, and personal relationships is what it means to be human and I never lose sight of that. That's why it's important that I stay in touch with the runners who've invested in me, and that's how a coach differs from online training programs. A coach has the capacity to sympathize or empathize with the circumstances surrounding the training and goals. Run and train because you want to, because you enjoy the activity for its own sake, and because you value a fit and healthy lifestyle. If you can do that and maintain whatever competitive edge you have and still strive toward goals, then more power to you. A good coach is there to help no matter where an athlete falls along that continuum.

Personally, I enjoy running for its own sake, so I'm already in a good mood as soon as I change into my running shoes. I'm able to adapt my goals to the conditions of the environment and/or my physical state. In this sense, I'm always aligning my skills to match the challenge, which is the hallmark of achieving flow. I keep good records of my workouts (not in an obsessive way and not all the time) and I include subjective data, so I can always go back during free time and compare a workout against the same exact one I did a few weeks, months, or years ago, and most of the time, I'll see improvement. You can always revisit old training grounds to note how far you've come. Additionally, have a special place to run whenever you want a good workout, as mentioned previously in the *Breakthrough Performances* section.

Not every race will be a PR, nor will you always get a medal, but most people begin the sport of running to simply finish a given race or distance. Then they are driven to seek out new distances and/or to do it faster. This is the nature of all individual sports and some would argue the nature of humans. You test your boundaries, you test your limits, and pass or fail, you're a better person for it, and how you specifically define "a better person" is up to you, and *unique* to you. It's not something I can give as a coach. From my high school cross-country coaching days, I still own a shirt designed by the kids that has this quote on the back: "Only those who risk going too far can possibly find out how far they can go"—T.S. Eliot.

Additionally, develop a HUGE vocabulary and you can use words other than "unsuccessful." Our thoughts are framed by the exact words we use. "We think in terms of language"—George Carlin. This is why elite athletes frequently use mental imagery and develop scripts for races. They practice the exact words/phrases (cue words) they want to say at various points in the game/race/course to keep the self-talk positive and task-specific. It is a skill that takes deliberate practice to develop.

HAPPINESS AND THE PROGRAMS

Let's bring this book full circle and come back to the programs again. The programs I create are there to offer guidance in terms of variety, challenge, performance enhancement, and injury prevention. The programs are *not* there to create an atmosphere of pressure. I'm a very mellow individual and my athletes gain that impression through the group workouts I coach and our weekly communication. The programs are not rigid or militant; we *must* have freedom of choice (autonomy) in what we do in order to keep it intrinsically motivating and fun. As you do more racing and harder workouts, don't lose sight of the fact that you still need to be in the running game for your own reasons. The athletes I coach are training with me for many different, equally valid reasons. However, I don't want them to view running, or even the weekly recaps, as *work*. The longer I coach an athlete, the less structured the programs become. This evolution is by design and is purposeful, and I used Phil Jackson as a premier example in the opening chapter. Additionally, I don't want my athletes to view the speed/track workouts as strictly "race preparation" because these workouts also function to offer variety and to improve health. It's nice to have the best of both worlds, so speed workouts shouldn't be viewed as a "necessary evil."

Every now and then I acknowledge that the same desire that makes an individual want to achieve a new level of fitness or certain accomplishment can sometimes bring anxiety. For instance, on one hand, without a coach there to assist, running may have reached a plateau and perhaps a runner then begins to doubt his/her own methods. On the other hand, the runner becomes fitter working with a coach; however—and the point I'm making—because the goals and fitness are escalating, there's now the potential to become nervous before a race or to feel guilty about missing workouts. I never ask athletes to do anything they can't do, nor want to do, and I admit that sometimes the goal time I give or the program I develop with them is off the mark. Adjustments are always made together between coach and athlete. A coach should demand honest feedback and then adapt accordingly. I like giving people the experiences of being an *athlete* (not just a runner), but nervousness and pressure do not have to be part of that experience. In fact, it's the great athletes (including many amateur runners, like us) that either diminish this pressure or eliminate it altogether. Again, "Keep It Simple and Stupid" is the mantra of sport psychology.

Above all else, the coach and athlete must be on the same page that running is enjoyable for many different reasons. A dose of structure, science, and objectivity—in trying to keep injuries away—shouldn't warp one's sense of enjoyment. It's unconditional love from my end, so I implore the athletes I coach to view happiness with themselves as the ultimate goal, even as I offer to shake up the routine a bit. Again, we think in terms of language, so if the term "training program" makes you react a certain way then call it something different, like "running schedule" or "active to-do list." Perhaps those latter terms will help dismiss any notions of pressure. Running is supposed to be a fun leisure time activity, with or without a term like "peak race season" in the lexicon. The professional runners, especially the ones with long careers, are the ones who keep the "love of the game."

I was once selected to be a Lululemon Ambassador because I "promoted a healthy, active lifestyle in the community while maintaining balance in life." Do I do that for the athletes I coach? Do I promote this message too much or not enough? Do I practice what I preach when I communicate with my athletes? Am I bias in my own way and therefore not seeing amounts of stress/pressure I might be sending? I attempt to balance my messages between freedom *and* accountability because I know most of the busy adults I coach want both. Having fun and being competitive (against yourself or others) are *not* mutually exclusive goals. In fact, isn't it fun to be competitive and set new PRs? Isn't it fun to place in your age-group at a race and win a gift card for socks or cupcakes? I hope so. I coach individuals, not a team, and I attempt to help each runner find a proper balance, which many times is simply defined as helping them alleviate perceived pressures. I often use a Rick Pitino quote, "All pressure comes from within." Get rid of the pressure by shaping the goals to match the abilities, the basis of flow.

My point is not to philosophize for the sake of philosophizing, but to remind all of us that the journey is greater than the destination. Remember why you began running, remember how it felt the first time you ran for an hour without stopping and take pride in knowing that there have been numerous instances when pain or discomfort made you say to yourself, "Wait, *why* am I doing this?" If you're still running and still pushing yourself, then you've no doubt found those reasons why. Remind yourself of those answers on occasion.

I can reflect upon the elements of running, training, and racing and all the milestones I hit along the way that used to be so very intimidating for me and how they seem so trivial now. I achieved milestones only because I tested my limits, thereby upholding the words of that T.S. Eliot quote. I genuinely hope that in sharing my thoughts and experiences as a coach that I've offered enlightenment on coaching philosophies, how to achieve running goals, and how to be happy doing so for a long time to come.

Enjoy the journey.

ACKNOWLEDGEMENTS

A SPECIAL THANK you to star runner and professor of English, Lisa Fox. There's no doubt that editing this book required a great deal of patience and a careful eye on her part. I am thankful for the re-education on the craft of writing.

I want to thank David Schwarz for helpful edits and his comments about writing.

I'm also grateful to Angie Marable and Matt Fay for their time and patience in helping to create the book's photographs and covers.

REFERENCES

Abshire, D. (2010). *Natural Running*. Boulder, CO: Velo Press.

Daniels, J. (2005). *Daniels' Running Formula*. Champaign, IL: Human Kinetics.

Dreyer, Danny. (2009). *ChiRunning: A Revolutionary Approach to Effortless, Injury-Free Running*. New York, NY: Fireside.

Epstein, David . (2013). *The Sports Gene: Inside the Science of Extraordinary Athletic Performance*. New York, NY: Fireside.

Gokhale, E. (2008). *8 Steps to a Pain-Free Back*. Pendo Press.

Larson, P., and Katovsky, B. (2012). *Tread Lightly*. New York, NY: Skyhorse Publishing.

ABOUT THE AUTHOR

MIKE HAMBERGER HAS been teaching sport psychology at Marymount University as an adjunct professor since 2009. He lives and works full-time in the Washington, DC area with his private coaching business, DC Running Coach, LLC, founded in 2006 (www. DCRunningCoach.com). Through his coaching, Mike has guided countless amateur runners and triathletes, members of military and law enforcement, as well as high school and collegiate athletes. He has been published twice as lead author in the *Journal of Contemporary Athletics* and as second author in the *World Leisure Journal*. He is frequently invited to speak at clinics and has been consulted by numerous publications, including *Runner's World* and *Competitor* magazines, and *The Washington Post*.

Mike received his Masters degree in Kinesiology (concentration in sport psychology) from the University of Maryland, where he will begin PhD studies in the fall of 2015 in Cognitive Motor Neuroscience. His education, combined with various coaching certifications, provided him the opportunity to be the head track & field coach and strength & conditioning coach at Sidwell Friends School for five years. He earned his B.A. in psychology at Widener University, where he was a 3-sport collegiate athlete, competing in football, rugby and as an All-Conference decathlete. After his undergraduate years, he competed in triathlon/duathlon for ten years, earning All-American honors and representing the USA three times at the amateur World Championships.

He believes that understanding the research in the field of social psychology unlocks the key principles of sport psychology, and that understanding human nature in this way offers much insight into the art of coaching and leadership.